Confrontin... or

THE AFTERMATH OF VIOLENCE

WILMA L. DERKSEN

Amity Publishers

ALSO BY WILMA L. DERKSEN
Have You Seen Candace?

© 2002 Amity Publishers
Printed in Canada
ISBN 0-9731557-0-1

TRAUMA AND RECOVERY
by JUDITH LEWIS HERMAN, M.D.
© 1992 by Basic Books.
Reprinted by permission of Basic Books,
a member of Perseus Books, L.I.C.

Design Susan McWatt FitzGerald
Blue Cherry Design
Photography PhotoDisc Inc.
Printing Derksen Printers Ltd.

Amity Publishers
Winnipeg, MB Canada
www.amitypublishers.com

INTRODUCTION

PART I: THE CRIME VICTIM DETOUR

CHAPTER 4
TERROR TRAUMA

Retreat

CHAPTER 5
WITHDRAWING TO MAKE SENSE OF IT

CHAPTER 6
GRIEF DISPLACEMENT

CHAPTER 7
TIME/MEMORY WARP

CHAPTER 8
SPIRITUAL CRISIS

5

CHAPTER 9
IDENTITY DEVASTATION

6

CHAPTER 10
FIXING THE HARM

Rectify

CHAPTER 11
DISABLING HARM | 7 |

CHAPTER 12
BLAME/GUILT CONFUSION | 8 |

CHAPTER 13
TRUTH DILEMMA | 9 |

Chapter 14
Uncontrollable Rage

| 10 |

Refer

Chapter 15
Credibility Crisis in the
Justice-Making Process

Chapter 16
Victim/Offender
Trauma Bond

| 11 |

Acknowledgments

THIS WORK IS THE COMPILATION of all that I have experienced and learned in my travels over the past 15 years.

I was compelled to take this journey more for myself than anyone else — driven to understand the plight of all victims. Now I feel that the learnings have become a gift that I have received and that I want to share.

I am grateful to the many victims of crime who gave me of their precious time and answered my many questions, for the participants in the audiences who challenged me pushing me to continue to explore, to my colleagues in the Restorative Justice movement who kept nudging me along and to the researchers and authors whose words and research have been so valuable in gaining understanding.

A very special thanks to Sue Simpson whose editorial assistance was invaluable. Her patience and diligence were truly extraordinary and without her consistent encouragement and belief in this project, this work would not have happened.

I am deeply grateful to Mennonite Central Committee Canada which had the wisdom and generosity to establish a victims' program where many of these ideas were tested and researched and to the *Pathways* Advisory Committee, Yvette Berube, Agnes Dyck, Heidi Friesen, Angela Funk and Sue Simpson, who explored the fifteen elements with me for four years.

I cannot overlook the first readers of this manuscript who plodded through pages and pages of disconnected thoughts and sentences and saw beyond, always encouraging me. Thanks also to the designer, Susan McWatt FitzGerald, for her creativity.

I reserve an abundance of love and appreciation for my husband, my children, and family for their encouragement and support. They have respected my need to take this arduous journey.

Lastly I thank the source of all wisdom, courage and goodness.

> *"We must expect insights from many*
> *different sources if our knowledge is to grow."*
>
> —*John Sanford,* Healing and Wholeness.

INTRODUCTION

THIS IS PROBABLY NOT GOING TO BE AN EASY
BOOK FOR YOU TO READ. There is something in each
of us, whether we are victims ourselves or caregivers of a
victim, that doesn't want to enter the horror of victimization.
To enter into it is to revisit the pain, the sense of powerlessness, the confusion, the fragmentation, and the feelings of
hopelessness.

At first when I was beginning to write this book,
I too wanted to avoid the reality of the violence. I kept trying
to minimize the horror. Then I came across an article by
Daniel Juda entitled, *Hearing the Horror*. In this article he
takes to task the American Psychological Association Task
Force for their clinical approach to victimization. He writes,
"We need to study the capacity of the human being to
experience soul death and act in a soul-killing manner....
We need to develop a new vocabulary to describe the
subtleties and nuances of horror."

This same need — to name the horror — was expressed
by the reader of the first drafts of this manuscript. "You
haven't made it strong enough," she said. "You're not quite
saying it yet." Because she is a mild-mannered, delightful
person, I didn't expect this comment from her. But I should
have. She had been raped by a stranger when she was thirteen, and more recently she had experienced the murder of
her brother. She was intimately aware of the dark side of
criminal victimization. She also knew the value of naming
the darkness and confronting it in order to dispel it. "If we
don't face our crap, it haunts us," she kept telling me.

My own horror began on November 30, 1984 when our
thirteen-year-old daughter, Candace, didn't come home from
school. After a frantic search that lasted almost seven weeks,
we discovered that she had been abducted, bound hand and
foot, and left to die in a shack in the plunging, freezing
temperatures. To this day, we still have no idea who would
have done this to our child — or why.

When Candace's body was found, my husband and I
thought there would be some kind of closure to our shattered
lives. But that same evening, we received an important visit

from a "parent of a murdered child" who told us how the act of murder had ruined his family, his life and his health. Because of the trauma around the murder he had developed a heart condition, lost his close family relationships, lost his ability to concentrate, and even lost the memory of his daughter. He told us that there was no justice. As he was talking, I realized the aftermath of a homicide or violent crime can be as destructive and deadly as the murder act itself.

After his visit, my husband and I decided that we were going to survive this trauma. We committed ourselves to fighting this horror and to find healing for the sake of our other two children, for each other and for Candace and her memory. At that time both my husband and I, because of our faith backgrounds, chose the word "forgiveness" as the word that would guide us through the aftermath. We hoped it would spare us some of the horror. It was a good word, a good goal, but it didn't spare us from anything. We still had to walk through the darkness of the aftermath of murder — a walk that was unimaginably horrific.

Since then I have met many other victims of serious crime and listened to their stories. What has struck me most in these stories is that, regardless of the victims' backgrounds, their age, socioeconomic status, race, or values, their stories of dealing with the aftermath of murder all described similar themes, similar conclusions and hurts. I have also continued to hear the words of our first important visitor, "There is no justice," echoed in their stories.

At the same time as I was trying to understand what was happening to our family and to other crime victims I was meeting, my colleagues in the Restorative Justice movement were constantly asking me questions. "What do victims need?"

Because of these two compelling pressures, I listened to the stories intently for clues that would unravel this horrific mystery. What was it about murder or violence that made recovery almost impossible? I found fifteen themes or "issues" that kept surfacing in the stories. I wrote them down. At first these themes were a scraggly list. With time the list grew, matured and became more organized. Soon I found myself describing them to others, eventually to audiences. It is these fifteen elements of the aftermath of serious crime that I will be describing in this book. I will be making general references to my story, but I will not be including the details. You can read my story in more detail in the book I wrote shortly after the murder of Candace, entitled, *Have You Seen Candace?* It is a description of our lives from the day of her abduction to the anniversary of that date.

The story that I will be using to illustrate the elements in this book is the September 11, 2001 terrorist attacks on the United States. Four planes were purposely hijacked and deliberately flown towards American symbols of power. Two planes crashed into the twin towers of the World Trade Center in New York, another into the Pentagon in Washington, and the fourth plane missed its target and crashed into a field in the state of Pennsylvania.

There are a number of reasons why I've chosen this story. The first is that the event was extremely well documented by the media — so well that all of us were able to see the planes actually fly into the towers the same day. The coverage was extensive, complete, and immediate. Newscast anchors were able to give us a detailed description of the events as they unfolded, various columnists the analysis, and talk show hosts, Oprah Winfrey for example, the individual pathos.

Another reason is that the impact of that crime affected all of us in so many ways. We were all victimized. Even those of us who don't live in the United States were emotionally, politically and even economically impacted. To this day, almost a year later, whenever I need to travel by plane, I am aware of the changes in airport security. The ramifications will be with us for a long time because there is little that we can do to change or undo the aftermath of violence. There is no escaping the immediate destruction of the aftermath of violence. We can't turn back the hands of time. We can only hope to survive the destruction.

We have a much better chance of survival if we confront the horror and learn to understand it. Understanding dispels frustration and conflicts. It enlightens us. It can empower us. It gives courage. It unites us and supports us.

Actually, to seek understanding is the first step in healing because it helps us to find meaning. And hopefully it is this quest for understanding that will make it easier for you to enter into this book's description of the horror found in the aftermath of violence.

"Neither the sun nor death can be looked at with a steady eye."
—La Rochefoucauld

Part One

THE CRIME · VICTIM DETOUR

THE FIVE STAGES	FIFTEEN ELEMENTS
React	1. Story Fragmentation
	2. Terror Trauma
Retreat	3. Grief Displacement
	4. Time/Memory Warp
	5. Spiritual Crisis
	6. Identity Devastation
Rectify	7. Disabling Harm
	8. Blame/Guilt Confusion
	9. Truth Dilemma
	10. Uncontrollable Rage
Refer	11. Victim/Offender Trauma Bond
	12. Justice Revictimization
Recover	13. Unsatisfactory Closure
	14. Recovery Controversy
	15. Paralyzing Despair

The Big Plan

MY CHILDREN SAID IT WAS IMPOSSIBLE. I WAS
DETERMINED. It was a twenty-five-year-old house that
hadn't been touched. Worn shag rugs covered the entire main
floor; the walls were covered with dated wallpaper and nothing
had been washed down for a long time. But we knew it was
the house we wanted to buy — grand cathedral ceilings, right
location, right price and, best of all, huge windows facing west.

They didn't think it was possible to redecorate and move
into a house in one week. But I was determined. The last
house we had moved into, we had redecorated one room at a
time which had taken ten years.

It took me an entire day to plan every detail of what
we have come to call "the big plan." Then we followed it
religiously. We color-coded the moving boxes, picked out
the rug and paint beforehand, arranged for the movers and
scheduled our friends who had offered to help. Fortunately
we belonged to a caregroup of six couples who were willing
to help us for a day.

We took possession of the house at 10:00 on a Saturday
and our caregroup came in at 12:00 to help remove the
wallpaper and wash down the walls. They were amazing.
One friend washed all the windows, another washed down
the kitchen, one tackled the bathroom, the other three
stripped the wallpaper. At 5:00 we had pre-ordered pizza.

My children were an immense help. Our son-in-law took
down the mirror tiles in the dining room; our daughter and
son continued stripping the third layer of stubborn wallpaper.
My husband did a bit of renovating around the front door.

Sunday night we pulled out the rugs. Monday we started
painting. Thursday the new rugs came in. Friday the furniture.
Saturday we did the final moving. Sunday we collapsed in our
new house — absolutely delighted and extremely proud of
ourselves.

What a rush! As a family, we still talk about how we
transformed an entire house within a week.

The plan depended on everything and everyone falling
into place. We were just fortunate that nothing went wrong.

THE DISRUPTED PLAN   Driving into work on the morning of September 11, 2001 I heard over the news that two planes had crashed into the twin towers of the World Trade Center in New York. By the time I reached the office, some colleagues had set up a television in the lounge and had gathered there to watch the breaking story.

By noon we heard that planes from all over the world were landing in Canada; some were arriving at our Winnipeg airport. That evening our family sat glued to a little television set and watched with horror as the two planes crashed into those towers over and over again.

Everything stopped as we ached for the people in the towers; we ached for their families at home; we ached for all the stranded passengers in our city; we ached for a country so privileged, so safe, which was now experiencing violence so publicly and so intentionally.

All of us knew that something had changed. We heard the words often during those days. "Our world will never be the same again." Violence changed something for us. Sometimes I wonder how many big wonderful plans were destroyed that memorable day.

In this book I will be dealing with something very similar to the September 11 atrocity, except on an individual level. Violence on a personal level has many of the same dynamics as violence on a national level. Regardless of our plans, the world stops.

One mother who lost two of her daughters in a murder described the aftermath in her city. "The whole city stopped. Everyone was stunned. How did it happen? When the police weren't finding anyone, that just added to the chaos." This statement resonates with what was said after September 11.

The first reaction to violence, whether it involves a person or a country, is that everything stops. Our life road is blocked. This isn't about the natural choices of life, a fork in the road as depicted in Robert Frost's poem "two roads diverging in the woods and I took the one less travelled on."

The impact of a crime forces the unsuspecting traveller to abruptly leave the main road, abandon all earlier plans, and veer off to the left or right. Whether we want to or not, we are forced to change direction immediately and enter a Crime Victim Detour.

Even a minor crime such as a break and enter causes us to stop. If we come home to a trashed house, we stop. Our adrenaline starts to pump. Our first thoughts are about safety. Is the offender still in the house? We report the crime and assess the damage. Maybe in the end we will be too frightened to stay in the house that was once our "safe place."

Unfortunately, crime is becoming more prevalent. In Canada, we had over two and a half million crimes reported in the year 2000 and 300,000 violent crimes in the same year. What is the impact of this violence on each individual? What is the impact of crime on the welfare of the country?

The Crime Victim Detour

After a presentation, I remember describing the aftermath of violence as an abyss to a small group of people. I said something about picturing all of us victims hanging on to our sanity at the edge of a dark abyss, afraid that we were going to fall.

I described how the crime of violence had a catastrophic impact on the lives of victims. That it created incredible pain, shock and harm. And it does. Eric Schlosser entitled an article about murder "A grief like no other."

According to Ronnie Janoff-Bulman, in her article on *Criminal vs. Non-Criminal Victimization: Victims' Reactions,* "...the victim of intentional harm by another person leads to unique challenges to one's beliefs about the world and oneself, and that these in turn result in particular coping difficulties for the crime victim." In other words, victims of crime face a much more serious challenge than any other victimization.

Off to the side, listening intently, was a tall, slender gentleman who was highly regarded in this group — a retired psychologist. "You should let yourself fall, you know," he said.

For him to offer such advice was uncharacteristic; I thought he was joking. "No," he said. "I'm serious. You need to let yourself fall to the bottom of the abyss and, when dealing with other victims, you need to let them fall into the abyss too. You might need to shove them."

With time, I've learned that he was right. Feeling too exhausted to hang on to the edge of the abyss anymore, I let myself free fall to the bottom of the darkness that was threatening me. The falling, the bottoming out, was not as bad as I had expected. Facing my demons turned them into paper tigers. It was the clinging, the resisting, fighting the inevitable fall that had been the worst.

Without choice, we have been thrown into an abyss of darkness, frustration, fear and fury. This is where we are going now — into the horror of the abyss. It is in this abyss that we need to confront our fear, our pain, our anger. We need to explore our guilt, our nightmares. We need to ask ourselves, "What is the worst case scenario?" We need to confront our enemy.

Hopefully you will discover as I did, that on falling into the abyss I really didn't have that far to fall until I hit the bottom. I was already at the bottom. The worst has already happened.

Carl Jung has said, "It is not by looking into the light that we become luminous, but by plunging into the darkness."

"Feelings cannot be fixed
as if they were a torn patchwork quilt
in need of a needle and thread.

> *Like a musty blanket, feelings require*
> *sunlight day after day*
> *until the fresh air has finally cleared*
> *the cool dampness away."*

—Anne Kaiser Stears

The Five Stages

As we journey into and through this abyss of the Crime Victim Detour, it's important to recognize some of the landmarks along the way so that we can orient ourselves accordingly.

Often the first thing I hear from victims is the question, "Am I going crazy?" No, crime will not make us go crazy. It might make us feel that way for a long time, but the craziness we feel is a normal reaction to an abnormal situation. Hopefully by recognizing the stages, it will help us to feel more normal.

Researchers have been writing about "stages" as long as they have been describing death and crime victimization, including sudden death or homicide. Most of us know about the Elisabeth Kübler-Ross stages: denial, anger, bargaining, depression and acceptance. Marton Bard and Dawn Sangrey are early pioneers in research about crime victimization. They refer to initial disorganization/shock, struggle/recoil and readjustment. Dr. Theres Rando speaks of three stages: avoidance, confrontation and re-establishment. Judith Herman talks about disconnection and reconnection. It's all right to think of stages if we see them as broad strokes, as descriptive rather than prescriptive.

The stages along the Crime Victim Detour differ from other models of recovery because they are imposed on us as the crime is processed through the criminal justice system, beginning with the police and ending with the prison term. Even if the offender is never apprehended and the crime is never reported, the stages might still play themselves out in our expectations of what we hope for as justice.

I used to visualize the Crime Victim Detour as beginning with an unexpected swerve off the main road of life and being plunged into an abyss that had edges as steep as Mount Everest to climb. But over the years as I have studied this material and listened to the stories of victims, I came to see the abyss as having five mountains within it. Then I saw them as five mountain ranges within an abyss. Needless to say, I believe this is not an easy journey.

But as I describe them, remember that every one of us will experience the stages differently. For some the stages might be a mere hill, for others a mountain, for others they might be a mountain range.

Description of The Five Mountain Ranges

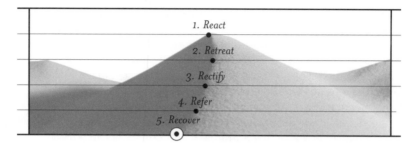

React The impact of a violent crime is immediate and disempowering. Since violence is a criminal offense, the first reaction to stop the violence is to involve the law enforcement agency. Once the police have been notified, we are part of their process. We can only react to these events as they unfold. The act of violence is happening to us. Our immediate need is to stop the violence because we want to feel safe again.

Retreat There is a natural pause after a violent act. People catch their breath and assess the damage. The police need time to investigate the crime. In homicide there is the funeral of the loved one that forces us into dealing with the death, if not emotionally (we might be too numb to realize the full impact of our loss), at least socially. In serious crimes other than homicide, there could be the necessity of cleaning up the crime scene. We might be hospitalized. We will need to recover.

Rectify The crime disables us. Before we can continue our lives, the crime needs to be addressed and justice restored. Our personal issues need to be dealt with: Who is going to pay for the loss? How can I fix this injustice and prevent it from happening again? How can I find justice? Hope for justice and the pursuit of it energize us. We are engaged in the process. If the crime hasn't been reported, we might decide to deal with these issues ourselves.

Refer The criminal justice system processes the crime. We are referred to the professional justice-makers. The justice-making process usually includes a trial or formal process of some kind. Often we find ourselves disengaged at this point because we become merely bystanders in the process. If the crime has never been solved or reported, we will need to come to terms with the lack of process.

Recover There is a conclusion reached after the crime. At some point, even a lack of resolution becomes a conclusion. Whether the conclusions are to our liking or not, we are forced to live with the aftermath of violence. Others expect us to come to a place of "moving on." We expect to put the crime behind us. Life goes on.

Remember these stages are a fluid organization of the victim's journey. Each journey along the Crime Victim Detour will vary depending on the type of crime, the length of investigation, the trial, and the offender. Not everyone will experience all these stages. For example, because there was never an offender found in our case, we experienced this Crime Victim Detour very differently than others where the offender was arrested, tried and sentenced.

The timeline of the Crime Victim Detour could look like this:

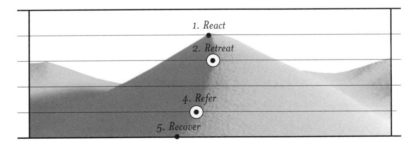

We might pass through some of these stages very quickly; we might linger in others for a long time, and at times we might find ourselves stuck in one.

The Fifteen Elements

As we wind our way through the Crime Victim Detour, we will experience some of the other elements that characterize the aftermath of violence. These are the obstacles that make mountain climbing hazardous. These are the issues that we have to face which could be compared to the storms and the wild animals we might encounter along the way.

I've organized these elements in a sequence along the Crime Victim Detour but I need to say again that this organization is only a suggestion. Life doesn't usually happen in such an organized way. These elements can be experienced simultaneously, sequentially as well as cyclically. The reason I've chosen to organize them in a sequence is that some of the issues come to the fore in certain stages along the detour. For example, fear may dominate the first encounter with the police, while anger may dominate when we encounter the formal trial process. However this does not mean that we won't feel anger immediately after the crime or tremendous fear during the trial. All of these issues are pervasive along the entire Detour. The organization is a way of eliminating some of the confusion as we talk about it.

There are fifteen elements. When we insert these elements into the ranges, the Crime Victim Detour could look like this:

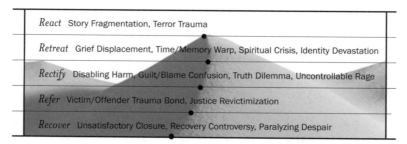

React Story Fragmentation, Terror Trauma

Retreat Grief Displacement, Time/Memory Warp, Spiritual Crisis, Identity Devastation

Rectify Disabling Harm, Guilt/Blame Confusion, Truth Dilemma, Uncontrollable Rage

Refer Victim/Offender Trauma Bond, Justice Revictimization

Recover Unsatisfactory Closure, Recovery Controversy, Paralyzing Despair

Most of us won't experience the Crime Victim Detour in this orderly manner. At the time of the crime, these elements might descend on us like an avalanche or we may experience them simultaneously like layers on top of each other. Sometimes they can be experienced randomly beginning with the last and ending with the first. An element can be forgotten for years and then suddenly emerge, stimulated by a new set of issues and insights.

Each element can feel like a different crisis. The element story fragmentation, for example, may feel like a flash flood; terror trauma may appear like a grizzly bear on the path ahead. We might experience grief displacement like the bottom of a canyon, the time/memory warp like a house of mirrors, the spiritual crisis like an endless labyrinth and the identity devastation like an earthquake. We might find that the disabling harm is similar to having both legs broken and being unable to walk, the blame/guilt confusion like shadow boxing with a ghost, the truth dilemma like walking blindfolded and our uncontrollable rage like experiencing a tornado. The victim/offender trauma bond might feel like being dragged at the end of a rope behind a galloping wild horse. We might find the justice revictimization to be an endless tunnel with no light at the end. Just when we think it can't get any worse, we reach the chute of unsatisfactory closure which slides us into the maze of recovery controversy where we wander until we eventually land in paralyzing despair which is similar to being mired in mud.

"It isn't for the moment you are stuck
that you need courage
but for the long uphill climb
back to sanity and faith and security."
—Unknown author

Alternate Applications of the Elements

Touring Labrador a few years ago, I was extremely hesitant in trying to apply these fifteen elements in a culture and place that were unfamiliar to me. I felt that there was something presumptuous about defining and labelling before understanding the context fully.

After one rather difficult presentation, there was a long, dreadful silence. I held my breath, hoping I hadn't offended anyone. Finally the organizer pointed at the overhead that listed the fifteen elements and said, "That describes the victimization of our people."

Since then I've heard the elements applied to terrorism, war, bankruptcy, offenders, natural disasters, divorce and cultural genocide. I welcome this application. If it brings understanding to any situation of victimization, that's wonderful.

The fifteen elements can also be applied to crimes of a less serious nature — though I've come to believe that all crime is serious. The first time we workshopped these elements, we had four victims, who were carefully chosen to represent different crimes — break and enter (B&E), domestic dispute, assault and murder tell their story.

We were all surprised when the victim of the B&E crime displayed the most trauma and was the best example of someone journeying through the Crime Victim Detour and the fifteen elements. Later in the book I will talk about some of the variables of violence that determine how we will experience victimization.

Even though I do not have the time or the space to apply the elements to every kind of crime or violation, I invite you to do the work of applying them to your personal situation.

The Victim Traveller

Who are the travellers on this journey? We are — you and I — and all those who have been victimized by a serious crime. The United Nations' definition of a victim, which I have adjusted to include only crime victims, is a wonderful one:

A victim is anyone who suffers as a result of a (criminal) offense, physical or mental injury or economic loss: or, any spouse, sibling, child or parent of the individual against whom the offense was perpetrated, or anyone who had an equivalent relationship, not necessarily a blood relative.

For our purposes, we are going to restrict our definition to victims of a violent crime with special emphasis on murder victims. I want to note that we are not dealing with the offender and his or her latent victimization. At the moment of the crime, the offender's past victimization is not an issue. There is never any rationalization that justifies a violent act against someone else. According to Ronnie Janoff-Bulman, "The primary defining characteristic that differentiates criminal from non-criminal victimization is the involvement of an intentional act ('ruthless design') on the part of a perpetrator."

The word victim is defined in the dictionary as someone who is "defeated, vulnerable and disempowered." These words aren't usually seen as very complimentary descriptors. None of us wants to be described as defeated, weak, or disempowered. Some of you might even object to the label victim, but I'm going to retain the use of the word "victim" to describe ourselves because there could be some advantages in being named a victim. For example, for family members of someone who was murdered, the victim status can offer them financial compensation. It is an official, legal designation.

The word "victim" has gained credibility with the public. As the entire credibility of the justice system is being questioned, there is evidence that victims have credibility with the public. When the public was recently polled as to whom they found most credible, the chief of police registered the highest at 67% and victims came next at 66%. Everyone else working in the justice system scored lower than 50%.

We need to be victims before we can be survivors. We can't talk about the issues around victimization if we are referring to ourselves as "survivors." After the act of violence, we aren't sure we are going to survive — not at first. We must enter into the abyss of victimization before we can come out claiming to have survived. Our purpose here is not to deny that truth, or hide it, but to explore it and possibly to redeem it.

The definition of victimization is particularly critical for those who have experienced the murder of a loved one. One man told me bluntly, "Surely the person killed is the victim — not you." But as the mother of a murdered child, I felt I was a victim. And I felt like a victim for a long time.

Research shows that victimization doesn't affect only those who are considered primary victims, but many others. In Lula Redmond's work with 300 families of murder victims, the average number of mourners for each murder included seven to ten surviving family members. "These are (other family) members who are experiencing acute and chronic long term grief reactions." This count did not include neighbors, friends, co-workers or others outside the family system. "Homicide appears to leave a wider range of affected survivors than from deaths by other causes. Many others experience reactions to the psychological trauma of murder in a community, who are considered to be outside the immediate circle of family members and friends."

If a bike is stolen, the bike isn't seen as the victim. The owner is the victim. In the same way, if a person is stolen either through murder or through some disability suffered because of a violent crime, the family will feel victimized; the employer who loses a valued employee will feel victimized in a very real way.

People whom others would consider just "slightly" involved in the crime, such as the store clerk who was the last to see the person before they were killed, may suffer extreme traumatization. Police officers, trauma counsellors, employers, pastors — many of these people experience more trauma than expected.

So, in the light of this research, I'm not going to differentiate between a "primary victim" and a "secondary victim." I would like to leave the definition of victim up to you, the reader. Do you consider yourself a crime victim? Do you feel the trauma of violence affecting your life? If so, under this definition, you could be a victim suffering primary traumatization.

Out of respect for the victims who have been murdered, I'm going to call them "our loved ones."

The Reader's Journey

I've tried to make this journey into the abyss of horror as pleasant and as comfortable as possible. For clarity, I've tried to remain organized and arrange the topics along the path of the detour as listed in the Crime Victim Detour.

The chapters describing the Stages (REACT, RETREAT, RECTIFY, REFER and RECOVER) are illustrated with the story of the terrorist attacks on September 11, 2001 that is presently being referred to as 9/11. Each of these chapters will also deal with descriptions of the main agencies, institutions or influences that you will need to deal with after experiencing a crime, and some suggestions.

The chapters of the Elements are organized into a consistent format that includes: a story from my own life, description of the fundamental value threatened by the crime, definition of the element itself, some underlying reasons for this element, consequences, suggestions and considerations.

Since I don't consider this to be an academic work, I haven't provided endnotes or an exhaustive bibliography. But for those of you who are interested in the research literature, throughout the book you will find quotes from authors and journals that will highlight recognized research that I have found to be helpful. In this work, I have relied heavily on anecdotal evidence that I've gathered through the stories of victims. It is also based on my own personal experience.

The main reason for writing this book is to provide words and labels that help organize the victim experience and dispel some of the myths and misunderstandings still surrounding the victimization resulting from violence. It is my response to the constant pressure that I have been feeling from others to "get the fifteen elements down" so that they can finally be available to a broader audience.

Thought for the Journey

We are truly, beautifully and wonderfully designed. There are two things I find admirable about the human race. The first is our ability to survive. Seeing the resilience, courage, faith and endurance in any human being is always amazing.

The second is that we are all connected. We are not alone. If we were alone, none of this justice talk would matter. But it does matter, because we need each other. What we do to each other matters immensely.

I hope that as we explore this victim's journey, you too will see not only the brokenness created by extreme victimization, but also the courage and the strength of those I've encountered along the way. At some point I hope the sun will shine through the horror.

"Outside, the morning was bright,
sunshine flooded the trees
and birds were singing;
inside the house was a scene
of horrible slaughter of a beautiful girl.
The mother saw the detective
directly in front of her move his lips
as though he were talking to her
for the longest time.
She heard nothing, she said after."

—A victim

CHAPTER 2: THE IMPACT OF VIOLENCE

Panic

THE FIRST REACTION FOR MOST US OF US ON
September 11 as we watched the horror of the terrorist
attacks unfold was: Who? What? Where? Is everyone safe?
The response in the trembling tower was immediate. Everyone
rushed for the stairwell. Everyone formed a plan of action;
some were successful, most of them weren't.

Survival is our first instinct. Even though we might already
be aware of loss, there isn't time to mourn during these first
moments. One of the survivors in the tower described it,
"People were rushing and merging together and going crazy."

High energy, quick thinking and quick movement characterize this time of reaction. This is the time when we hear of
indisputable heroic acts by "saviors" who chase the offender
during a crime. People will act with clarity and call 911 —
and stay until the scene is contained. Even though we all react
differently to a crisis, we will all react.

There is tremendous fear. Not until we are safe and we
know everyone we love is safe, can we settle down. Even
then, when the violence has been contained, the fear continues. Professionals swoop down offering trauma counselling.
The media is at our door. Or we might be alone and choose
to be alone.

Those first moments are etched into our minds forever.
Whether we are the first on the scene of the crime, whether
we are the ones who experienced the assault ourselves or
whether we were notified later of the assault against our
loved one, we will never forget those first moments.

Often in serious crime the reaction to violence can
last a long time. In our case, Candace disappeared for almost
seven weeks. During the entire time, I would say that our
whole family, and to some degree the entire city of Winnipeg,
was in a state of emergency. Stopping the violence, finding
Candace, took priority. Even Christmas took a back seat in
our family to the search for Candace. It never left our minds.

The intense memory of those first moments of reaction, together with the memory of the emotions accompanying all the events, becomes part of the enduring trauma.

First Stage — React

The impact of a violent crime is immediate and disempowering. This the first imposed stage of the Crime Victim Detour. To experience a violent crime means that someone, an offender, has broken the law, and has through physical force caused us as victims tremendous harm. Our immediate need is to stop the violence because we want to feel safe again.

According to the dictionary, laws are "binding customs or practice of a community, a rule of conduct or action and the whole body of such rules." Laws also refer to sovereign authority which implies a legal system. Breaking of this sovereign law is considered a crime, a gross violation of the public law. The harm created by crime is not only against us as victims but against society as a whole.

The whole world took notice of September 11. When someone has committed an offense that violently injures another person, it involves all of us. Every murder in our city hits the front page at some point. As a healthy community pursuing safety and security we can't tolerate murder or an unprovoked assault.

On an individual basis, the act of violence happens and then continues to happen to us because the assault isn't only physical, it is psychological. When we are assaulted or a loved one is murdered we have immediate feelings of being out of control. Violence challenges our basic assumptions of life. "The victim's assumptions about a moral universe are shattered," Ronnie Janoff-Bulman writes in her article exploring the difference between criminal and non-criminal victimization. "Once again, it is a matter of salience, for we might all say that we know evil exists. Unfortunately, it is not until its existence is made hedonically relevant to us that our assumptions about order and morality become truly disrupted."

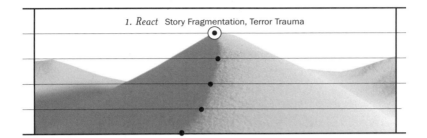

1. React Story Fragmentation, Terror Trauma

This encounter with an outside force of evil which has gained control of our world might feel like an insane explosion in our otherwise orderly and safe world. The first reaction to this explosion is one of fragmentation and terror which are the two issues that we will be exploring in this stage.

Story Fragmentation The reaction to something as horrific as a violent crime is disconnection, shock and numbness. This shows itself in our inability to find the right words, our inability to make sense of what is happening about us. When everyone around us, such as the police and the media, is demanding answers, we have none.

Terror Trauma Fear resulting from a violent crime will show itself in severe physical, mental and emotional traumatization. The terror of murder or an assault or threat of any kind strikes fear in our hearts before we can even formulate words. We will experience extreme fear until the offender is apprehended or until we find a safe place.

Law Enforcement Officers

We assume the role of the police is to intervene during a time of crisis, restore public safety, apprehend the offender and begin the investigation. Often we see the police as the saviors. They are looking after us.

During this time it is good to remember that even though the police are on the side of safety and the public (they usually have a police victim service unit which will guide us through the interaction with the police force) they are not necessarily there to look after us. Often during this time, the police are investigating everyone. It is good to remember that even if we feel innocent and have been the obvious victim, the police might also be investigating us.

It is important to remember that a case is being made to be presented in the courtroom. "Whatever you do or say could be held against you." Exercise openness but also some caution. If you feel uncertain about giving your statement to the police, ask a friend to be there with you. If they ask to interview your children, insist on remaining with them. And if that is not possible, suggest that a friend be there.

Also remember that if you want to know details about the investigation, you will have to ask.

Media

In dealing with the media exercise discretion. It is the role of the media to write about every serious reported crime incident in the community in order to alert the other citizens to exercise caution. They are the red flag raisers.

Often we are afraid of the media. We have seen news reporters attack politicians and misrepresent some facts. We have no desire, especially in our traumatized state, to expose ourselves to that kind of pressure.

Consider carefully your response to the media. It is true that you don't have to talk to a reporter; you always have a choice. But remember there are times when having the public know about what has happened to us or our loved one might be advantageous. The time of the crime, or shortly thereafter, is the only real time the victim has a voice. During the terrorist attacks of September 11, our attention was on the victims for only a brief moment. In the first moments of crisis we wanted to know: Who were they? How were they doing? Shortly thereafter, we turned our attention to Osama bin Laden. Probably for the next ten years, we'll be talking about the war in Afghanistan and we will remember only the victims who spoke out publicly during the time of crisis. If there is something that needs to be said about your loved one, the time of crisis is the time you need to say it.

Remember that reporters can be very supportive of victims. The reporter who might tear apart a politician is sympathetic to victims at heart. Journalism gives voice to the victim.

Remember that reporters will report the story regardless of your cooperation. Ask yourself, "Which story do you want printed?" If you are unable to be a spokesperson for your family, you might want to consider appointing someone who will help to get the story correct the first time. It is very difficult to correct a front page story a year later when you might finally be ready to talk. Your communications don't have to be lengthy.

If you choose a spokesperson, choose someone who can express himself or herself well and has a strong loyalty to you and your family.

"The story doesn't end with her murder,
and it didn't end with his apprehension.
It didn't end with his confession
or all the stuff that led up to him
pleading guilty to first degree murder
or when he tried to have that overturned.
It never ends."

—Victim whose mother was murdered

"Stories compose the real world.
We cannot form a picture
of our experience without them.
The least livable life is the one
without a coherent story."

—Daniel Taylor

| 1 | STORY FRAGMENTATION |

An Old Bear Rug

NO ONE HAD TALKED ABOUT IT FOR YEARS. It was a vague dark memory, the hidden room where we played as children.

"Do you remember grandma's attic?" someone asked.

There was a collective smile in the room full of cousins. Then the stories began to pour out. One person remembered the closet full of old clothes; someone remembered the old gramophone; some even remembered the songs on the records that we played on it. Others remembered the boots, the books, the window overlooking the orchard, and the floor boards, worn smooth. All of us remembered the old bear rug with the head still intact, the glass eyes — and yes — even a stiff dry tongue. And how the older ones would somehow make it come alive again, appearing out of the dark shadows waving its long, stiff tongue, to scare the younger ones.

We talked about the old chestnut trees that we loved to climb. We couldn't help but remember the day one of the cousins fell from the highest branch, landing on his back, traumatizing all the aunts and uncles — and destroying our entire Sunday afternoon.

Even though many of us hadn't seen one another for years, at the end of the evening we felt close to each other again. Over and over we talked about how much we had enjoyed the evening, as if it had been an evening at the movies or some other professional entertainment. But it wasn't a performance — it was just the power of story.

Words and Story

Words and stories are important to us. "I love words," writes
Macrina Wiederkehr in her book, *A Tree Full of Angels.* "How full of
power they are. What a source of healing consolation and joy, hope
and encouragement they can be for others. People can die for lack
of words. They can starve just longing for a human voice. Think of
all the words that have been spoken, written, and sung throughout
the ages. The human story is continually told through the great
works of literature, history, psychology, science and so on. Our
response to all words, if we want them to feed us, is to listen and
connect them to our lives."

After any event, the words that describe the event are almost as
important as the experience itself. Most everything we experience
needs to be sifted through the screen of words to be understood
fully, to be experienced again, to be ordered, to have meaning and
to become a reality in our lives.

Personal narratives are a way to know and understand each
other more completely. Words help us understand ourselves.
Kay Pranis in her article, *Telling our stories and changing our lives,*
says, "Telling our story is like holding a mirror up in front of
ourselves — a mirror in which we realize others can see our reflec-
tions. Our way of constructing our story, which shapes our view of
reality, becomes more transparent to us when we speak out loud
to each other."

We are constantly called on to tell our stories at different times
and in many different ways. When we meet someone new on the
airplane, even the most fleeting introductory pleasantries are full
of our story. Who are you? What do you do? How many children,
grandchildren do you have? If we are unhappy or insecure with
any part of our story, it becomes a problem to even begin some of
these conversations.

We need true stories. We read the newspaper every day,
many versions of the same story to get at the truth of it. We need
fictional stories filled with imagination that speak of the truth in
a less threatening way.

In the introduction to his book, *The Healing Power of Stories,*
Daniel Taylor writes, "You are your stories. You are the product
of all the stories you have heard and lived — and of many that you
have never heard. They have shaped how you see yourself and the

world.... Our greatest desire, greater than the desire for happiness is that our lives have meaning. The desire for meaning is the originating impulse of story. We tell stories because we hope to find or create significant connections between things. Stories link past, present and future in a way that tells us where we have been, where we are and where we could be going."

STORY FRAGMENTATION

Yet the first reaction to something as horrific as violence and murder is a disconnection, shock and numbness. This shows itself first in our inability to put words to what happened. Many victims talk about being lost in a state of fluid emotion with no words, just darkness. Many talk about a disconnection, a fragmentation.

Gerald Flood in his newspaper column the day after the U.S. terrorist attacks wrote, "Never has a blank page loomed so large. Never have words seemed so inadequate. Never has the contemplation of expressing — what? outrage?– seemed so puny and unworthy. Never has it been said that anything that could be said has seemed so utterly trite — all bombast and nonsense.... We are reduced to tears, to rage, to bewilderment, all of it everywhere the same at once so that it seems banal, impotent, ineffectual. We don't even know whom to blame or to console."

Harlan Ellison probably says it best. "I have no mouth and I must scream."

When we face a violent act, the loss of words is a normal reaction. The confusion is always valid. The gaps are legitimate. This confusion is a symptom of the event rather than the person's ability with words.

In the book *Trauma and Recovery,* Judith Herman captures this inability to find words in her introduction to the book when she says, "Certain violations of the social contract are too terrible to utter aloud: this is the meaning of the word unspeakable."

When we are traumatized our stories will have obvious inconsistencies and lack chronological cohesion. We might lapse into lengthy descriptions of simple details and reflect defensiveness. Our story might come out in spurts and end in long silences. We will be fumbling for words.

Some of us stick only to facts in our story and express no feelings. Others dramatize their emotions with few facts. Some of us might talk about going crazy, not remembering anything or not being able to function.

Ever after we tell our stories and organize events as "before and after" the violence.

Myrna Klassen explains this in her story after her husband had burned down their house killing her oldest son.

"The first time I told my story was just hours after my son was killed. I needed to tell it to make sense of what was happening to me and to keep the facts straight. Sometimes I would try and fix things in my story; so I told it over and over again. I also didn't want my son, Gary, to be forgotten. I told my story to strangers. Sometimes I made mistakes in telling my story. I used to overwhelm people with it. Now I'm learning to unload my grief in little bits and pieces. It's a fine art — it really is."

I remember so clearly how words failed us the day Candace disappeared. Around 9:00 we had exhausted all our leads to find her and so we called the police. When they came, I laid out Candace's picture on the dining room table with a few descriptions of what she was wearing. I expected that they would take it, make posters and plaster them all over the city.

But they didn't. They said, "Don't you know that we haven't had an abduction in Winnipeg for the last seven years? Don't you know that every missing thirteen-year-old in this city is a runaway?"

We thought Candace had been abducted; they labelled her as a runaway. It was only the beginning of a constant struggle to find words for ourselves and then communicate them to the people around us to convince them.

For someone who wanted to be a writer and a communicator, the inability to tell my story was probably the biggest shock. I remember shutting myself away from the world and desperately trying to journal but I couldn't even describe the events to myself; I didn't have the "right" words. The fumbling for words, the lack of them, all added to the trauma.

Underlying Reasons for Story Fragmentation

The issue of Story Fragmentation is probably one of the first things we as victims need to deal with. Sometimes it can begin at the time of impact. When we need to call out for help, we can't remember the numbers 911. When we telephone our friends to tell them, we can't find the right words. When we have microphones stuck in our faces asking us how we feel, we can't find the words. There aren't any words.

If we aren't able to express our story or tell it, the story can continue to haunt us for years. It can act as a ghost, uncontrolled, a force seeking to be exposed. For some of us, the story becomes our albatross that we share with friend and stranger alike. We look for the words that will make our story acceptable and for people who will accept our story. We practice telling our story over and over again.

As Judith Herman writes, "…far too often secrecy prevails, and the story of the traumatic event surfaces not as a verbal narrative but as a symptom."

Here are a few reasons why you might be having difficulty:

Violence threatens everything we hold sacred. It violates our sense of safety, our morality, and our sensibilities. The images of blood and murder weapons are abhorrent, gut-wrenching and distasteful. In the movie theater when the violence becomes too much, we can close our eyes. In life we can't. Our initial reaction to anything so incomprehensible is shock, denial and numbness. Putting murder into words creates a reality for which we might not be ready.

We might not feel safe enough to tell our story. As Marton Bard and Dawn Sangrey describe in *The Crime Victim's Book,* "Because crime is an interpersonal event, the victim's feeling of security in the world of other people is seriously upset. The crime victim has been deliberately violated by another person. The victim's injury is not an accident: it is the direct result of the conscious, malicious intention of another human being. Some people can't be trusted — again we all know that, but the victim is confronted with human malevolence in a very graphic way." There is good reason for us to not feel safe.

We might not have a safe place to tell our story. When we feel uncomfortable with the story of our lives, we need time and safe places to practice telling our story repeatedly. In the beginning we might share too much or too little and be misunderstood. The failure to tell our story right the first time might discourage us from continuing to search for the right words.

We simply might not have the terminology or the confidence to label something so foreign to us. How many of us have studied policing, nursing, criminology, and psychology? Murder requires that we become an expert in each of these fields. To do this we need to learn another vocabulary that includes medical, theological, psychological and justice terms such as: medical examiner's office, Armenian and Calvinistic, post traumatic stress disorder, second degree, manslaughter, plea bargaining, retribution, restitution, restoration.

Those around us might use words to minimize what is happening to us. We ourselves might use words to minimize what is happening. Daniel Juda confronts this impulse in his article, *Hearing the Horror.* "To avoid discussing such horrifying occurrences is understandable. It hurts! It terrifies!.... But to be helpful (and to fully understand) we must develop the capacity to capture... the unspeakable." The healing journey can begin only when we deal honestly with what is happening to us and use the words our heart is using. That might mean becoming comfortable with words we find offensive.

There might be a great deal of pressure to remain silent. If both the victim and the offender are from the same community, the offender family might act as a silencing agent. Secrecy and silence are the first line of defense for an offender. Many victims find themselves caught in this covenant of secrecy that can be imposed by the defense, prosecutors or law enforcement agencies. In any kind of investigation there might be a need to hold some things in confidence, but remember that we as victims can always talk about how we feel.

Our stories might be too confusing and full of gaps to be able to tell them the way we would like to tell them. We might have huge gaps where we simply don't know what happened or why. These gaps in information might be inaccessible to us for a long time. They could be in the police file, in the offender's memory, or no one might know. They might be "why" gaps. The inability to understand or make sense of what happened might deter us from wanting to tell our story or knowing how.

Our stories might be too revealing or make us feel too vulnerable. Violence not only violates our physical bodies or lives; it has the capacity to rape the private parts of our story. We might have family secrets, unresolved relationships or just "baggage" or "stuff" we don't think anyone has the right to know or needs to know. Yet when a crime happens in our lives, suddenly our entire lives are on display. The police in their investigating need to know all the details of our lives. Telling the story of the crime might reveal some of this "stuff" that we haven't resolved for ourselves. We might have latent regrets, guilt, unresolved anger, embarrassing failures, uncontrollable anger or grief that the telling of our story forces us to lay bare. Telling our story might arouse emotions that we don't want to deal with just yet.

Our story might not fit the norms of those around us. Our story might feel different than the stories of our friends. It might feel unacceptable at a dinner party. When our story makes us stand out and feel different, it might not feel safe to share it.

Just remember these are only a few reasons; this list is not complete. You might have your own reasons why it is difficult to tell your story.

Consequences of Fragmented Story

Our inability to tell the story of our lives after murder can become a critical factor in the way we deal with the murder. Our society often bases a person's credibility on the ability to tell his or her story coherently, concisely and spontaneously. A person who can't tell his or her story can be held suspect and often is.

Crisis demands clear thinking and the integration of fact, story and reason. At a time when we need to make critical decisions based on all the facts, we might not be able to access all of them. This can leave us feeling vulnerable and we might defer decision making to someone even less capable or to someone who is self-serving.

Repressed parts of our stories have a way of haunting us. They will find a way of interrupting our everyday lives and emerge as images of fear in our nightmares.

Healing our Stories

As difficult as it will seem, in order to feel completely whole again, free and content, we might have to learn to tell our stories and integrate them again. We need to begin the journey by healing our broken stories. We need to find the words to tell our own stories — words that reflect not only the event, but the truth of it. "We need to understand exactly what happens to the relatively naive self when it is forced to witness or participate in an act of evil," writes Daniel Juda.

There are many different ways to tell our stories. I know of one woman who told her life story through a series of gorgeous quilts. I've heard of a gentleman who knit his story into yards and yards of an over-sized afghan. Another person found a great deal of comfort in cutting out memorial poems from the obituary section of the newspaper every day. I recently read about a judge who turned from the language of legalism to poetry when he encountered tragedy. Use whatever works. We might need to search for stories that help us make sense of what is happening to us.

It takes time. It took Harold Kushner fifteen years to write his book, *When Bad Things Happen to Good People,* in order to make sense of his grief. It could take us longer.

Our story does not necessarily need to be public. We can tell our story to select friends and feel it is enough. We might need to be able to tell the story only to ourselves.

How we tell the story is important. It will need to be complete.

We might want to start by telling our story as a chronological outline. What happened? The more details of the event we uncover, the better we will be able to put it into context. Simultaneously we might begin to look for the words describing the feelings that accompany the story. Some of our feelings might be hard to understand or unacceptable, but that's all right. We need to find the right words so that both our heart and our mind will be satisfied. We might need to acknowledge severe anger towards people close to us. We might need to feel hate for the offender, confess the pain of being misunderstood, express the guilt for all the "should haves."

Remember that each one of these processes begins with a single word — and we will end with a woven story.

As Judith Herman writes, "People who have survived atrocities often tell their stories in a highly emotional, contradictory and fragmented manner which undermines their credibility and thereby serves the twin imperatives of truth-telling and secrecy. When the truth is finally recognized survivors can begin their recovery."

Cathy Caruth says in her book, *Trauma: Explorations in Memory,* "In listening to testimonies and in working with survivors and their children, I came to believe that survivors did not only need to survive so that they could tell their stories, they also needed to tell their stories in order to survive. There is, in each survivor, an imperative to tell and thus to know one's story, unimpeded by ghosts from the past against which one has to protect oneself. One has to know one's buried truth in order to be able to live one's life."

In whatever way we choose, whether it be through art, words, actions, pictures, poetry, confessions, prayers, or just through silent processing, we need to put words to what we are experiencing. And remember they have to be our words, uncensored and honest, that come from our mind and heart.

Considerations

Cherish your story. The crime doesn't diminish you or your story. Your story is important.

Tell your story in your own way. If this is difficult, find a safe place and a safe way to express yourself. You might want to find someone you trust. You might want to schedule a regular debriefing time for yourself with them.

(If safety is an issue, logging the events as they happen or as they happened might be critical evidence later in the justice process.)

If your story is incomplete, research the parts that are missing. Don't be afraid to ask the "stupid questions." You have every right to know. Ask for the medical examiner's report, pursue getting the transcript of the court proceedings, if you need to. If you need a book of courtroom definitions, ask the local victim services for one. Ask for resources that will help you put words to your experience.

Take the time to write notes to yourself. Initially you might find that you can't remember everything that is happening. Make lists. Write down names and addresses. Your memory will come back later. You might want to journal your way through the event. Writing down your first thoughts in the morning or the last ones at night can be a way of organizing your life again.

(One word of caution, if you were to be called as a potential witness, remember that the journal could be subpoenaed. However, it is always safe to express how you feel about each day and about the events as they unfold.)

When dealing with the media, write out a short description of what happened from your perspective and give it to them. You could include a fact sheet for all the people in your family who are linked to the crime, their names, ages, and specific facts you think are important to the telling of your story. If you find that you can't manage this, you might want to ask someone to help you. It's okay to not know every detail. Say you don't know, if you don't know.

You may want to write an impact statement and submit it to the Crown Attorney through the victim/witness assistance program or to the National Parole Board for the next parole hearings. Remember that anything you write will be read by the offender. You might want to ask someone to review your story to make sure you are not revealing too much or too little.

If you find yourself repeating the story over and over again, try telling it in three different distinct ways. Answer the questions:
- what happened
- what the feelings were that accompanied the events
- what impact this had on you and on those you love.
  If this arouses new emotions, find a safe place to tell the story.

Collect all the memorabilia of your story: press clippings, photos, and letters. Even if you can't read them now, save them for the future just in case you need them some day. This might also be a good task to delegate to a friend who is wanting to help you in some way.

"Words are a form of action, capable of influencing change."
—Ingrid Benglis

*"It takes a thousand voices
to tell a single story."*

—Native American saying

2	TERROR TRAUMA

Adopted Cat

WE HAD HEARD MUCH ABOUT ARIA, BUT HAD NEVER MET HER. "Where's Aria?" was our first question as we entered our daughter's home for Sunday lunch.

We found her curled in a tiny white and orange ball in the warmest corner of the kitchen under the table, sleeping. Hearing her name and our strange voices, she opened her beautiful chestnut eyes, stretched luxuriously as only cats can do, then padded out to us on her oversized white paws. She looked us over, then went to swirl herself around my daughter's feet.

Only a week before, my daughter and her husband had picked this kitten up from a farm where it had spent the entire four months of summer holed up in a farm machine shed. Never having interacted with humans, all of the kittens were wild. When caught, this tiny kitten had trembled with fear and had been ill on the ride home. Completely terrorized, the kitten had spent the first two days hidden in the darkest corner of the basement, coming out only once in a while to cry. With treats and patience, my daughter had coaxed her out and began to pet her. In three days, the kitten had made the adjustment and became part of their home.

This was our first visit to see Aria. After a few minutes of assessing us, she came to us, chasing the little string toy we dangled in front of her.

All afternoon she stayed with us, watching us while we had lunch, swirling under our feet as we cleaned up the dishes, then coming to sit on our laps as we watched the football game.

No fear. We had been worried that she would still be traumatized. No fear meant that we could enjoy each other. No barriers, just trust.

Safety and Security

We function best when we feel safe. Some time ago at a meeting I asked everyone to describe a place where they felt safe. It was interesting watching the expression on their faces as they went back in their minds to a safe place. As they visualized the place, there was a look of peace and happiness that crossed their faces. Most of them talked about feeling safe in their homes, in their beds, with their partners, asleep, and with special "safe" friends. Just talking about safety made us feel safer.

Poet Ann Kiemel describes this sense of safety in her poem, *magic of life:*

> *to know my way around the city, to feel comfortable with my job, to like my new sandals, to be asked to play tennis, to ride my bike on a warm evening with a friend...*
>
> *to have a cousin, a brother, a mother, a family...*
> *to say something innocently, and suddenly see it make people laugh — and then i laugh because it's so wonderful to see happy people....*
>
> *to have someone reach out and touch me, or look*
> *at me with dignity and respect, to have one person*
> *like my sister that I can be totally free with...."*

We long for this poetic safety. Basically we feel safe when there is no threat of physical danger, when we feel in control of our lives and when we feel empowered to make the right choices for ourselves.

We spend a great deal of time and effort in creating a place of physical safety for ourselves. Advertisers have keyed in on this need. They know we will buy "safe" cars, "reliable" brakes, "secure" mutual funds and "bottled" water. After a "break in" they know that we are susceptible to buying any gadget that will make us feel safe again. We will spend any amount of money to feel safe again.

We will put a great deal of effort into whatever we perceive will give us more control of our lives. If it is money, we will work hard at our employment so that through financial empowerment we can determine where we will live, who we'll associate with and what we'll do with our time.

The word "control" can be seen as a negative, and it is negative if we use control to hurt others or ourselves. But taking control of our lives in a healthy way can translate into feeling more safe, more confident, more comfortable, and therefore more generous, more understanding and loving. We learn, play, and manage our lives better when we feel safe.

In her article on criminal victimization, Ronnie Janoff-Bulman writes, "Although people generally recognize that bad things happen to people and even happen relatively often, they simultaneously maintain a belief that 'it can't happen to me.'" Safety is one of those things we take for granted until we don't have it anymore.

TERROR TRAUMA

2

Our feelings of safety are destroyed when we experience violence or the threat of physical violence at the hands of another human being. We also feel extreme fear when someone close to us has been violated or murdered.

This fear will show itself in severe physical, mental and emotional traumatization that can last for the rest of our lives in varying degrees, making us susceptible to post traumatic stress disorder.

Fear causes an adrenaline rush, an accelerated heart rate that provides a new surge of strength to our extremities. Because our body will want to be light and quick, making it easier for us to run, it will eliminate all unnecessary fluid — like the coffee we just had. We might feel nauseous. Our minds will be on red alert and we will experience exaggerated startle responses, alertness to any lingering danger long after the initial danger has disappeared. In trauma, the mind becomes selective of what it chooses to notice and absorb. We become very focussed on survival.

There are fears of every kind: fear of abandonment, fear of pain, fear of death, fear of violence, fear of the perpetrator, fear of our own emotions, fear of shame, fear of rejection, and fear of fear itself. But the fear of death or annihilation is the fear that underlies all fear in this terror trauma after violence. As Elisabeth Kübler-Ross writes, "Death is still a fearful, frightening happening, and the fear of death is a universal fear even if we think we have mastered it on many levels. It is inconceivable for our unconscious to imagine an actual ending of our own life."

The best way to picture the reality of this fear is to imagine meeting a grizzly bear on a path. Our minds would either begin to spin, or freeze. We would all react differently. One thing is certain; none of us would be able to "carry on" as if nothing was happening. We would not be able to sleep, eat, enjoy intimacy, read or visit with a friend. Our lives would stop!

We saw a graphic example of this after the terrorist attacks on September 11. None of us ever imagined that the United States would be able to clear its skies of all airplanes that quickly. It is amazing what fear can do following the moment of attack. Then the fear lingered, causing a huge drop in airline ticket sales.

After an assault, we no longer have any illusions of safety. We no longer have the luxury of thinking "it won't happen to us." We know it can. According to Janoff-Bulman, there is evidence that the more invulnerable one feels to misfortune prior to victimization, the more difficult the psychological adjustment will be afterward.

Following an assault, we have also learned the dreadful truth that we cannot identify a "murderer" or an "assailant" beforehand. After the terrorist attacks someone said, "The terrorists were living in our apartment house, and we didn't know they were terrorists." The fact that people with evil intent could not be identified beforehand was the basis for her fear.

Because human nature is unpredictable, there is no way that we can prevent what happened from happening again. We know that there aren't prison walls high enough or a criminal justice system strong enough to keep us safe from someone who intends to harm us.

In the face of this lingering fear, some of us will insist on bandaid symbols of safety. We might want to keep our lights on, build a fence around our yard, insist on not being left alone, become very protective of other members of the family. (Some families will never sleep in their bedrooms again; they fall asleep in the living room in front of the television.) Many can't watch violence on television or even watch the news. We often develop a generalized fear of impending doom. We might experience anxiety attacks, irritability, flashbacks, and numbness. These are all normal reactions to violence.

Frank Parkinson says that re-experiencing the trauma and the initial fear is a normal part of trauma. "The trauma-inducing event can be experienced again hours, days, months, or even years later. The feelings and emotions which were generated at the time of the crisis can be felt as if they were happening now, in the present. The sensations and emotions felt at the time of the incident have been repressed and pushed down into the depths of the mind, but emerge and come to the surface when least expected."

Unchecked fear can show itself in severe long-term physical, mental and emotional stress.

Physically, this new level of fear can alter our entire lifestyle drastically and permanently. Often victims will complain about having trouble sleeping, eating, and concentrating. Not being able to carry out these normal daily functions can eventually leave us dependent on our friends, family or state. We might begin to suffer from illnesses as our body begins to complain about the abnormal stress.

Mentally, being on constant alert creates a very tired nervous system. If this heightened fear reaches paranoia levels it can restrict our freedom and create conflict in our families. For example, victims of a break and enter crime might find it difficult to leave their house after their home has been violated. Parents who have suffered the loss of one child to murder might impose unreasonable curfews on their teenagers which can result in family conflict.

Emotionally, extreme anxiety can rob us of the ability to relax and not being able to relax can inhibit us from enjoying playful times that refresh us. Victims often have a difficult time conceptualizing and planning a vacation because of this. Eventually if we can't enjoy ourselves or those who are close to us, we will find all of life less satisfying. If we are filled with anxiety we will not be able to fully participate in an intimate moment with our partners.

Judith Herman, who is considered one of the leading writers on trauma, says in her book, *Trauma and Recovery*, "Traumatic reactions occur when action is of no avail. When neither resistance nor escape is possible, the human system of self-defence becomes overwhelmed and disorganized. Each component of the ordinary response to danger, having lost its utility, tends to persist in an altered and exaggerated state long after the actual danger is over."

I remember the fear in our lives after Candace's body was found. Because we have never found out who took Candace, we have had no way of containing our fear. Who did it? Why?

When our second daughter was old enough to attend high school and planned to attend the same school Candace attended, suddenly I could not face the possibility that she would be walking along the same road at the same time that Candace walked home the day she disappeared. I just couldn't go there. I could not live through that. So we decided to move. It wasn't a good time to move. We certainly didn't spend a lot of time thinking about the place we were going to move into. We just moved. There is nothing rational about the fear we experience.

Pseudo fear might have a place in the fun rides at carnivals and horror movies. But when fear becomes a reality, fear can be completely incapacitating.

"No man can hide from his own fears.
For they are part of him and
they will always know where he is hiding."
—Anonymous

Underlying Reasons for Terror Trauma

Life is our most precious possession. The natural death of a
friend can be traumatizing because we have to face the issues of
our own mortality and our own vulnerabilities. This natural fear is
heightened when we face the possibilities that we can experience
violence, murder and the threat of injury at the hands of another
human being.

**The realization we are living in a hostile world and that some-
one wants to harm us is traumatizing.** "Victimization represents
a dramatic recognition that people can be malevolent and hurt
others. Suddenly, the entire world of people becomes suspect.
Who can be trusted? Who is completely safe?" write Andrea Medea
and Kathleen Thompson in their book *Against Rape.*

The inexplicable nature of violence of any kind terrifies us.
We gain a great deal of security and safety from our belief that
there is a cause and effect rule of law. Knowing the relationship
between events gives us a sense of control, prevention, and security. When we encounter a senseless act of murder and violence,
it destroys the security of this illusion of cause and effect. We can
no longer believe something bad won't happen to us.

We fear pain. Murder is usually violently inflicted by gunshot
wounds, beatings, and stabbings. Pain is associated with any
assault. All of this terrifies us. The degree of trauma that we
experience when someone is murdered can correlate to the
degree of violation the body of our loved one suffered before
death. We fear the pain our loved one went through. We fear the
pain of the memories. The images of violence can run through our
minds over and over again, like television reruns.

We fear losing control. Murder, violence and intimidation
rip the controls out of our hands. The fact that the police are in
control of the investigation and the media take control of the story
of our lives doesn't help us establish controls in our lives. We feel
powerless.

Even if we can resolve things in our mind, our body remembers. Our body can respond to trauma triggers without us understanding why. We can experience memory flashes that take control of our body and our lives at the most inopportune times.

We can't easily confront this fear. We could understand the rush of fear if we were to meet a grizzly bear on the path. We would deal with it and be personally involved with the solution. A serious crime, even a simple break and enter, can produce some of the same fear reactions as meeting a bear. Yet, because we call the police who deal directly with the offender, we are sidelined and are often not directly involved with solving the situation. Because of this we often have no way of confronting our fears. Murder or violence replayed in our minds is never over and therefore the fear is never contained.

The worst fear is that we will not be able to prevent it from happening again. A guest on the Oprah Winfrey television show who had lived in the same building as two of the terrorists kept saying, "I lived so close to evil, but didn't know it." The fact that we can't predict an act of violence makes us feel guilty and powerless. If cold-blooded killers can look exactly as we do, there is no way of identifying murderers. How can we feel safe if we can't identify our enemies before they act?

"We cannot escape fear.
We can only transform it
into a companion that accompanies us....
Take a risk today —
one small or bold stroke
that will make you feel great
once you have done it."

—Susan Jefferson

Consequences of Terror Trauma

Even though our fears are valid, the tragedy of murder is compounded when the fears rob us of enjoying our lives.
It becomes a real challenge to create safety for ourselves again.

Jerilyn Ross, author of the book, *Triumph over Fear,* says it best. "Over the years I have been repeatedly saddened by the stories of wasted years, wasted lives... of people trapped in fear."

The consequences of not dealing with this fear can be enormous. The trauma triggers that victims experience can be as traumatic as the actual event. Being in this constant state of terror and fear over an extended period of time can lead to post traumatic stress disorder which can result in severe physical deterioration. If the terror produces panic, the fear is compounded by developing into a fear of fear itself.

Bottling up reactions can be the worst response. It can be like trying to keep the cork on a fizzing bottle of champagne. As Frank Parkinson writes, "Sooner or later the champagne will explode and blow the cork high into the air. Human emotions can be the same."

Confronting our Terror Trauma

Judith Herman says that we need to recreate safety to recover from trauma. "Establishing safety begins by focussing on control of the body and gradually moves outward toward control of the environment. Issues of bodily integrity include attention to basic health needs, regulations of bodily functions such as sleep, eating and exercise, management of post-traumatic symptoms and control of self-destructive behavior.... Because no one can establish a safe environment alone, the task of developing an adequate safety plan always includes a component of social support."

In order for us to feel safe again, these fears need to be acknowledged, honored and respected as being real and valid. We need to identify the source of our fears and then begin working with them, examining them, dealing with them, and eventually modifying them so that they don't hinder us from continuing our lives.

Realize that fear causes your body stress and that you will need to will yourself to relax. Remember to take a few deep breaths to relax yourself throughout the day. Good nutrition, adequate sleep and moderate exercise always help.

Create routine. So often when we feel stress, we want to pamper ourselves and not do anything, yet our bodies and our emotions will feel more secure in the comfort of our usual rhythm of life. Our children feel especially safe when life has a routine, when things are predictable.

Recognize your stress triggers. When you do have a flashback, give yourself time and space. Realize that you won't be able to function in peak form for a while.

In the case of trauma images, find someone you feel safe with and go back to those pictures and see them as part of a slide show. Start to insert happy pictures alongside the trauma images.

There is no complete cure for fears. But we can make them work for us rather than against us.

Considerations

Talk about your fears. Don't be ashamed of them. Acknowledge them.

Inform yourself. Gather information about the things you fear. Identify your enemy. Often by isolating your fears and analyzing them, they will lose their power over you.

Do something about your fears. Create a plan of safety. Confronting your fears needs to become as routine as your trauma.

Identify your trauma triggers. Usual trauma triggers are anniversaries, birthdays, holidays, (especially any significant holiday), revisiting places that hold memories and certain friends who remind you of your loved one or who remind you of the offender. Anticipate these trauma triggers.

Look after your body. Eat nutritious food. Take the time to do moderate exercise. Take time for yourself. Know that your fears have a real impact on your body. Take control of your body. Slow it down through breathing exercises or walking.

Revisit your values and your basic assumptions about life.
Do you need to readjust your world view? Are your ideals of safety realistic? Do you need to come to terms with your fear of death? Take the time to find your inner peace. What are some things you value that no one can take away from you? Build on these values. Find your strengths and build on them.

Prepare yourself for times of anticipated trauma. In ancient days, tribes getting ready to fight participated in elaborate rituals that helped them overcome their fears and feel brave again. After September 11, the people in the United States did some of this. They used their national anthem to give them courage; they waved their flags, and they spoke words of encouragement to each other. Find out what makes you feel strong and what songs inspire you. Surround yourself with things that make you feel safe.

If you feel stuck in severe terror trauma, you might need to seek professional help.

"Every waking moment is filled with the pain of that moment. Every night is filled with terror and with fear."

—Ann Weems

"Make friends with your fears."
—Yvette Berube whose brother was murdered

CHAPTER 5: WITHDRAWING TO MAKE SENSE OF IT

Shattered

A WEEK AFTER THE TERRORIST ATTACKS, the front page of our local newspaper showed people in tears. Some of them were clutching roses, some carnations. Some were hugging their friends; others were sitting quietly with their heads in their hands.

The following days, the pictures of mourning were replaced by pictures of a country reestablishing its national pride. In one edition, I noticed the slogan "God Bless America" across the entire front page. The colors that were predominant, even in Canadian newspapers during this time, were the red, white, and blue of the flag.

Inside these newspapers were many references to God and prayer. Prayer services were held in Washington.

Crime on a personal level has some of these same dynamics. After the crime, we are stunned into silence. Characteristic of people in grief following terrible violence is the "trance-like stare" that gives the appearance of being haunted. We need time to retreat into ourselves, regroup, recoil, and deal with private issues. We need to decide how to deal with the loss. We might need to talk to our close friends and our God during this time.

Second Stage — Retreat

There is a natural pause after a violent act. "The survivor withdraws to make sense out of the tragedy. There is no emotional energy to direct to others," writes Lula Redmond in her book, *Surviving: When Someone You Loved Was Murdered.* "The state of the survivor is analogous to that of a wounded animal who withdraws to lick one's wounds, retreating deep in the forest of one's own self-imposed isolation." The emotion is one of overwhelming pain and suffering.

Some other reasons for this time of retreat may be that we are too vulnerable to deal with the crime. The child who has been sexually abused might need to grow up into an adult before he or she can confront the crime.

The police need time to investigate the crime; this forces victims to be sidelined for a time. Our friends might need to put the crime on hold, return to work, and carry on with their lives as they wait for the trial which can take up to one or two years for a serious crime. We ourselves might need to put the crime on hold for a time. Sometimes it is easier to retreat than deal with the crime. We might prefer to deny or avoid dealing with the impact of the crime. It is easier to repress it. The negative aspect remaining in retreat mode too long is that we might need the offender apprehended and sentenced in order to feel safe. We might need to have preventative measures taken, such as a denunciation of the crime in a public court. Seldom does the timing of this stage of the Crime Victim Detour coincide exactly with our needs.

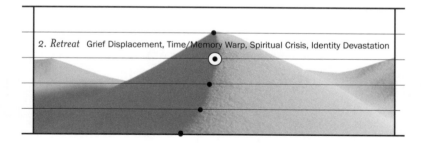

2. Retreat Grief Displacement, Time/Memory Warp, Spiritual Crisis, Identity Devastation

Not only is our outside world shattered, our inside world has also been demolished. We are facing emotional losses, disorientation, questions regarding our world view and lack of confidence. We will be exploring these four issues in this next stage.

Grief displacement Since the grieving process is one of vulnerability, pain and sadness, it is natural for us to replace the grieving emotion with anger or numbness. At a time when we need to mourn, the offender often intrudes into our quiet time.

Time/memory warp The trauma of violence can disrupt our ability to reason, concentrate, remember or manage our time. Because the inner controls of our minds are overwhelmed and disoriented, the trauma can rob us of our ability to learn, dream creatively or plan in advance.

Spiritual crisis An encounter with violence will often leave us feeling insecure about our spiritual beliefs and our understanding of a Higher Power. The criminal violation of society's moral code and social contract calls into question the order and control of the entire universe. We wonder "why?"

Identity devastation Violence changes us. Our world is turned upside down. Our values, interests, lifestyle, attitudes and habits can be so drastically altered that we become unrecognizable to ourselves and others. Society's tendency to "blame the victim" can also cause us to question our identity.

Needing Help

During this time, most of us aren't functioning very well.
We might be absent minded, emotional, unfocussed, overly sensitive, and confused.

I remember how I'd try to clean the house, and then right in the middle of a task, I would wander off to make a telephone call. There were times when I didn't want to leave the house, times when I put coffee into the coffee maker but not the water. I didn't feel like making any meals. We need very practical helps at this time. We might need someone to go grocery shopping for us, clean the house or sit with the children.

If you find a true friend during this time, you are very fortunate. Treasure those who help you. Be open with them about your needs. Don't be afraid to seek professional help if you need to.

At the time of Candace's disappearance, we had wonderful friends who formed a "search committee" and who continued to support us even after Candace was found. We are still grateful to them.

Discerning Help

One word of caution. Be aware that some of the people offering assistance may have motives for doing so that will interfere with their being helpful to you.

Many times, victims have complained about being taken advantage of during this time by either very well-meaning friends or relatives, or not so well-meaning acquaintances. Some people have been hurt and judged by friends and drained of energy by others; some have become dependent on professionals. Some were blatantly "stolen" from; others were betrayed.

The best way to remain balanced is to have a few people helping you with different areas of your life. Consult widely. Get second opinions. The best relationships are those that are mutually beneficial. On the other hand, no friend is perfect. A balance of imperfect friends is better than no friends at all.

Be aware that there are at least five different kinds of helpers who might offer to help you. Charlotte Hullinger, co-founder of Parents of Murdered Children identified three. I've added a few to the list:

The rescuer helper. They want to be the hero. Rather than listen, they make suggestions that encourage dependency. It is hard for them to see people in pain and feeling helpless; so they want to fix things.

The hostile helper. They want to find a cause for the crime. They may want to blame you. They speak with judgment and try to distance themselves from your victimization. They are afraid. They claim it would never happen to them.

The helpless helper. Their own needs overwhelm them. They seek you out, not to help you but because they want you to listen to their story. These are the energy-drainers.

The opportunistic helper. They aren't motivated by caring, but by greed. They see an opportunity to either feather their own nest or steal some of the spotlight from you. These are people who make their living off victims.

The agent helper. These caregivers are loyal to the organization they work for. If they are working for the criminal justice system, they might be more loyal to the offender than they are to you. They might come alongside with the pretense of consoling and comforting you, but in fact they will put subtle pressure on you to cooperate, to remain silent, to accommodate and "to not make any waves."

The martyr helper. These caregivers are always there to assist and do. However, they then complain to others about all they have to do for you. If these comments get back to you, they add to your pain. It's all about their image of themselves.

You can probably add others to this list. You might even experience some who are a blend of two or more.

The main point of these descriptors is not for you to avoid everyone with any unsavory motives (there is actually no one who is the perfect helper) but to be aware of their flaws and to trust them accordingly.

*"In some ways you never
'get over' a significant loss.
It inevitably changes you.
You can only choose whether
that change is for the better."*
—Karen Katafiasz

3	GRIEF DISPLACEMENT

Hidden Treasure

ROCKY STAGGERED UP THE STAIRS FROM THE basement and sprawled on our kitchen floor, unable to get up. He wailed in pain.

Rocky was our rather nondescript, grey and black pet cat that we had adopted when our son was about five years old. My husband and I considered him a great investment since he seemed to entertain the children but leave us alone.

Now as he wailed in pain, we wrapped him up in a blanket and took him to an emergency veterinary hospital. The diagnosis was that Rocky could have one of five diseases. Three of these diseases were leukemia-like and terminal. The other two diseases were treatable but had a high risk of failure. To find out which disease it was would require that he be tested. These tests would cost $300.

My husband and I come from farming backgrounds where pets are inexpensive mousing devices, or a child's toy. To consider spending hundreds of dollars on a cat was unthinkable. In addition, the cat was aging.

But then we looked at our son who was thirteen at the time. Tears were rolling down his cheeks. Without words, he pleaded with us to save his cat. Somehow the two had become one.

We had no choice. We laid down the $300 and desperately hoped that the cat would live. Suddenly, what we had thought was just an ordinary animal living with us in our house had become extremely valuable. Somehow our son's happiness and emotional well-being were tied up with the cat. Ours was tied up with our son.

Our cat lived and continues to be loved.

Mourning and Grieving the Loss

We become attached to things we love. On national holidays we celebrate love for our country. We have birthdays, anniversaries, memorial days — they all bring us together under the banner of love.

We have a right to be attached. In our *Canadian Charter of Rights and Freedoms* we are promised that everyone in our country has "the right to life." And most of us take that to mean not only "life" but "a life." We not only want to breathe and survive, we also want the freedom to love, to choose our own destinies and to cherish things that belong to us.

A British psychiatrist, John Bowlby, devoted much of his professional career to studying the area of attachment and loss. He says that we become attached to anything that ensures that our needs will be met. The best illustration of this is the attachment of a baby to its parents, to its mother in particular. The mother represents survival to the baby. We are attached to everything that sustains us.

Abraham Maslow in his study of the hierarchy of our needs writes that our first basic needs are physiological. We first need to have our physical needs for food, water and safety met. If these needs are filled, then we will seek to have our need for belonging met. To feel loved and respected are also basic emotional needs for survival. Our children, our home, our friends, our extended family, our community and our work are not extensions of our lives, they are our lives.

Just because we don't always see the attachment between a father and son, doesn't mean it doesn't exist. In many ways it exists in the same way that an arm is attached to the shoulder. To sever an arm results in tremendous pain. To sever a relationship is the same. If we lose anything to which we are attached we will feel incredible pain.

Many parents of murdered children describe a pain in the heart similar to that of a heart attack or a stab in the heart. But when they went to see their physician, there was no visible wound. The pain of losing a child is as real as that.

We would find it unimaginable to expect a person with a severed arm to continue functioning as normal. We would know that they need a time in bed, somewhere to mend and gain strength. We would know that they would need a rehabilitation program.

An aboriginal elder once said that animals knew that they needed to retreat to heal for a time after being wounded. It was only humans who kept running when they were hurt — bleeding in public. In the past, there was a better understanding of this need for a time of mourning. For example, after a woman lost her husband, she would retreat into an official year of mourning.

The pain of a wounded heart takes time to heal. When we are in mourning we need a safe place to cry, to remember, to nurse our wound, to contemplate life and muster the courage to live again.

As Lula Redmond has written, "We grieve for our losses, whether they are the loss of a treasured timepiece, loss of a camera, loss of our possessions through purse snatching, loss of a home and possessions from a fire, loss of a loved relationship by estrangement or divorce, or the ultimate loss of a loved one by death. There are multiple reactionary behaviors, physical, emotional, cognitive and social in each situation. When it is the irreplaceable loss of a human being, the loss of a person for whom we have an emotional attachment, we experience multiple normal reactions."

During this time of mourning we will need time to do the tasks of mourning which are to detach from that which we have lost, face the finality of the loss, experience the painful emotions of loss, remember and ritualize the memory of the love, learn to live with the loss, and fill the loss with something new.

Mourning is characteristically a time of low energy with sadness and minor symptoms of depression. It is a time when we are highly sensitive and vulnerable. It is a time of ritual, and a time of vulnerability where we take tentative steps. We might take two steps into the past then three baby steps into the future. We mull, we process, we weep, we talk, we visit the grave site, we pray, we cry, we light candles. We might find that there are times of confusion in our adjustment — times when we can't remember what we had for breakfast because we are absorbed in our grief. There might be times when we don't care what happens in the outside world, times when we don't care what happens to us, times when we just want to withdraw. We feel vulnerable. We fear losing more. We fear the intensity of grief feelings. Grief is rarely considered a good time or one that is easy, successful or full of creative energy.

But mourning is necessary. Mourning is meant to take the painful endings and losses and slowly turn them into good memories. After a time of mourning, the memories of our loved ones should come back and comfort us, energize us, and give us meaning. We want and need positive memories. It is called life experience. At the end of our lives, it is the good memories (which will all contain some element of loss in them) that will satisfy and sustain us.

GRIEF DISPLACEMENT

Yet the first reaction to something as horrific as a death resulting from violence is grief displacement, the constant disruption of our mourning process. For obvious reasons, this element applies particularly to homicide. The loss of a loved one, whether a friend, husband, neighbor, child or public figure, can lead to a grief that is complicated because of the violence of the death.

Losing a loved one through homicide is one of the most traumatic experiences that an individual can face because it is not only the person who is taken from us but everything that person represents. After experiencing a violent crime, many victims talk about a sense of having been changed from the person they used to be.

They experience:
- Loss of control over their lives
- Loss of independence
- Loss of friends' support or social standing
- Loss of sense of safety, security or well-being
- Loss of spirituality
- Loss of trust
- Loss of beauty
- Loss of financial security

There are so many other insidious ways that murder or a violent act can continue to rob us of enjoying our lives.

We once renovated a house that had experienced a fire. We thought we would only have to fix the hole where the fire had burned through the roof, but it wasn't that easy. The fire had raced along the wires inside the walls and maliciously started to feed on the wood in the most unlikely places. The smell of burned wood was pervasive. The fire had stained everything with black soot that wouldn't wash off. It had weakened the frame of the house and totally destroyed the plaster. The water that had been used to put out the fire had done nothing but create more damage. The fire damage was permanent.

Violence not only destroys the life of our loved one, it also races through our own lives and eats at the trust, the sense of safety and well-being. It races through the community. And murder isn't the only way to destroy someone. There are many ways to rob someone of life. Physical abuse, slander, rape, trashing a home, stealing money – all of these forms of violence can lead to disabling someone from continuing to live his or her life. These losses too need to be mourned.

Mary Bessette says it best in her interview with *Pathways*. In describing the aftermath of murder she says, "You've been totally robbed, you know. Your life is kind of taken away. Total happiness is never going to happen again." Then she told us how, after the murder of her son, she stopped taking family pictures. She notes that this is a loss that people don't often think about but one that is very significant.

After a murder act, the mourning process can be deliberately repressed until the trial has taken place — which may be one to two years later. Since some issues of murder are never resolved, it is not uncommon for grief to be permanently lost in the aftermath of murder.

It might not be safe to mourn. Many victims talk about not being able to be sad, or not being able to cry. They can feel only anger, fear or numbness. They feel that crying is a sign of vulnerability. They can't afford to be vulnerable when they are still experiencing so much fear and anger.

Some victims talk about not being able to disassociate the offender from the victim. In that case, their process remains focussed on a justice issue alone.

We all react differently. Some victims can't cry. Some can't stop crying. Some will avoid any talk about their loved ones. Some won't stop talking about them.

Gwen Thiessen, whose niece was killed, didn't have a memorial service for her until after the murder conviction — six years following her disappearance. While this feels natural, six years is a long time to have grief build.

Sylvia Isaak, who lost her mother to murder, says, "It's like things build up. Especially when you speak of murder and you're talking for two or three hours with the investigation team. And they're telling you who the prosecutor will be and what they're going to do with the case and when they think it's going to come to trial. You talk to the media, go over the funeral, and when all is said and done — I just miss my mom."

I remember so vividly the day of my daughter's funeral; what should have been a time of sadness and mourning was almost a public spectacle. The media wanted to be present and, because they had been so helpful to us during our six-week search, we wanted them to be there to thank the public for us. The police escorted us and protected us from the crowds. I'll never forget seeing three officers standing in the swirling snow and saluting Candace, as we drove by. After the funeral, the police took the guest book. Even though all of it was necessary and expected under the circumstances, it still intruded on the moment of mourning.

Underlying Reasons for Grief Displacement

In the aftermath of murder, we not only lose our loved one, we also lose our sense of safety, our privacy, our friends, our own story, our place in society, and control of our own lives. Many of these losses can be life-changing.

One woman said, "I didn't just lose my fiancé. I lost my entire dream for the future. I lost my sense of well-being and of safety. I lost my faith in humanity."

Janice Lord in her book, *No Time For Goodbyes,* describes grief spasms for people experiencing trauma. "Survivors are often surprised to find that in the midst of a series of good days something may bring on a spasm of grief."

In Lord's book *Beyond Sympathy* she writes, "It is important to understand that the sudden killing of a loved one is an extremely draining and compelling experience. Many feel almost driven to 'do something' although they don't know what. They cry out for justice as a way to make sense of a senseless act. Helping them to obtain copies of police reports, investigations, and autopsies can facilitate understanding. Obtaining materials about the criminal justice system and criminal code books from a university library can be helpful too."

Lula Redmond in her book, *Surviving: When Someone You Love Was Murdered,* writes, "There are varied reasons for the delayed, exaggerated and complicated bereavement reactions experienced by survivors of homicide. The lack of familiarity with and support by law enforcement, the criminal justice system and media intrusion lead to bereavement complications. The delays in resolution of the murder conviction, lack of adequate punishment for the crime, and lack of acknowledgment by society heightened the feelings of loss and control."

The natural inclination for all of us is to avoid places of pain and uncomfortableness. We can be easily distracted from what we need to do. The aftermath of murder provides us with many legitimate distractions. Yet, we need to remember that if the mourning process is suppressed, the entire healing process can also be sabotaged.

The intensity of the emotions might be so overwhelming that we feel we can't be in control of our feelings; so we prefer to repress them. They are called grief spasms. Since a murder is so public, the time of mourning can also feel very public. This can make us reluctant to venture out into public for fear that we will "lose control."

The continuing presence of an offender (dead, alive, or unknown) can also stifle the grieving process. The rituals of mourning and the eulogizing of the victim or loss can feel like a judgment on the act of murder and the offender. Often pastors and well-meaning friends will focus on the need for harmony and peace in the community and talk about forgiveness at the time of the funeral. Yet grief demands that the loss of the murdered loved one should receive full attention. A good funeral and a healthy expression of mourning can be the first necessary acts of justice making. It is a natural way of re-establishing society's broken moral code by saying that violence, in another person and in ourselves, is always wrong.

The sadness characteristic of a mourning period can feel very vulnerable and vulnerability can feel very unsafe in the face of murder. Sadness and pain can easily be replaced with the more empowering emotions of fear or anger. Hysterical laughter can be a substitute for crying.

During the grieving process, the attention given to the crime, the violent images and the offender can overshadow the memory of our loved one. It becomes difficult to separate our loved one from the presence of the violence. The investigation, the trial, the police presence can all disrupt the natural flow of grief.

Investigators and other justice professionals can intimidate us by insisting on secrecy and confidentiality prior to the trial. We might feel that since we need to keep some secrets, we should remain completely silent and in this way the secrecy can inhibit our grief. We need to remember that normal grief expression will not distract from the justice process.

Losses in serious crime are often compounded by many other losses. There is the loss of a loved one, but there is the loss of safety, loss of trust in human kind, loss of privacy, loss of control of our story and loss of sense of family. There is often a loss of job or a job change that can cause tremendous financial loss. There is a great loss in the sense of physical well-being.

"Respect the power of grief."
—Karen Katafiasz

Consequences of Displaced Grief

Grief cannot be easily put on a shelf. If it is, one of the consequences is that it will surface at the worst time — just as fear and anger do. For example, we will break into tears at an inappropriate moment.

Since grief manifests itself as a low energy time of mourning and healing, this low energy can revisit us years later. Often those who take on the role of caring for the entire family will begin to grieve when everyone else is finished. They will suddenly not be able to carry on working, cleaning the house or whatever they usually do, and no one understands that it is simply their time to grieve.

Unacknowledged grief can manifest itself in some of the same symptoms as trauma: irritability, emotional instability, and anger. Judith Herman in her book *Trauma and Recovery* writes, "Atrocities, however, refuse to be buried. Equally as powerful as the desire to deny atrocities is the conviction that denial does not work. Folk wisdom is filled with ghosts who refuse to rest in their graves until their stories are told. Murder will out."

Unexpressed grief can keep us stuck. If we avoid the memories of our loved one too soon and move on too quickly, the memories can take on a grotesque distortion later on and haunt us as flashbacks or anxiety attacks.

On the other hand, it is easy to be caught up in creating the "right way of doing mourning." I know that lighting candles is in vogue right now — but some of us don't feel comfortable doing that. We might visit the grave site. Some of us prefer to do our memorializing through writing. Pressure to conform does not help the process. Whatever process we choose has to have integrity; otherwise it becomes another burden with which to deal. We will never do it right, so we should give up that expectation.

Grieving the Loss: Mourning the Memory

I remember hearing someone say that we have all been given a few buckets that we must fill up with tears. My mother didn't cry during Candace's funeral or at the time of my brother-in-law's death. She was a calm, composed presence throughout, except that she often said she didn't understand why she couldn't cry. Now, years later, she is crying. Mourning takes on different forms. But we need to mourn all the losses we suffer in order to feel the pain, to cleanse and heal our souls.

These are the tasks of grieving:

Dissociate the loss from the crime. The violence, the police investigation and the criminal justice process can be a welcome distraction from the reality of losing someone we love.

Face the finality of the loss. It is common for the body and the mind to continue to fantasize that the loss isn't real. We yearn and ache for those we've lost. The criminal justice process can give the false hope that it will provide closure in a trial and that somehow a sense of justice will be restored.

Acknowledge and experience the pain. It is instinctive to avoid pain. It is so much easier for grief to be replaced by anger, the more empowering emotion. We need to mourn, to feel the pain, to relax in the pain.

Eulogize the loss. The memory of the loss needs to find a place. It is important to talk about the loss and the value of the loss. The larger the loss, the more we need to remember and memorialize the loss.

Learn to live with the loss. Life does go on even after a horrendous event such as murder. The details in life will suddenly seem unimportant but they are important. It will take time to rehabilitate and to carry on with the mundane routine of life. It is important to make the changes, to adjust, and to try to go through the motions of routine and life.

Fill the vacuum left by the loss. Nature abhors a vacuum and will fill it. The emptiness of the loss will be filled. Be proactive about it. Make a conscious effort to fill your life with good things.

Considerations

Take the time to grieve your loss. Collect poems about grief or songs about grief, and give yourself a time out to appreciate them. And cry. Manage your grief times. As you continue to uncover other losses, you might need to take time to mourn them also.

You might want to reclaim the site of the violence by holding a private memorial service there with an even smaller group of friends with whom you feel safe. Some examples of "reclaiming ceremonies" have been a healing circle, a charismatic exorcism ceremony, or a prayer service. One woman went to the place alone, lit candles and cried. Others have reclaimed the site with a wreath of flowers. One washed the room with bleach. We all need to do it differently.

A memorial service is extremely important in helping you make the necessary adjustments to your loss. If you are memorializing a loved one, make sure the service focusses on the memory of your loved one, celebrating their goodness, smiling at their humanness. This is the time to sing their favorite songs and cry. It is a time to allow others to tell their stories of the "good times" and hint at a few of the "other times." You will need the memory of a good service to comfort you during the hard times ahead.

However, remember you can't ignore the fact of murder in a memorial service, otherwise it will have an "unreal" quality about it that hinders the expression of genuine sorrow. Somewhere in the service you might want to include a very brief but succinct report on what has happened to date in the case. This is also an opportunity to correct any untrue aspects of the story that are already circulating in the community. You can help create a climate of justice by starting to tell the truth of how you feel.

Some ministers will be tempted to use this public platform to further their own agendas which might be to evangelize to the community or to bring peace to the community. Some of them ask for prayers for the offender. If this is offensive to you, let them know in advance what your wishes are. Be clear about the boundaries.

If there are public issues surrounding the death of your loved one, you might want to hold two services, a private one for the family and another one for the public.

Memorialize your loss. You might want to plant a tree, collect a pile of rocks, or write a letter to someone about your loss. In murder you might do this by publishing a picture of your loved one in a local newspaper or in selected magazines. Create a scrapbook about the funeral. Fill a book with notes of sympathy. Put the effort into creating a lovely headstone.

If there is an important event coming up, like a wedding or Christmas, light a candle for your loved one during that time so no one forgets about what happened or feels guilty about not saying anything. Talking about it is a way of freeing everyone to talk about the tragedy or loss. Say just a few words of explanation.

One year after the murder have another private memorial with some friends.

Journal about your grief.

Don't be afraid to mention your feelings when it is appropriate in a conversation. Share your grief. Often others around you will be hesitant to open up the subject of your grief for fear of hurting you more, so it is often up to you to initiate conversations.

"It's the neverness that is so painful.
Never again to be here with us —
never to sit with us at table,
never to travel with us, never to laugh with us,
never to cry with us....

All the rest of our lives we must live
without him.
Only our death can stop
the pain of his death."

—Nicholas Wolterstorff

"The tears...streamed down,
and I let them flow as freely
as they would, making of them
a pillow for my heart.
On them it rested."

—Augustine

| 4 | TIME/MEMORY WARP |

Time Capsule

IT WAS LIKE OUR OWN FAMILY TIME CAPSULE. When my elderly parents moved into a personal care home, my four siblings and I had to sort through the house where they had spent the last thirty years of their lives.

We knew our father was an amateur historian who had documented and collected memorabilia and pictures of our cultural heritage. In our family room he had built a large wooden picture album that stood in the corner and glass cabinets along the walls that displayed old china and tools my grandfather had made as well as scrapbooks of important immigration pictures.

But we had never guessed how historically aware my mother was. As we went through the boxes we found that she too had been a collector, storing family memorabilia that documented our lives. She had preserved every letter we wrote, every gift we gave, and every card we sent.

As we went through the house, we were impressed again and again at how orderly they were with their belongings. In my father's workroom every tool had a place; most of them hung carefully on the wall. Every container was neatly labelled, and the large equipment was cleaned and ready to use. My mother's kitchen was the same way. Her recipes were all filed away with small notes as to how good the recipe was, on what date she had made it and to whom she had served it.

It brought back so many memories of how they had lived their lives. The house was never messy. Mom always put everything away that she used, cleaned the house every Saturday, washed the clothes on Monday. A former mechanic, my father maintained the car religiously. In the car trunk we found tools for every kind of car breakdown — and a box of cash — just in case. They were never unprepared.

It was no wonder that we remembered them as living a life of peace and harmony.

Life Experience

Memories are valuable life experience. When our experiences are well organized and labelled, they can become like tools that can be used efficiently and effectively. When we see a scissor near a toddler, we remove the scissor immediately. From past experience, we instinctively know that a scissor represents danger to the inexperienced. The past is valuable because it informs the present.

None of us is quite sure how our mind works. Unlike my parents' house, we can't see how we store things, label things or priorize in our minds, but we know that's what we do. We know when our minds are cluttered and when they feel clear and organized. We know that when our minds are busy puzzling over a difficult problem we don't function as well. We know our minds work best when we have control over our time.

Most of us can process a day's experience consciously before we fall asleep and allow our unconscious to do the rest while we sleep. All of our experiences need to be labelled and processed. We ask ourselves questions. Where should we file it? Under "danger?" Under "guilt?" If we've had an especially wonderful conversation with a friend, we might file it under "do again often."

But if we've had a particularly dreadful board meeting, it might take us a long time to sort through the discussion as to why it turned against us. We will need to answer the questions: Who supported me on that motion and who didn't? How could I have done it differently? If we can't understand it, we might sleep badly that night and need to talk to someone the next day to help us understand. It might take two or three days till we finally come to a resolution. If we can't solve the problem, we will uneasily put it into the file "hold to reconsider." Either way, we will resolve the problem or develop a plan of action.

As we get older, we are expected to have accumulated more and more of these life experience memories which allow us to process the day quickly and function more maturely and wisely.

Time/Memory Warp

4

At the most critical time in our lives, when we face the after-math of murder or any other serious crime, our minds are so traumatized we lose the ability to process what is happening to us.

Many victims describe this trauma as being unable to control their minds. Abtfam Kardiner described it in similar terms. "When a person is overwhelmed by terror and helplessness, the whole apparatus for concerted, coordinated and purposeful activity is smashed."

There might be too much information being thrown at us.

Spinning is one way for our minds to deal with this overload. We can't focus on one thought. The mind keeps reviewing every-thing at once. It becomes a torturous replay that can't be stopped. This kind of spinning can result in a constant need to tell the story indiscriminately, constant crying, or constant nervous energy. We saw this happening on September 11. We needed to watch the planes crash into the towers over and over again as we tried to make sense of what was happening.

Shutting down is another way to deal with information overload. Some describe this as sitting in a trauma trance for days. We can't deal with all the fear stimuli, the conflicting stories, the elusive facts, or the overwhelming flood of emotions. We are defeated before we begin. The only way we can handle it is to shut down. It's a way for the mind to protect us. Judith Herman writes in *Trauma and Recovery,* "This altered state of consciousness might be regarded as one of nature's small mercies, a protection against unbearable pain."

Constriction is another way to gain control of our trauma. We focus on one thing at a time. After September 11, a columnist in the *Winnipeg Free Press* headlined his column, "There is other stuff going on," then proceeded to say that September 11 "had not just taken over the front page of the world's newspapers but most of the inside pages as well." He then enumerated all the other important political events that had happened while our attention had been on the tragedy. Our focus on the terrorist attacks had excluded everything else.

This time/memory warp is really like having a clean desk one day, a normal life, and suddenly overnight, after murder has happened to someone we love, our desk is loaded with letters, notes, pictures. Our receptionist has tried to sort some of them and has labelled them from top priority to urgent. Every last piece of paper has "urgent" written on it. Everything we touch pertains to life and death issues in our lives. We work feverishly all day and all night. The next day we are given another load and it continues like this until our whole office is overwhelmed with "urgent."

When everything is ringing with alarms, a minor incident like brushing our teeth can suddenly be labelled with fear. It's as if the red ink of urgency spills onto everything. There is great danger during this time in labelling a minor experience and flagging it with traumatic emotions. Being unable to process or put the memories away in an orderly but accessible way leads to continuing disorganization. Everything remains on the desk till eventually there is no clear distinction between past, present and future.

Losing our ability to anticipate the future means that we can't plan. It takes good planning to budget, diet, organize a holiday. No future means we are susceptible to depression and may become suicidal.

When the present is interrupted by the unprocessed past, we suffer from intrusive memories, nightmares, flashbacks, anxiety attacks. We will find that we don't have enough memory for the details. We can't remember names. We can't remember what we did during the day. We are absorbed entirely by the trauma to the point where some people around us might call us "self absorbed." In this state, we have very little ability to empathize with others or listen to their stories. We can't concentrate. All we experience is the constant rerun of the violence that replays itself over and over and over again in our minds.

Some victims talk about a "noise" in their heads that is so loud they can't hear others speak. Their anxiety pounds in their ears.

Deborah KiiskeeN'tum describes how, after the murder of her stepson, she sat in her chair for a year and didn't move. It was as if she was in a trance.

"I remember being unable to write or read during that time after the murder. I couldn't remember names, couldn't remember addresses. Some days I couldn't even remember whether I had made my bed or not.

"It took a great deal of effort to listen to other people's stories because my own mind was so full of my own thoughts. It was almost as if I was living with a constant noise in my mind of my own train of thoughts."

Not being able to feel in control of our minds results in a tremendous loss of confidence.

Underlying Reasons for this Time/Memory Warp

Violence assaults us on every level. It is overwhelming. If we take any medication to see us through this time (even though it is prescribed by the doctor and for our own good), it will numb us for a while and contribute to this warp. If we self-medicate (drink too much or take sleeping pills), the escapism we need or seek will also contribute to this time/memory warp. When we are overwhelmed it is natural for our minds to shut down and give us space to recover somewhat before reality assaults us again.

Violence is interruptive and unexpected. We can't prepare for it. Someone doesn't come to our home with a Power Point presentation to give us an orderly report on what happened or how this is going to affect our lives or what to expect. For example, no matter how much we train police officers to give the most sensitive notification, there is always going to be a feeling of confusion, avoidance, and inability to comprehend. Violence never makes sense.

A violent crime presents us with an impossible learning curve at a time when our minds are often preoccupied with many personal issues. I remember logging thirty telephone calls one day when my daughter was missing. Calls from the public, the police, friends, and investigation tips were all coming in — and I didn't want to miss one of them. At the end of the day I couldn't remember who called or why. It was just too much.

We might be exposed to parts of life which we feel are inappropriate, distasteful and embarrassing. Most of us avoid what we consider to be the dangerous criminal element. Now we might find it in someone close to us, or at least in a group of people who intruded into our territory. We don't want to go there. We might hear and see things that we find repulsive.

Because of the confidential nature of the investigation, we are often denied access to the very knowledge we seek that might help us organize the information overload that happens in our minds. For instance, many of us organize our lives around our time schedules. Yet the scheduling of a trial can be complicated and elusive. We need information to understand a problem before we can solve it; yet professionals often refrain from giving straightforward answers for fear of hurting us.

"The most creative power given to the human spirit is the power to heal the wounds of a past it cannot change."
—Smedes

Consequences of Time/Memory Warp

**The trauma of violence can rob us of the ability to manage
our lives.** Our mind can feel out of control. Our experiences come
back to us in the guise of trauma triggers, intrusive memories,
nightmares, flashbacks or anxiety attacks. Intrusive memories are
memories of the murder that intrude into our everyday experiences
without warning, forcing us to relive all the trauma of the initial
impact of murder. These memories can ambush us at unexpected
times and send our bodies into the initial trauma stages.

The trauma of murder can erase the past. We might experience
an inability to remember things the way they were before the
murder. One father said that the murder of his daughter had
robbed him of everything, even the memory of his daughter.
Another parent of a murdered child said that she couldn't remember her daughter. She could only visualize her with the two men
who had killed her, standing on either side of her. Murder memories can be so traumatic they take over all past memories.

The trauma of murder can erase our short-term memory. We
lose memory capacity. Medical research has proven that people
who have experienced trauma lose the ability to remember details,
for a time at least. Many victims have said that this inability to use
their memory impaired their ability to work and carry on their everyday duties.

We lose our ability to plan for the future. To think of the future
we need a sense of hope, security and anticipation. If we can't feel
hope and joy, it is difficult to want to live and plan for tomorrow.
Many surviving victims harbor deep-seated death wishes. Having
no sense of future leaves us feeling as if we have no anchor, no
sense of direction. Time has become a burden, not a joy. We have
lost our ambition.

Murder becomes the defining moment of our lives. Murder
divides time. We begin to order our personal history around the
event and classify memories in terms of what happened before the
murder and what happened after.

The justice agenda can rob us of time, not only the actual time we spend sitting through a trial, but the time spent needing to process it afterwards. Tending to the details after a crime could become a full-time job. Processing the experience also takes time. We need to debrief.

The management of our own scheduling might slip. Since we've lost control over the timing of events, we might lose control over our own schedule. Time will leak. We might suddenly "be late" or "forget" an appointment. We might forget the date, the day of the week. People might complain that we are becoming forgetful.

We might even lose control of our bodies. Many of the stories I hear tell of someone experiencing stress, tensions and not knowing why till they look at the calendar and realize that they are two weeks away from the anniversary of the day that the murder happened. This can serve as a trauma trigger. Others find the month of November, before Christmas, laden with fear and dread. At first they might not understand why, but their body does.

"The only way I could deal with anything was to keep my mind as active as possible.... If I ever let myself, even for a second, slip into that dark hole then I couldn't make it stop."
—John Walsh

Managing the Time/Memory Warp

It is no easy task to manage the Time/Memory Warp.
We will need to be patient with ourselves. Time will help to heal.

Memories cannot be "willed" to do anything. Usually if they keep intruding on our lives, it means that there is something in the memory we need to resolve, fix or reframe. Instead of spending a great deal of energy trying to forget or avoid the trauma triggers, it's much more beneficial to do some intentional remembering. We need to take the time to sort through our memories and become comfortable with them.

We need to memorialize the good memories, process the bad memories, forgive ourselves for the guilty memories, address the injustice in some of them and become comfortable with all of them. This is no small task. It will take time, effort and careful thinking. Start with the easy memories — the good memories. We can hold onto our loved ones by talking about them, telling their jokes, looking at photographs and keeping them part of ourselves. This is the part of remembering we need to do.

Often there is no way to get around this memory warp without revisiting each event of the violence and putting a rational perspective on it. We need to replay the events and consider them carefully.

More than anything else, victims say that the simple passing of time will begin to help us sort through the mess in our minds.

Anticipate your trauma triggers, such as anniversaries, places, holidays or people. Being prepared for them by surrounding yourself with support will help to alleviate some of the stress of going through these events alone.

A certain amount of discipline will help. Try to consciously make an effort to do a few things that are "difficult." Don't do them all at the same time. Do one a day.

Just remember that for any of this to be helpful, we need to be authentic. "If amnesia is imposed, it won't hold," says Judith Herman.

Considerations

Don't be alarmed by your inability to control your thinking patterns. Remind yourself often that you aren't going crazy. Feeling different from your normal self is common after an assault or murder. It is an impossible task to sort it out all at once. Other victims who "look" as if they are all together most likely don't feel that way at all inside.

Prepare for trauma triggers as much as you can. Surround yourself with support. After the event, allow for some extra time to go through the "down" periods. Anticipate that you might feel tired and low after a stressful time. Take time out to recover.

Try to physically organize your traumatized mind. Get out an old scrapbook and paste all the newspaper clippings or pictures into it. Date the scrapbook and put it away. Any kind of simple organization of memories like this will help your mind to put things into order.

If you can't, get your friends to help you organize your life again. If you can't bring yourself to read the newspaper, ask your friends to clip the articles for you and keep them.

Don't hide your lapses of concentration. Be up front about them. Ask professional offices to call you to confirm appointments. Once others know how to help you, they will be glad to help.

Make lists. Write things down. Don't rely on your memory when you know that it might be faulty.

Take one day at a time. Try focussing on the present.

Talk to someone regularly to try and organize what is happening to you. If this isn't helping, seek professional help.

<table>
<tr><td>5</td><td>SPIRITUAL CRISIS</td></tr>
</table>

Chocolate and God

I'M NOT SURE HOW WE HAPPENED ON THE CONVERSATION. It was one of those magical evenings when dinner continued forever. The daylight faded unnoticed and we were still talking over a cup of strong coffee diluted with rich cream and some kind of decadent chocolate. A candle, dripping with wax, was burning in the centre of the table.

"How does God talk to us?"

"A small voice in my heart," said one guest. "If it tells me good things then I know it's God…."

"When I'm walking in the woods," said another.

"When I'm driving," said another. "Through music."

As we delved into the topic, the stories of experiencing God as a presence in our lives sent shivers through us. The conversation was intense, satisfying somehow.

"Why don't we want to talk about this more often?" I wondered out loud.

"It's a little scary," said one.

I wondered if everyone experiences God in the same way. The next day in a meeting with a writer who had been a self-professed atheist ever since I'd known him, I asked quite bluntly, "Does God talk to you?"

"Not God," he said with disgust. "I'm not religious."

"I know. But what about a higher power — a presence?" Then I waited, allowing the question to hang in the air. He contemplated it for a long moment. "When I was young, on the fields, I could see him in the prairie fire. Judgment."

"What about now?" I asked.

He shifted his eyes. "Much later after I had left the church, I realized a presence again. Now I think we're all connected," he says, "to the universe."

I waited for more.

"I have felt the presence, in my room, touching my shoulder, but I haven't paid much attention."

"Why not?"

"I think it needs to be learned — to listen....
But I haven't exercised this. I haven't listened much."

The next day I asked a friend (again we were having chocolate), "Does God talk to you?"

"Yes," she said. "When I see the northern lights dancing, I see God."

And that led into another wonderful discussion.

Spiritual Resources

One of the world's most mysterious paintings by French artist Paul Gauguin (1848-1903) depicts a group of people who stand or sit in a kind of timeless primeval world, arms lifted up to the sky. Gauguin painted the work toward the end of his life and considered it to be his masterpiece. The title of the painting is *Where do we come from? Where are we going?* — the eternal questions. We are spiritual beings who seek answers to these questions. Perhaps the most basic function of religion is to respond to our natural wonder about ourselves and the cosmos — the answer to the musings that happen when we admire a starry night.

Spirituality involves the recognition and acceptance of a Higher Power that is referred to in many ways: Tao, Great Mother, Divine Parent, Great Spirit, the Ultimate, the Absolute, the Divine, the Holy, Creator, Supreme Being, etc.

In his book, *Anxiety and Phobia,* Edmund Bourne explores how spirituality helps those suffering tremendous fear. He writes, "Spirituality involves the recognition and acceptance of a Higher Power beyond your own intelligence and will, with whom you can have a relationship."

Spiritual stirrings come when we experience an overwhelming feeling of awe as we fly over the snow-tipped peaks of the Rocky Mountains or stand in the middle of a prairie plain on a starry night. During these moments we feel the presence of something more powerful than ourselves.

Bourne also says, "This Higher Power can provide you with an experience of inspiration, joy, security, peace of mind, and guidance that goes beyond what is possible in the absence of the conviction that such a power exists."

Most of us want to know a loving God because, with God on our side, we would be assured of a beautiful harmony in our lives. We would have peace in the midst of danger, importance in the midst of defeat, and a sense of control and understanding when the world is falling down around us. This is what we look for in spirituality.

According to Michael Molloy in his book, *Experiencing the World's Religions,* "Religion helps us cope with death, and religious rituals offer comfort.... Religion offers companionship and the fulfillment of belonging to a group. Religion stimulates art, music, and dance, and has been the inspirational source of some of the most imaginative buildings in the world. Religion helps us relate to the unknown universe around us by answering the basic questions of who we are, where we come from, and where we are going."

SPIRITUAL CRISIS

5

Experiencing an assault violates all of our spiritual hopes and beliefs. This is why it is common to experience a spiritual crisis after an act of violence or murder. The most common questions we, as victims, ask are: Why my loved one? Why me? How could God let this happen to us? Who is in control of this world? And why is it such a mess?

Lula Redmond confirms this in her book, *Surviving: When Someone You Love Was Murdered.* "Murder is a violation of everything we have been taught to be right, honest, fair, or unexpected in life. (Murder) is a personal violation for each one's values and belief system. We value life and believe if we are good people, do not hurt others, and practice our Judeo-Christian beliefs, that life and God will be fair to us."

After the September 11 terrorist attacks, the Americans revisited their beliefs. Our local Saturday paper on September 15 had the bold headline, "God Bless America." The front full page picture featured a woman bowing her head in prayer with a red, white and blue U.S. flag draped beside her. On the second page was an article describing the national mourning ceremonies held at the Capitol. Together with President Bush, a Muslim cleric, Imam Muzammil H. Siddiqi, and the well-known Christian evangelist, Rev. Billy Graham, addressed the people. Graham was quoted as saying, "We're facing a new kind of enemy. We're involved in a new kind of warfare. And we need the spirit of God."

In the October *Time* magazine there was a story about a Manhattan minister, Gregory Keosaian. The Sunday following September 11 he was surprised that his church was full — and that the attendance has continued to grow. However he found that the sermon that he had prepared was not appropriate. Victims in a spiritual crisis didn't want the usual platitudes. "I learned the hard way," he said, "that the needs of the people are so intense at a time like this, so different, that there is almost nothing you can say or do that can be right."

Our spiritual crisis will be directly related to our beliefs. Most of us aren't even aware of our beliefs until something like this happens. Here are some common beliefs that are threatened when violence happens to us.

For those of us who believe strongly in a loving God, it will suddenly seem incomprehensible how a loving God, who is so powerful as to create this earth, could allow something as evil as murder or violence to happen to our loved one. The act of violence is irreconcilable with our notion of a loving God. If this is our belief, we will be questioning God's very existence and God's intentions towards us. We might want immediate answers to our confusion yet the answers that we receive from our friends might seem hollow, inappropriate, and shallow. This will only intensify our confusion. We might find we have no patience for anything that doesn't fit with our reality. We feel spiritually alienated.

Those of us who believe that there is a cause and effect relationship between doing good and being rewarded will question the "good" that we were doing and wonder why it wasn't sufficient to protect us. We will question ourselves to find out what hidden sin we have committed for which we are being punished. We will feel we have failed God and our loved one. If this is the case, we might recommit ourselves to our faith and find a place of comfort in confession and forgiveness.

For those of us who doubted there was a God and who wondered about the ability of a Higher Power to control this world in the first place, we will be more convinced than ever that God is irrelevant. We will wonder if there is any meaning in life. There will be no place to go with our fear, no place to go with our anger. We will feel disconnected and alone.

Whatever our belief system, we will probably find ourselves going through a time of re-evaluation. Victims who experience this crisis often talk about their inner spirituality as being disconnected, empty, purposeless, and dried up. They talk about feeling old, worn-out, tired or thirsting for something more. Victims in the midst of their tragedy will often use desert language. It is natural that after the violence the trust between ourselves and our God is tested severely.

During this time many victims will also describe a time of heightened sense of the "afterlife" or the "supernatural." *Hello from Heaven,* a book written by Bill Guggenheim, details some of these experiences which he calls After-Death Communication (ADC). During one of the workshops for bereaved parents which I was able to attend, he asked how many of the participants had experienced an ADC; almost all hands were raised.

Many of the victims I have talked to tell me stories about feeling the presence of their loved one. Some of them experience supernatural occurrences such as the television turning off and on at the same time as something meaningful concerning their loved one was being experienced. Many talk about dreams where they meet their loved one in a beautiful place and talk with them. Usually these dreams feel very real and reassuring.

All of us will react differently to this kind of spiritual crisis. Some will move away from the church or faith community; others might begin to attend again. But whatever we do — something will have changed in us.

This change in our spirituality is best expressed by a pastor, Rev. Dale Lang, who lost his son in a school shooting. "I can't play church anymore," he told me. "I can't practice church for the sake of religious practices anymore. I don't want nice church services."

His life changed. "I spend more time seeking God and being in his presence than I do planning a sermon."

Spirituality in many ways remains an unexplored frontier of our lives. But we are spiritual beings. For us to really come to peace with what has happened, we will need to continue to explore this part of ourselves until we find the answers.

Underlying Reasons for this Spiritual Crisis

Murder is an out of control act of violence against another human being and brings into question all the control issues; the biggest of these is "Who is in control of this world?" If a loving God is in control of this world, how could this have happened? If God isn't in control — then why bother? Huge impossible questions.

The religious community often presents itself as having the answers to all spiritual questions. In reality, we might find that the church is often more comfortable with quick and simple answers rather than addressing the hard questions. The quick platitudes of "all things work together for good" and "love your enemy" don't have the same meaning for us as they did before.

It may not be in our religious experience to understand the questions of our own souls. We might not have the vocabulary to put our doubts and questions into words.

Members of churches and faith communities might not be comfortable with our presence. We might violate their own beliefs that nothing bad should happen to good people. If we are good, that belief is wrong. If the belief is right, then all victims are bad. The congregation might reject us.

Spirituality is a very personal journey. Answers that satisfy others might not be enough for us. And it will take time and thought to rethink our faith.

Re-evaluating our faith also means re-evaluating the faith of our loved one who has passed on. To change or question our belief systems might cause guilt for not having paid more attention to this before.

At the time when we feel the need for faith, for strength from a Higher Power, we might feel confused as to whom we can really trust.

Violence often becomes the focus of the spiritual battle of good and evil. In this scenario evil feels as if it has won and is in control. Goodness and hope are shattered.

Murder or the threat of death forces us to think about the hereafter. Is there a heaven? Is my loved one in heaven? How can I continue the connection with my loved one in the hereafter?

Consequences of this Spiritual Crisis

We can experience church withdrawal during the aftermath of murder. Going to church and being constantly exposed to what we perceive as the shallowness of the usual Sunday morning services might prove to be too much for us. Seeing others all dressed up and families sitting in a row singing might remind us too much about our own loss. We might find it difficult to listen to the platitudes of friends that promise sunshine after every storm. We might feel the condemnation of some who feel that we are somehow responsible for the misfortune that has happened to our family. We might want to avoid people who try to be helpful by imposing simple solutions by encouraging us to "let go," forgive and move on.

It is not only the victim who has problems with church; the church has problems with the victim. In his book, *Toward a Justice that Heals,* Morton-MacCallum Paterson writes, "But the most shocking thing of all was the discovery that the faith communities typically freeze out crime victims as effectively as they do offenders. The 'taint' of having been bloodied by violence is as offensive to religion as when it is on violent hands." He calls it the leper status of crime victims.

We can lose our desire to communicate and pray to God. Some of us go through a time of withdrawal from God. We can't relate to anything about God. Even the mention of God can cause the person to revisit all the pain of rejection.

Many victims complain about being in a state of confusion and feeling stuck when it comes to their faith. We might feel alienated from God and the church but cannot find it in ourselves to have the desire to return to our faith or engage with the church or faith community. We feel frustrated that we have "lost" our faith as we once knew it. We want to "regain our faith" but we do not know how. Victims often express nostalgia for the "safe and secure" faith that they once had.

Finding Healing in our Spirituality

As victims we need to remember that questioning God is not unusual or blasphemous. Questions can lead to new understandings and growth. It is more important to remain honest about our feelings and doubts than to conform to other people's expectations and allow our spirituality to become a sham.

If we feel that our faith or spirituality has let us down during the crisis, we have every right to reassess and reevaluate it. A relationship with a Higher Power is not meant to cripple us or leave us feeling deserted and a failure. It is meant to give us strength. Surely our God, Higher Power, Creator will be able to take all our doubts and fears. In fact, there is much evidence that God enters into our grief.

To re-enter into the new spiritual understanding that happens after murder, we might need to change our expectations. Instead of seeing God only as the protector, the controller, the miracle maker, it is probably healthier for us to begin to see God as a guide. We will feel increasingly safe if we begin to believe again that there is a source who can help us through the difficult times — not protect us — but help us.

Most religions have a belief in the afterlife. This long view of life helps us deal with the unfinished justice issues that occur in murder. A healthy concept of the afterlife will help us deal with unresolved justice issues. "'Vengeance is mine, I will repay,' says the Lord" takes on a new meaning after we have experienced violence. We will find meaning by learning from an experience, preventing it from happening to others, and finding opportunities to help others.

In his book on fear, Edmund Bourne says of spirituality, "Of all the methods and guidelines suggested in this workbook, a personal spiritual commitment is likely to reach the deepest in helping you overcome your basic sense of fear.... A number of my clients have experienced major turnabout in their condition as a result of cultivating their spirituality."

Considerations

Don't hide your spiritual misgivings. There is no shame in questioning your beliefs in God, in the church and in yourself at a time like this. It is perfectly normal.

Tell your Higher Power, God or Creator how you feel. Take some time to go somewhere alone and lay it out as plainly as you can. Tell God all about your disappointment and your feelings about the act of injustice that has interrupted your life.

Spend some time listening to your heart cry, listening to your heart plead with God, and listening for God's answer. A word of caution: a time of listening can be quite traumatic if you experience new insights and need to deal with new issues. It is a good idea to have someone near to support you and listen to you if you need to talk to someone after a period of listening.

Find a spiritual mentor whom you can trust. Take time to meet with this person regularly.

Continue to practice what you know to be right, even though you might not feel like it. For example, continuing to attend church or a faith community is a way of holding onto your faith until you can understand again. Continue to read the Bible or sacred scriptures from your tradition. Continue to search.

Enter into spiritual lament. There are many good books on this subject. Psalms in the Bible are an excellent expression of lament. Spend time in nature. Gardening or climbing a mountain are wonderful ways to experience a sense of awe.

Be open to new understandings. It is not unusual for people who have lost someone to murder to experience a visit from the spirit of their loved one. It is not unusual for victims to experience a long spiritual desert before they arrive at a new understanding of God. This might be very different than the one they had before but

"We are not human beings having a spiritual experience, we are spiritual beings having a human experience."
—Dr. Wayne W. Dyer

6	IDENTITY DEVASTATION

To Be or Not to Be!

WHEN A GROUP OF US WERE ORDERING LUNCH at a local restaurant, we noticed one of our friends carefully studying the back of the menu, the section reserved for children or seniors. We teased him about wanting to be a child; he only smiled.

As we shared our selections and choices, he pointed at his choice from the seniors' menu and described the meal, saying that as a senior he had a much better selection. We were stunned. "You aren't a senior yet, are you?"

He was too close to our age. Yet when we looked at him, we did notice that his hair was grey, so was his beard, and yes, he had a few smile crinkles around his eyes.

"I am 55," he said. "And why shouldn't I order from the seniors' menu? The prices are better and so is the selection."

We studied the back of the menu. He was right.

"Will they ask you for your ID?" we asked. For us it was a novel idea that at some point we would have to show our ID again.

"I don't know. This is my first time."

When the waitress came, we watched the interaction with great interest. When she didn't ask him for his identification, he confessed that there was something unsettling about that. We all quipped that she would have asked us for ours!

Identity, Belonging and Acceptance

As human beings we are born with a social interest.
According to psychologist Alfred Adler, "All humans need to live in harmony and friendship with others." It is important to stress here the need "to build, first and foremost, a healthy and solid social self (a persona)" as John Monbourquette writes in *How to Befriend Your Shadow*. We are social beings who are connected with those around us in important ways. This social connection is not an option; it is part of our identity. We want to belong.

Our identity is a set of behavioral or personal characteristics which makes us recognizable by the group to which we belong. Most often we inherit part of our identity from those who have given us birth and molded us in our formative years.

The reflection of our primary family grouping is often how we begin to think of ourselves, our status, our role, and our belonging to the rest of society. One author speaks of an "existential loneliness" that permeates every human spirit, a kind of unnamed pain inside, deep within us, a restlessness, an anxiety, a sense of "all aloneness" that calls out to us. We have an ache to belong to community.

In his study of the hierarchy of our needs, Abraham Maslow says that belonging, esteem and love needs are second in importance, following our needs for safety. According to Maslow, we need "friends, companion, a supportive family, identification with a group, and an intimate relationship. If these needs are not met, the person will feel alone and empty."

There is a whole raft of words to describe how we attain worth. We need love, importance, self-esteem, value, position, role, appreciation, inclusion. If we are fortunate to experience all of these, we will feel emotionally happy and secure. If we don't, we will search until we find this worth in a group. Just as we can't survive without food, we can't survive without worth. Very few of us can continue to feel good about ourselves if the group that holds the making of our identity continues to reject us. We will begin to feel unacceptable. Our self-esteem will plunge. No matter how much we want to deny it, we are all susceptible to the same longing and pain of rejection.

This was brought home to me when, as a journalist for a small denominational publication, I needed to attend a trial involving a conflict in the Hutterite community.

Hutterites are usually a private communal people. They are probably best known for their expertise in agriculture and their distinct style of dress. The women wear ankle-length cotton skirts, colorful blouses, black jackets, and usually a head covering of some kind. The bearded men wear homemade black suits, and white collared shirts.

The case that I was covering delved into the practice of excommunication or shunning of a member in the community. Sitting with the people of the community day after day, I soon lost all my journalistic objectivity and began to hurt along with them as every detail of their private lives was put on display.

After a particularly long day of court proceedings, I happened upon a few of the Hutterite leaders outside, on the steps of the courtroom. As a journalist I wondered if they would clarify a few questions I had, but they turned their backs to me. Soon after, I noticed that another man who approached them was also ignored. It was understandable that they ignored me, a journalist, but I couldn't understand why they so obviously ignored the other man. It was evident that the man was shaken.

Since both of us were waiting for a ride, the man began to vent his frustration about the trial and about the Hutterite colonies. I discovered that he was an ex-Hutterite who had been excommunicated from the colony years ago and had slowly and painfully assimilated into the mainstream of society. He was now working in a bank not far from the courtroom. He had come to watch the trial purely out of interest.

I continued to be curious as to why he was so upset; so I asked, "Why do you care what happens in this case? You have been excommunicated by the colony. They rejected you — and this doesn't involve you."

"You don't understand," he said mournfully. "Most people don't understand. But when you have belonged like we did, and you have been rejected, you never get over it. You never get over being rejected by your community. It is my identity, my worth."

Adler writes, "It is almost impossible to exaggerate the value of an increase in social feelings. The mind improves, for intelligence is a communal function. The feelings of worth and value are heightened, giving courage and optimistic view, and there is a sense of acquiescence in the common advantages and drawbacks of our lot. The individual feels at home in life and feels his existence to be worthwhile just as far as he is useful to others and is overcoming common, instead of private feelings of inferiority. Not only the ethical nature, but the right attitude in aesthetics, the best understanding of the beautiful and the ugly, will always be founded upon the truest social feelings."

IDENTITY DEVASTATION

6

Yet an act of violence or a murder can change us and make us unacceptable to society. One of the first comments we heard on September 11 was "everything has changed."

Americans instinctively knew that their position in the global community had changed irreparably. Before the terrorist attacks, the United States was perceived as powerful, unconquerable, and invincible. When the planes crashed into the twin towers, the world suddenly knew that the Americans were vulnerable. Within a day, their identity changed from an unquestionable world power into a victim country.

Most of us know instinctively that to become a victim is not a promotion. It is a helpless, disempowered and isolating state in which to be. Our fear of being abandoned and rejected has a good possibility of becoming realized.

Eric Schlosser in his published article on murder in *The Atlantic Monthly* writes, "The victim is a defeated soul, a loser in this contest of strength. Perhaps it is easier to identify with the murderer. To do otherwise means choosing the side of the powerless...."

A victim is a "loser." To be a loser in today's society is the worst possible designation. I heard from an inmate that if someone wanted to instigate a fight in prison, all he or she had to do was call the other person a loser. No one wants to associate with a loser.

"Becoming a victim frequently shatters positive self-perceptions," writes Ronnie Janoff-Bulman in her article on criminal victimization. "People generally see themselves as decent and worthy, victims seriously question their self-worth and often perceive themselves as weak, needy, and unworthy."

After a crime, many victims express feelings about being alone and isolated in their grief. Some complain about not being understood by their friends. They complain about feeling as if they are being watched. They complain about feeling "different." All of this amounts to rejection. Being rejected is an ongoing wound that will remain with us forever.

Judith Herman in her book, *Trauma and Recovery,* says that it is the "emotional distancing of others and stigmatization that leaves the survivors of homicide feeling abandoned, ashamed, powerless and vulnerable."

Society as a whole finds victimization very difficult to deal with. According to Lula Redmond in her book, *Surviving: When Someone You Love Was Murdered,* there is stigma in murder. She believes it rests in society's belief that "those who are murdered have in some way led to their own death. By this explanation, a protective shield is set up within the mind of the observer that the circumstances are such that the tragedy would never happen to them."

She adds that this blaming the victim is in actuality "… a superficial aura of personal security" not based on the reality that victimization of any kind can happen to anyone at anytime. None of us are immune to violence, but the people around us don't want to believe this so they blame us for our own misfortune. We are labelled as victims. We are stigmatized along with the offender.

Unfortunately in every act of violence and murder there is an inherent conflict and conflict threatens social unity. For a community to remain alive and a functioning social organism, it needs to be unified. Conflict forces members of a community to choose who is the victim and who is the offender. If the community believes the offender rather than the victim, the victim will feel revictimized and hurt again. This is the hardest rejection to take.

Victims who experience this kind of rejection often rail not only against the offender but also against the community that has rejected them. They will feel the need to constantly vindicate themselves.

If the community does not want to choose, it might reject both the victim and the offender. Both are stigmatized.

Often victims simply reject society. As Ronnie Janoff-Bulman observes in her article on criminal victimization, "The entire world view of the victim is colored by the experience of victimization, and the perception of the world of people in particular gets tainted by the rude awakening of the victim to the malevolence in others." We can no longer trust our community as we did before.

For whatever reason, suspicion between the victim and the community can become a difficult obstacle for victims to overcome. Some might never regain their feelings of worth and place again. This is devastating for anyone.

I think Terry Brunsel said it best. "I was sixty-five. I had lived through everything, children with medical problems, a husband with a heart condition. I thought I could handle anything. But when it came to this, I completely shut down. My former experiences counted for nothing."

Darlene Rempel says, "My family didn't understand — didn't talk to me."

William Niederland, in studies of survivors of the Nazi Holocaust, observed that alterations of personal identity were a constant feature of the "survivor syndrome." While the majority of his patients complained, "I am now a different person," the most severely harmed stated simply, "I am not a person." Encountering murder can have the same result.

I remember the moment I was first labelled. It was the evening of the day that Candace's body was found. A man came to our door, identifying himself as the "parent of a murdered child." He said this in a way that included me in that identification.

I remember an actual physical reaction to the words. The blood literally drained from my head and puddled in my toes. Eighteen years later, I am often introduced with much the same words.

Underlying Reasons for this Identity Devastation

The violence we have experienced suddenly overshadows everything we were before the event. Many of us build our identity carefully by attaining an education, marrying someone acceptable in our society, belonging to the right organizations, and behaving in an admirable way. When murder happens, the murder cancels out all of that. This can be devastating.

There is a stigma attached to violence. Society often blames the victim for the crime. People want to believe that the victim deserved what happened to him or her. It allows them to hang on to the false illusion that if they don't do anything wrong, "nothing bad will happen to them."

Media has tremendous power to make or break our reputation by the way our stories are written. Usually the first version of the story is told by the police at a press conference. Often the offender's version of the story is already known. In this case the loved one, who has been murdered and therefore silenced, is often accused of having been the one who provoked the attack. These kind of insinuations, though never proven, can cloud and damage a reputation very quickly. These false understandings are hard to correct.

The inherent conflict of good and evil in an act of violence forces people to choose between the victim and offender. Those who choose the offender (because it is often easier to side with the more powerful) will reject the victim. Some will choose to reject both so as not to "get involved." Either way, we as victims remain the loser in the conflict.

We change. We can turn from being compassionate and understanding to being angry and traumatized. "Most radically traumatized is the victim's sense of community. The social order of one's immediate world has been disrupted.... Reciprocity among citizens no longer is taken for granted," writes C.T. Fischer in *A Phenomenological Study of Being Criminally Victimized.*

Our values might change. Let me give you an example.
One Sunday, we spent time with friends who listened carefully to
our story for most of the afternoon. When it was their turn to tell
us about their lives, they started by complaining bitterly about the
postal carrier who was ruining their lovely lawn by walking on it and
creating a path. We couldn't relate. Their loss of a lawn couldn't
compare to our loss of a child.

**We might also change in a way that devastates our image
of ourselves.** If we have always perceived ourselves to be "nice"
people, loving, forgiving and generous, to find ourselves filled with
anger, fear, and lack of forgiveness will have devastating effects
on our view of ourselves.

**We might make significant changes in our lives that change
our role in society.** Victims often move from the house where
they had lived to escape the memories. Many change jobs. Some
tradespeople decide to learn more about what is happening to
them and move into social services. Others who are in social
services find they can't empathize with the people around them
and move into trades. All of these changes in our lives also change
who we are and to whom we relate.

**It is difficult to initiate new relationships after a traumatic
event.** If we do not work aggressively at seeking out people, we
will naturally suffer from a world that is getting smaller. After an
act of violence, every new or old relationship is approached with
the implicit question, "Which side are you on?" This isn't conducive
to friendship making. We become afraid to enter into the social
network.

We withdraw. Because we lose our ambition and our desire to fit
in, we no longer make any effort to belong. Victims do this physically,
socially and emotionally. This can lead to becoming more and more
socially alienated.

We begin to find the word "victim" offensive. We reject parts
of our own identity and withdraw.

Consequences of this Identity Devastation

These identity changes can leave us feeling insecure.
We might find ourselves asking the questions: Who am I now?
Am I still important? Who are my true friends now?

It can lead to lack of confidence. Not knowing who we are
can lead to strong feelings of insecurity. In this competitive world,
confidence is everything. We might find ourselves incapacitated
with self-doubt at a time when we are dealing with a very aggressive criminal justice system.

We withdraw to safe places. We might find it difficult to go
to parties, attend church or sports events, participate in faith
communities, or go to any place where we can be seen and
watched by society.

Others of us begin to fight back. We might force ourselves
to continue to go to work and act as if nothing has happened.
When our friends withdraw, we will still want to relate to them.
We might find ourselves forcing relationships and begin to make
social errors.

We might react strongly to anyone who identifies us as victims
or slights us in the tiniest way. When we openly and forcefully
demand respect, this can lead to further alienation.

This isolation and withdrawal is not healthy. It is very common
for someone who has experienced this trauma of rejection to
entertain suicidal thoughts.

"Belong to people.
Accept pain as part of your life.
Know that you have made a difference."
—Harold Kushner

Recovering our Confidence: Recovering our Self

Probably the best advice I received during the time of identity devastation in my own life was from my mother. Someone had just told one of my friends that I was heavily medicated which explained my calmness during my television appearance. I resented being perceived as "overly calm" and I resented being accused of "being on drugs." I wasn't sure what I wanted people to say about me, but it wasn't that. Seeing my agitation, my mother calmly said, "Don't worry about what others think. Just as long as you know the truth of who you are." In reality it doesn't matter what others think. Even though we need to be part of the social fabric, "who we are" is not based only on what others think. We can become more selective about those with whom we want to associate.

We need to realize that we are important to society in a new way. The victims of the terrorist attacks on September 11 brought the Americans to a new understanding of themselves. They suddenly became spokespersons for what happened. One of the victims, Lisa Beamer, whose husband fought hijackers on the doomed Newark to San Francisco flight, got on a plane one month later on October 19 to model how the American people could deal with their fear. Her actions were a front page news story.

We need to reclaim the word victim. As I said earlier, it is true, the word victim describes someone injured, destroyed or sacrificed — someone of disempowerment. But it is also true that victims, in their time of brokenness, have an important role to play in the justice-making process. Our new found knowledge of criminal behavior, of the justice system, of our own victim journey are important stories that society needs to hear.

We need time. When we made the transition from teen to adult, it took time. We had to experiment with our new mature bodies. We had to fail. We had to find where we could succeed. Moving through the victim role is a similar time of transition.

We need to continue to try to relate to those around us. Even though there is a general stigmatization of victims, don't assume that everyone is doing this. Because we are highly sensitive to everyone around us, we might misread someone's good intentions. Continue to reach out.

Remember who you were before you became a victim. Even though we now have an additional role to play, we are still and always will be more than a victim. We can be many things at the same time. We can be a wife or husband, mother or father, at the same time as we are the manager of a store. We are the sum total of everything we care about and in which we participate. We need to continue to strive for balance.

The last thing is to give yourself a lot of room for error. There is no one who has yet been able to "do this victim thing" right. Most of us cry when we should be holding it together, or we are too controlled when we should be crying.

Considerations

Cherish who you are and who you are becoming. Embrace the role of victim for the time being. Explore the issues because in them you will find the meaning and healing.

Allow yourself to be more than a victim. No matter how much people want to box you into being "just a victim," remind yourself of who you were before the crime, and retain that part of your identity. Know that even though your world is changing, you are becoming better. Realize that you are more than the tragedy. Find someone who reflects you the way you "were" and visit with them regularly.

Allow yourself time to make these adjustments. Every transition takes energy, time and determination. I've known a few friends who, when going through extensive counselling, prepared themselves for the tiredness after each session and took time out for themselves. It is important to manage the process of recovering your identity.

Find a support group of people with the same experience.
It is often comforting to meet others who are going through the same thing as you are — and surviving. It is sometimes sobering to find others who are dealing with worse situations. It will be very important for you to regain your trust in people and be with people you can trust again.

Find biographies of others who have survived atrocities.
For example, Viktor Frankl's book, *Man's Search for Meaning,* that describes his experience in a concentration camp was extremely important for me when my daughter was murdered.

Correct your story. Don't be afraid to clarify your story or explain the circumstance of the murder to those around you who find it difficult to understand. If the media gets it wrong, write it out for them. If you don't have the energy, find someone to help you write it out. Continue to correct your story. Monitor it.

Inform your friends. Help your friends to understand you. Realize that some of their mistakes are made because they truly don't know how to help you. During this time when you are vulnerable to criticism, you might want to avoid people who are being vindictive or nasty. Allow your friends who are truly trying to help you, to help you.

Don't withdraw. Even though it is uncomfortable, continue to go to parties, church, faith communities and social functions. If it is difficult, stay for only a short time. It will become easier with time. Realize that you have an important role to play in society.

CHAPTER 10:   THIRD STAGE — FIXING THE HARM

Importance of Justice

WE KNEW THE PRESIDENT WOULD TAKE ACTION.
Three days after the terrorist attacks, the headlines in our
newspaper were already hinting of a war. A front page picture
of President George W. Bush was captioned "Bush readies for
war." It is clear from the picture and stories that he has moved
to a new position of purpose. "We have just seen the first war
of the 21st century. This country will not relent," he said.

A little more than a month later on our Canadian
Thanksgiving Day, the United States declared war on the
country of Afghanistan. We were enjoying a lovely turkey
dinner, listening to the news. Nothing seemed right. We
understood the need for justice, but we weren't sure what
justice should look like in this situation. The fact that food
parcels were dropped along with the bombs only added to
our confusion.

Justice is a wonderful word that promises us restoration
of safety, property and good will. The scope of the word
justice is best found in Proudhon's quote from *De la Justice
Dans la Révolution et Dans L'Eglise*. "Justice under various
names governs the world — nature and humanity, science
and conscience, logic and morals, political economy, politics,
history, literature and art. Justice is that which is most sacred
among ideas, and what the masses demand today with most
ardor. It is the essence of religions and at the same time the
form of reason, the secret object of faith, and the beginning,
middle and end of knowledge. What can be imaged more
universal, more strong, more complete than justice."

Other words for justice are: fairness, righteousness,
equity, moral goodness, rectitude. The word justice fills
us with pervasive good feelings of social healthiness. It is
our universal vision statement. It is the over-arching social
contract that ensures fairness, goodness, respect, integrity
and freedom. We know that if we have justice, we can live
together in peace, trust and harmony. Justice allows us to love
and live with dignity.

Preparing for Justice

Rectify is the stage in the Crime Victim Detour where we as victims want to fix what has happened to us.

We want justice.

It might surprise you to realize that the over-riding characteristics of this stage — especially as we move to the pre-trial time — can be excitement, determination, high energy and optimism. In comparison to the previous two stages, REACT, which is dominated by fear, and RETREAT, which is dominated by sadness, RECTIFY, which is dominated by anger, is the most comfortable place to be. Rectify is a place of great anticipation. We are going into a battle to restore justice and fix our lives. We are filled with the powerful emotion of anger. We arm ourselves with grandiose arguments that build us up. We believe that we can win. That's a wonderful feeling.

In the same issue of the newspaper that announced the war on terrorism, there was an article buried further on entitled, "Bush is finally looking more presidential." The article described Bush during the first three days after the attacks as being more like a governor consoling the people after a disaster. Then something shifted. "Now he is embracing the more profound of presidential roles, contemplating a congressional declaration of war, an address to a joint session of the legislature and the constant national visibility that will inevitably accompany a major military campaign." He was getting ready for war.

I remember when this change of mood happened in our family. For six weeks we had been in the React stage, looking for Candace. Then we had retreated for a day when her body was found. The next day as we were talking to the police, I said something about being so relieved that it was over now. Cliff straightened. "It isn't over. It has just begun." There was a new glint of determination in his eyes.

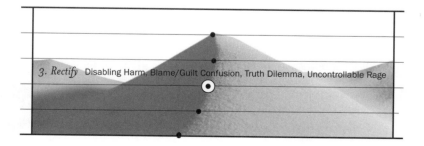

3. Rectify Disabling Harm, Blame/Guilt Confusion, Truth Dilemma, Uncontrollable Rage

The exception to this process if we as victims are still too traumatized by the crime and are still caught in the Retreat stage of the Crime Victim Detour, we will not feel that we are ready for the Rectify stage when the case goes to trial. If we are in a state of grief, we will want to retreat and not participate. We don't care about justice.

If a trial takes place when we are still in the React stage, a state of fear and trauma, the courtroom will feel extremely unsafe. But if we are ready to Rectify it all, we will be ready to fight and find our anger hard to control especially if we are not allowed to participate in the trial or if we feel slighted or insulted in any way. At some point these stages collide, intersect or overlap, and when they do, we will find ourselves extremely confused about what is happening.

Remember that even though we are assuming that there will be a trial at this stage in the Crime Victim Detour, this might not be the case. The offender might not be arrested or convicted. For example, our own case never went to trial because the offender was never found. However, just because there is no structured justice process does not mean that we easily "let go" of our justice expectations. In fact it can complicate our issues even more. At some point we will want to Rectify the injustice that has happened to us.

Justice-Making Process

Justice-making isn't foreign to us. We do it all the time. Being a parent could be compared to being a full-time justice-maker. We as parents try to be fair to our children, balancing their needs, their personalities and their conflicts with each other. We do it from the day they are born to the day we die.

All of us constantly do justice in all of our relationships. We are forced to face justice issues when someone breaks into the line at the grocery store in front of us. We do it when we are in the parking lot circling for a stall. We do it in the workplace when we share a printer and someone steps out of line. We do it every time we experience an injustice or the threat of an injustice.

Inherently we know how to create peace and do justice. We do it with little children all the time. Done right, it has wonderful possibilities of fixing broken relationships.

As a quick reminder, let's review the justice-making process that a mother might use with two children who are quarrelling and fighting. This process is also used in conflict resolution.

The children have quarrelled. We find Mary in tears with a bite mark on her arm, Betty standing to the side, shaking with rage. Mary's five dollar bill is missing. Betty has just bought herself some chips and pop. There is conclusive evidence that Betty has taken the money and then in denial, picked a fight with Mary and has bitten her.

Victim Perspective

First of all the victim needs to identify the "harm" or the loss. We as justice-makers begin by exploring what happened. When? Where? Who? As justice-makers, we ask the victim of this crime to tell us exactly what happened. Both Mary and Betty will want to give rationalizations, but we make them stick to facts the first time around. We reconstruct the crime scene. We then clearly identify the crime and the loss.

Second we need to allow the victim to confront the offender and describe how he or she feels about the offense. We tell Betty that she needs to be quiet while Mary tells "why" she is crying. Offenders, young or old, are rarely able understand why the victim is making such a big deal about it. "She deserved it." But in doing this, we allow the victim to play an important part in socializing and sensitizing the little offender to the extent of the damage that he or she has done.

At this moment it is Mary, who has the pain, the anger and the emotion to not be afraid and say it the way it is. When we allow her to express her shame and humiliation, we allow her to vindicate herself, confront Betty and lay the responsibility on the appropriate person. By doing this Mary regains her sense of fairness and safety.

Guilt and shame in this context are used in a positive sense, to help Betty gain a sense of empathy, let her feel the pain she has caused and in that way to stop the violence. The purpose of this is not to label or destroy Betty as a bad person, but to help her develop a sensitive and wonderful conscience that will keep her from hurting other people in the future, possibly her own children.

After the victim has finished, we as justice-makers comfort the offender. We need to restore dignity to Betty, to restore her confidence.

Third we need to explore the causes of what happened.

This is when we turn our attention back to the offender. Hopefully by this time Betty has gained a new perspective on her actions. Hopefully she has been able to listen and see how her actions have affected Mary. If she has been sensitive, she will be remorseful and open to suggestions. This is the perfect time to ask the "why" question. Ultimately we want prevention. The "why" question after the offense often leads to good suggestions of how the event could have been prevented.

During this time we need to allow both Mary and Betty to take any responsibility they had for the outcome of the event. Often if the offender is remorseful, the victim will begin to take ownership of his or her role in the offense — that is, if he or she had one.

This exploration process needs to be done carefully so that it doesn't in any way rationalize the wrongdoing or blame the victim. If done properly, it will help to separate Betty from her offense and help her regain her dignity. Peace and harmony will give a feeling of safety back to the victim.

Fourth we need to know who will pay for the losses.   If the offense was stealing five dollars, the stolen money has to be given back to the rightful owner. We need to ask the practical questions: Does the offender still have the five dollars? If not, who will pay? Often as parents we look at the plight of the two little ones; we, who have the resources, will step in and make sure the victim is not the one who is "out" the five dollars. We might take twenty-cents off the offender's allowance for a while. Once this has been done, there is still the trust that needs to be restored. It takes time to rebuild trust. The offender will need to submit to a probation time of accountability. The victim is asked to be patient and give the offender a second chance.

If we as justice-makers have enough power over both the victim and offender, we ask them to say kind things to each other, shake hands or even hug if they are sisters because we want peace in our families. If they aren't part of a family relationship, we might make them both promise that they will leave each other alone.

Offender Perspective

From Betty's point of view, she needs to know that if she doesn't cooperate she will be in disfavor.

First of all Betty must willingly confess to the wrongdoing. Offenders need to fill in the details of the crime so that the victim will understand why it happened. The victim during this time is allowed to ask the questions; the offender must tell the truth. If Betty should tell a lie, she needs to know that there will be continuing consequences for telling a lie.

Second Betty must give full attention to Mary while Mary is expressing her feelings, crying or venting about the humiliation she suffered and all the subsequent losses. Offenders must show recognition of how the wrong has affected the victim and show remorse. If they express their apologies, they need to be acknowledged for doing the right thing.

Third Betty must explore the reasons why she did it and offer ways to help solve the "why." Both the victim and the justice-maker help the offender see what the underlying issues are and how to solve them. This means a change of behavior.

Then Betty needs to compensate for the losses. The offender must do penance, if necessary.

Betty needs to know that she is as valued and loved as Mary. She needs to know that it took courage to go through the process and set things right. She needs to know that everyone at one point or another is an offender. She also needs to know that every time she offends, she needs to go through this process.

Making justice happen is not an easy process. It's amazing how mediating even the slightest infraction can require a great deal of energy from all those involved. As the process begins, the air is tense. The victim is angry, the offender resentful. Everyone in the process wonders, "Will the process of reconciliation work this time?" When it does, there is a sense of peace and relief. Many call it a minor miracle every time peace happens.

As parents who love our children and live with them every day, we have (hopefully) an advantage in "doing justice." We truly want our children to be treated fairly, respectfully and lovingly. This goes a long way in ensuring that justice will happen. In talking to my adult children and reviewing some of our own "justice" moments in the past, I discovered that even though I didn't always get it right, the process and the attempt somehow settled things between them.

Criminal Justice

Even though we know that everything is much more intense and serious in a crime that includes violence, we still expect some of the same processes to take place. As victims we know the power of truth to hold the offender accountable. We know we have a right to feel angry and to give the person who has hurt us a piece of our mind. We know the need to go to the root causes. We ourselves want to know why. We also want to prevent something like this from ever happening again. And we hope that somewhere someone will help us to recover from this injustice through compensation or at least through sympathy and understanding.

We need to remember that justice isn't only about giving a stolen five dollar bill back to the person from whom it was stolen. It is about mending the broken relationship and restoring trust.

Violent crime is about hurting someone physically, spiritually, and emotionally. Crime steals from us our safety, our dignity and our trust. Therefore to really do justice, it is more than simply establishing who did the crime and compensating the victim; it is about restoring the safety, dignity and trust.

A New Zealander, Judge James Rota, a descendant of the indigenous people from Mauit said it best. "Justice must elevate the human spirit or it isn't justice."

Third Stage – Rectify

Rectify is the third imposed stage when the crime needs to be addressed and justice restored. Unfortunately a satisfactory justice-making process is extremely rare these days. We have lost the ability to "do justice."

Disabling Harm The intentionality of the violent crime can threaten our beliefs that the world is a safe place and that all members of society are valued and trustworthy. The shattering of these basic assumptions of safety, value and trust can disable us so completely that we are unable to remain functioning and contributing members of society.

We hold the offender responsible for the loss resulting from the crime, but we expect a justice process to recognize our need to be restored to the lifestyle and life we were leading before the crime. When these needs are not met, we are left with a long-term disability.

Blame/Guilt Confusion Our first instinct is to identify the primary cause of the harm. If the cause is not immediately identifiable, we will find a target for our blame. We want to hold the person responsible for the crime accountable so that he or she has to take the responsibility for fixing everything that has been broken in our lives. What we thought of in the beginning as an easy process usually turns out to be much more complicated than we anticipated — hence the confusion.

Truth Dilemma To make sense of the violence, to restructure our lives and to build preventative safeguards, we need to answer the five basic questions: who, where, what, when, and why. Unfortunately in the aftermath of violence these answers are not often accessible. Being left with more questions than answers, we are faced with the dilemma of not knowing the truth.

Uncontrollable Rage The natural feelings of anger resulting from experiencing injustice can take on unusual proportions after experiencing violence or murder. Disempowering justice processes and a general lack of understanding of our needs can exasperate this anger until it escalates into an emotion that feels uncontrollable.

7	DISABLING HARM

One Hundred Kisses

MY SISTERS WERE AS DIFFERENT AS NIGHT AND DAY. The older one was dark, the younger blonde. The older one covered her bedside wall with pictures of spirited horses, the younger with plans of her dream houses. The older was the gregarious one, the life of the party, totally uninhibited. The younger one was the quiet one, who loved intimate conversations and was extremely modest.

Their differences were never as apparent as when they came home from a "Young Peoples" gathering at the church. Since we all slept together in a large upstairs bedroom with three single beds, I soon learned that if I pretended to sleep, I could hear all about their evening. Since I was five years younger than they were, there was simply nothing more intriguing than hearing about their teen life.

The younger one was usually horrified at the antics of the older one, and inevitably began the debriefing with "I was so embarrassed when you…." "Did you really have to get onto that table and make a spectacle of yourself?" The discussion would go on into the wee hours of the morning, with neither one really understanding or winning.

One evening the older one had had enough. She confronted the younger with the question. "Do I ever tell you how to act? Do I ever intrude on your life?"

The younger one was silent.

"I'm sick and tired of this. If you do this again — I am going to…."

She paused. In our family we didn't have many threats available to us. Our father did not allow any of us to shout, punch or show any signs of aggression toward each other. I don't remember my mother and father ever disagreeing in our presence. Not that we didn't have conflicts or problems, we were just expected to deal with our conflicts in a non-violent way.

Peeking from underneath my blanket, I could see her thinking hard.

"If you ever bring this up again — I'm going to give you a hundred kisses."

Needless to say for the younger sister, who never allowed anyone to touch her or touch her things, there was absolutely nothing worse.

It was an uneasy peace till two parties later when the younger one couldn't maintain her silence. "Did you really have to chase the boys around the church?"

"That's it," the older one exclaimed. "I told you if you ever said anything again I would kiss you a hundred times." With that she flew into action, jumped onto the younger one's bed and gave her a kiss. "One," she said. The younger sister struggled violently.

It was bedlam. The fight was wild. The younger one, trying to escape, jumped from bed to bed; I cowered in the corner watching in amazement. Smack, smack, smack. They were hardly kisses anymore.

"Eighty," the older one said triumphantly. Smack, smack, smack.

The door at the bottom of the stairs opened. The two of them stopped in mid air, panting.

It was my father's voice. "What are you girls doing up there?"

My father rarely opened the stairs door. We were all going to be in trouble. The last time when they did something wrong, even I was implicated. Our hearts were thumping loudly.

The older swallowed…. "We're kissing each other goodnight," she said.

There was a long pause filled with questions and bewilderment. "All right," he said. Then he closed the door.

"Eighty-four." And the struggle continued, a little quieter but just as determined till finally the two of them landed on the floor with one last resounding smack. "One hundred," my older sister pronounced and then sat back. Then they giggled with relief. When they caught their breath, both of them were emphatic that this had not been a good experience for either one of them, and that it would never recur.

Looking back, life was simple then. Imagine fixing something with a hundred kisses.

The Good Life

We all want the "good" life. Some of us think the good life was the past when we could leave the doors of our homes unlocked and when the only violence we encountered was a reprimand from a parent or a problem with a sibling that could be fixed with a hundred kisses. For some, the good life means something more extravagant like a cruise on a yacht in the Mediterranean. We all have different dreams of what "the good life" would be.

Goodness as defined in the dictionary, describes bountifulness, something full of beauty, kindness, conforming to the moral order of the universe and a feeling of well-being. If we don't have the good life, we have the hope of attaining it. Even if we will never have a luxurious lifestyle, we still hope for freedom, safety, respect and justice. Compared to some other parts of the world that are embroiled in war, most of us are experiencing much of that in our lives already. Our lives are predominantly good.

Research shows that for us to feel good about ourselves, we need to feel that we can exercise some control in our lives, make choices and be self-directed. We expect safety, we expect order, and we expect to be valued and respected. When something does go wrong, we expect to enter into a fair process of justice. In a good life we expect a certain amount of good will, even from strangers.

An example of this good life can be seen in a simple trip to the grocery store. When we enter the store, we expect to be able to wander freely down the aisles, choose from a selection of brands, push our cart to the cashier and be waited on in turn, pay the amount on the price tag, even if it differs from what is programmed in the cash register. We expect to leave without encountering danger of any kind. We assume this because we haven't ever experienced anything different.

These "assumptions" are important to us. "The assumptive world is the only world we know and it includes everything we know or think we know," writes Murray Parkes in his paper on *Psycho-social Transitions.*

Those who have had a "good life" have three basic assumptions. The first assumption is that we are invulnerable. Most people believe that bad things happen to other people, and that they themselves are relatively invulnerable to violence.

The second basic assumption is that the world is meaningful and that things happen for a reason. There is a cause and effect relationship in our lives. For instance, if I work hard, at the end of the month I will receive a pay check.

The third assumption is that people and life are valued in our country. We expect to be treated with respect. We have rights. When we have been wronged, we expect justice.

We also feel that we are entitled to pursue the "comfortable life." Most of us interpret this as being able to buy a car, a house with heat and air conditioning, a good television set and that perfect sofa. We feel that we are entitled to be owners and to live in our little space without intrusion.

In our pursuit of this good life, we look for safe places that promise us this goodness. We look for good people who treat us with respect, jobs that give us the ability to afford that new car, and if we can't do it all at once, we count on the promise of a good future to take out a loan. Our expectations of goodness are almost as important to us as the current goodness we are experiencing.

"Crime is deeply traumatic because it undercuts fundamental assumptions of autonomy, order, and relatedness."
—Howard Zehr

Disabling Harm

7

A violent act that flagrantly breaks the laws of our country shatters all the three assumptions of goodness. Violence disables us and prevents us from continuing our lives as we were accustomed and pursuing our dreams. Some of these harms are obvious in our lives, like the crumbling of the towers of World Trade Center. Some are less visible, like the children whose parents were killed in the terrorist attacks who will continue to feel loss for the rest of their lives.

In a crime such as murder, the obvious loss is that of a life. In other violent crimes, it might be physical harm, property harm or emotional harm. After a crime, the harm is immediate and visible. Life stops for us. We can't return to work the next day, we might land up in the hospital, we might be incapacitated at home, we might be without a vehicle. We are disabled immediately after a violent crime in some way.

As a result of the initial harm caused by crime, there are a series of less obvious spiraling losses that we will continue to experience. For example, the murder of our daughter robbed us of future grandchildren. We didn't recognize this loss until her friends began their families at least ten years after the murder.

A criminal act also violates us in unseen ways. For instance, violence robs us of our control of our life, shatters the very foundation of our feelings of security and goodness, and destroys our sense of well-being. It isn't only the obvious violence like the gun to the forehead, the slashed throat, the smashed car, or the rape that harms us, it is also the violation of our world view that disables us.

"People's basic assumption about themselves and their world are seriously challenged and/or shattered by the experience of victimization," Ronnie Janoff-Bulman writes in her article *Criminal vs. Non-Criminal Victimization.*

When our first assumption that we are secure and safe is shattered we feel vulnerable. We often expect things to get worse. Many of the victims I have encountered over the years talk about feeling "stalked by death" after their loved one is murdered. They can't go through a day without feeling that something dreadful is going to happen. These feelings of foreboding are not insignificant and cannot be easily dismissed; they are feelings of impending doom. I know that when our second child turned thirteen, the age at which Candace was killed, I had this uneasy feeling that she was not going to live to see her fourteenth year. My assumptions, based on what I had experienced, gave me feelings of doom not hope. There is a feeling that "bad luck" is targeting us. Misfortune happens in groups of three.

When our assumption of law and order is violated, we might be less respectful of the law or those who police those laws. It's more difficult to stick to the speed limit of one hundred kilometers per hour when everyone is passing us at one hundred and twenty kilometers per hour. Modelling of any behavior, good or bad, does influence us. When this lawlessness is not confronted in a formal way, we might question the validity of the entire justice system.

When unwarranted violence shatters our ability to predict what is going to happen to us, it robs us of our ability to plan and prepare for the future. If the cause and effect relationship is broken, we feel that we can no longer control our lives. Feeling powerless, we can become apathetic. When someone approaches us to make a difference, to change, or to contribute, we as victims can feel "what's the use?" We can no longer hope to effect change if there is no relationship between cause and effect. We have learned that we can be kind and loving and good, but that's not going to save us from harm.

If we have faced the intentional violation of another human being, we question the value of life or relationships. Murder or bodily assault has a clear message. "You are not worthy. I can hurt you. You don't matter."

This flagrant disregard for our welfare leaves us wondering about the goodness of others. Are other people trustworthy? Do they have my welfare at heart? Will I be violated again? This lack of respect for us and our loved ones will leave us filled with shame and humiliation. We have been publicly insulted by violence. Someone didn't honor us. We in turn find it difficult to trust another human being or honor someone else.

Even our sense of ownership is violated. We are territorial by nature. We want to own a house, own a car, own a lawn or garden. When someone intrudes into our territory and violates us in our space or in someone else's space, our relationship with the material world is also violated. When the pride of ownership is shattered, we wonder, "Why should I continue to look after my yard when it will just be violated again? Why should I look after my things when they will just be stolen?" We can no longer afford to care.

All of the above — the extreme fear, the lawlessness, the humiliation, the lack of caring — can lead to more losses. Because we tend to focus on what we have lost, we might not pay as much attention to those we love. We might lose our marriage, our job, our friends, our faith community, our position in society. The spiralling losses continue.

Violence is a form of intimidation that affects us physically, emotionally, intellectually and spiritually.

As we reel in pain from the aftermath of a violent or serious crime, our first response is to want it solved. We want it fixed and we want it fixed fast. We want to get into a program of rehabilitation. Yet the reaction to a violent crime is one of disassociation from the process of solving the problem. We have lost the capacity to recreate or repair.

Without a strong rehabilitation program, the disabling harm can continue to remain unaddressed for years, crippling an entire family.

The first parent of a murdered child, whom we met the day our child's body was found, was a prime example of this. He came to warn us that there is no justice. For two hours he described how he had lost the ability to work, to relate to his family and to concentrate. His health had been affected. His time was consumed with the endless trial, his emotions tied up with finding the offender. He eventually died of heart failure. His family is now suing the criminal justice system for the harm they have endured over the years.

As a victim of an abduction writes, "The fact that he got away without having to pay anything makes me really angry. He took so much from me, and I've felt like he needed to have things taken from him."

Underlying Reasons for this Disabling Harm

It is the intentionality of the act of violence that is hardest for us to comprehend or accept. "The actual design of the perpetrator is to harm another, either by taking something away or physically hurting the victim. Victims of crime have been singled out for injury (physical, psychological, or material) by another person, and this has implications for the reactions of crime victims.... It is the ruthless design of a perpetrator, the ill intent preceding the misfortune, which leads the crime victim to confront the existence of evil," writes Ronnie Janoff-Bulman.

It is this encounter with what many victims call "evil" that is the greatest cause of the disability and our inability to heal and "get over" this crime.

Violence shatters our assumptions. For most of us, our assumptions are based on a world that is good. After we experience violence, the balance of good and evil shifts in our world view. Evil now feels dominant. We feel vulnerable and doomed. We feel we have lost. "And the victim is likely to perceive him or herself as a loser, particularly in the case of criminal victimization, in which one has 'lost' to another human being," writes Ronnie Janoff-Bulman.

The intentional taking of control by a perpetrator, whom we perceive to be "evil" and "intending to do us ill will," leaves us with control issues. In other forms of victimization, such as in a flood, we all have a sense of being out of control. We know we can't truly control nature. But when it comes to another human being, we believe that another person can control his or her behavior. A criminal violation of the law does not feel like an accident or an act of God. It feels evil.

We need this imbalance of control to be corrected and goodness restored in order to feel safe and good again. We hope and wait for a justice-making process to denounce the evil and restore the good. If there is no place for the harm of the crime to be addressed, we do not gain a sense of "procedural justice" nor do we regain our sense of control and power.

In serious crime such as murder some of the losses are irreparable. The life taken can't be returned. There are no solutions to some of the problems caused by the crime. So much has changed — our priorities, our values, our lifestyle, our sense of self. We will not be able to go back to the way it was.

The losses resulting from the harm in an act of violence are hard to determine. How can we measure the value of a life that is lost? How can we measure the trust that is lost? To even try to attempt to compensate is impossible. Time and money are the currency we use in our daily lives but these are inadequate in compensating for life. Does another person's time in prison really satisfy the value question of losing a loved one to murder? In one case when the offender was able to offer money to compensate for the lives he had taken, the victim recoiled in horror and called it "blood money."

There are often not enough resources to tackle the overwhelming task of rehabilitation for us as victims. The criminal justice system has directed all of its resources to defending and holding the offender accountable. In order to qualify for compensation, the victim needs to apply and "prove" they are a victim.

Victims are not prepared for the losses resulting from a crime. Most of us believe that the criminal justice system, for which we pay taxes, performs the same functions as motor vehicle insurance. We assume that if we have been criminally victimized, we will be looked after in the same way as if our car was stolen. With horror, we soon realize that we do not have any crime insurance system that resembles motor vehicle insurance. Ezzat Fattah makes a poignant point in his essay, *The Sad History of Victim Assistance,* when he says, "Over the years I have repeatedly proposed a universal state insurance system for crime victims similar to traffic accident insurance, labor accident insurance, unemployment insurance, but the idea was always summarily rejected as a utopian dream. So while almost all other risks are covered in the welfare state by some form of insurance or another, the risk of becoming a victim of crime is not."

There is a great deal of societal disapproval around crime victims seeking compensation or justice on their own. The very act of seeking compensation is met with suspicion that the victim is trying to gain from the act of crime. Victims are often seen as opportunistic if they sue.

Consequences of this Disabling Harm

Criminal victimization has long term ramifications. We might be physically disabled if we have been assaulted. We might be emotionally crippled for the rest of our lives because of serious trauma of the violence. If we have lost someone we love, we will never completely fill the loss. Encountering violence will change us in some way. It will be a different world.

Many of us remain caught in the angry feeling that "someone has to pay" for this loss. We might want to "make someone pay."

If we are caught in the question of "Who is going to pay?," we might find ourselves waiting and depending on others. We will feel that it is not up to us to fix what someone else has destroyed. While we are in this waiting mode, we will feel as if our lives are in limbo. We are stuck and we don't have the energy, ambition or knowledge on how to proceed. We are incapacitated.

One fellow whose fiancée was killed was unable to continue his university studies and dropped out of school. The next year, because of the impending trial, he thought that he would still not be able to study and went to work instead. The trial was delayed for two years; he waited. In the end, he waited for three years, critical years in the life of a student, and never did continue his studies.

Some of us will become reckless. Having encountered someone who has no regard for the law, we too lose our respect for the law.

The shattering of our assumption of security can leave us unable to trust other human beings. We might never be able to enter into another intimate relationship.

Dealing with the Harm: Filling our Lives Again

After a serious crime we might need to consider a time of complete rehabilitation in the same way as if we were suffering from a physical disability.

We might need to reconstruct our shattered assumptions. After an encounter with evil our values might have shifted, so we might need to revisit our sense of right and wrong. We will need to regain empathy for other people again, our compassion.

We might need to work on our self-control. Life will feel like we are climbing uphill. Nothing will come easily for awhile. Grief, mourning, rehabilitation are all just plain, hard work. We will need to "choose" to take control of our lives again — turn the tide, and work at discipline in order to get our lives in control again.

We might need to look for compensation. However, remember that looking for compensation can represent a trap. Judith Herman warns us in her book, *Trauma and Recovery,* that the fantasy of compensation, like the fantasies of revenge and forgiveness are often "formidable impediments to mourning. Part of the problem is the very legitimacy of the desire for compensation." She writes, "Prolonged, fruitless struggles to wrest compensation from the perpetrator or from others may represent a defense against facing the full reality of what was lost." It can also be fuelled by the desire for a victory over the perpetrator or from others that will erase the humiliation of the trauma. She adds, "Though the fantasy is about empowerment, in reality the struggle for compensation ties the patient's fate to that of the perpetrator." Paradoxically, the patient will liberate themselves only if they renounce the hope of ever getting any compensation from the perpetrator. It is critical that we determine if compensation in our case is a destructive fantasy or a realistic, constructive goal. If it is realistic, consider it.

It is common after a crime to focus on what we have lost and lose interest in what we have left. As difficult as it might be, we need to cherish what we have. For me it meant pulling my focus away from Candace whom we had lost, and enjoying our other two children. I was amazed at how difficult this was. You would think that, being a mother and having lost one child, I would want to mother and cherish my other two children even more, but for me it didn't work that way.

If we are going to regain control of our lives, most of us need to reassess our own values after an encounter of violence. Do we want to emulate the perpetrator and answer evil with evil?

"We need to confront the existence of evil," writes Janoff-Bulman. Do we need to find alternative ways to deal with this evil?

Don't expect miracles overnight. Remember that it takes approximately twenty-one days to turn an action into a habit. It will take even more time to confront our feelings of unease. If we have encountered a gunman during one of our grocery shopping trips, it will take more than twenty-one trips to return to a feeling of safety and routine when we enter into the same store.

Considerations

Be careful to not minimize the harm done to you. Identify your losses. Be open and clear to those around you about your disability. You might need some very practical helps.

Take time to assess the assumptions you had in life before the violence. Are your assumptions accurate? Just as we were wrong to assume that bad things never happen to good people, we are equally wrong if we think that everything bad is going to target us now. We need to begin to assume that the good and bad are intermingled. We need to realize that there are people who intend harm and people who intend good, and to begin to recognize the difference.

Maintain your relationships. It is common to want to be alone when you are hurting but don't ignore those around you who continue to love you. Spend time with them. If you can't give them the attention they need, take the time to explain why. They will wait for you if they know you still care.

Manage your physical health. Be careful about becoming reckless with your own life. Eat carefully. Drive carefully.

Manage your time and work. If you aren't performing up to expectations or to your past record, talk to your employer. Tell the person about your feelings, then come up with a plan that will satisfy you both. You might need an advance of funds. Take time off. You might not be able to work for an entire day but you may feel that staying at home all day isn't healthy either. Explore the possibilities of working part-time hours for awhile.

Manage what you have left. Try not to compound your losses with financial mismanagement. Unwatched money has a way of disappearing. Simplify your money management and your lifestyle. Find someone you trust to help you. Income tax time, which is a time of year when everything becomes a reminder of the losses, might be difficult for you. Have someone help you organize your paperwork.

Don't make rash decisions about anything based on your feelings. Don't feel guilty about claiming compensation or insurance money. You might want to wait a little before you change jobs or move to another house. Don't throw away money to relieve your guilt. Your feelings might be unreliable ways to make decisions.

Don't try to absorb all the losses by yourself. Seek out compensation programs. Apply for them. If you can't fill out the forms, have a friend do it for you. Be open about your losses with your friends. They might have helpful suggestions for you. If there is no compensation coming, be persistent. Don't wait too long. Often the struggle to become financially viable again is exactly the struggle we need to help us heal.

"*Fear alone is a form of victimization.*
The expectation that one might
be injured, raped, robbed or even killed
not only causes anxiety and even panic
but often generates a broad range
of avoidance behaviors."
—John P. J. Dussich

| 8 | BLAME/GUILT CONFUSION |

Tasty Mangoes

IT WAS MONDAY MORNING. My son came down the stairs from his bedroom, his face aflame with the most unusual rash.

There had been no indication the day before that there was anything wrong with him. In fact it had been a delightful summer day spent barbecuing in the backyard with friends and good food. The special dish of the meal had been a beautiful fruit platter that featured mangoes. My son, who had never tasted mangoes before, loved them.

As we looked at the rash, our first thought was that it might be a form of measles which was making the rounds in the neighborhood. He did have a hint of a rash on his torso. We immediately took him to the doctor who was also truly mystified by the concentration of the rash around the mouth. But he drew the same conclusion as we had; it must be measles. The result was that my son stayed home from school for an entire week.

We were still slightly suspicious the next time we served the ever-popular mangoes. I told him that perhaps this time he should be careful to eat the fruit with a fork and knife. He was extremely careful, but still indulged in what he claimed was his favorite fruit.

The next morning he emerged from his bedroom looking like something from a horror movie. His face had swollen to twice its normal size and was covered with a scaly, red rash. We took him immediately to the doctor. This time we all agreed it had to be the mangoes. We bought some salve for itchy skin and wrote a note to the teacher saying that he would have to miss another week of school.

The allergic reaction had doubled from eating the mangoes the first time to the second time. The process of recognizing the problem, identifying the source of the problem, and then solving the problem, was extremely important to us. Identifying the source of the allergy was critical.

Friend or Foe

We have a powerful passion to protect ourselves and to survive. We are born with many skills to do this. One skill that we don't often talk about is the ability to discern what will enhance our life or destroy it. It's an important skill because not all aspects of life that we encounter are friendly or life-giving. There are animals, foods, weather and people that will destroy us if we are not careful. For instance if we are going to forage for mushrooms, we need to be able to distinguish between those that will nourish us and those that will kill us. It's as simple as that.

We are born with the need for a "friend or foe" detector; I think it's officially called an "enemy perceiver." In elementary school it was easy and fundamental. All boys had fleas and they were easily identifiable. As for others, the girls who came to our church were friends; the rest were suspect. We called those who were our enemies names, avoided them or threw things at them to keep them at a distance.

Recently I flew into Ottawa. At the airport I noticed that staff were trying to determine if I was friend or foe. First of all at the ticketing desk they asked me some very pointed questions about my baggage and made a point of looking straight into my eyes. Then I went through security where I placed my carry-on baggage on a conveyer belt and I passed through a metal detector. As I boarded the airplane they checked my identification. Security is much heavier since September 11, the day we discovered that the enemy can live within our country.

We all have different perceived enemies. Anyone who threatens what we value becomes an enemy. For the poor, the rich are the perceived enemy because they are hoarding the wealth. For the rich, it is the poor because they might steal the wealth. For the politically left, it is the right; for the right, it is the left. For the environmentalist, it is the corporations; for the capitalist, it is the environmentalist. Everyone who has a cause or a goal has someone or something against whom they are fighting.

So we surround ourselves with family because we have an unspoken loyalty that unites us. We find friends and people who will enhance our lives. We join groups of like-minded people. And very subtly we work against those whom we have determined to be the enemy of the common good or at least our good.

Most of us don't really "go to war" with our enemy; we prefer to ridicule, demonize, diminish, lock away — or support someone else who is fighting the same war we are. The most common way to deal with that which irritates us or threatens us is to distance ourselves from it.

Most people have a good offensive and defensive strategy to succeed. In order to play a good game of hockey, football or any kind of competitive sport we need a forward line that scores the goals, and a good defense. It is elementary that we need to know who the opposing team is and know that our team supports us. Then we need a good offense to score the goals and a good defense to help defend our own goal.

Hopefully as we mature, we become more sophisticated in our discernment of what is good for us or not good for us. We no longer blame irresponsibly; we hold those who have done wrong, like breaking a law, accountable for what they have done. As we become adults and more secure in ourselves we become more gracious and compassionate, realizing that the challenge is not to eliminate everything that threatens us or that encroaches on our territory but to share what we have and learn to live together.

"Where there is no shame,
there is no honor."

—Ethiopian Proverb

Blame/Guilt Confusion

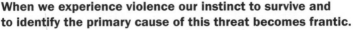

When we experience violence our instinct to survive and to identify the primary cause of this threat becomes frantic. In order to stop the violence and survive, we need to act quickly. We need to identify the enemy and form two strategies on how we are going to deal with this enemy — the offense and the defense.

This powerful emotional response to survive can suspend our ability to be rational in this matter. We often choose our target based not on reason or evidence, but on safety and vindication. This desperation combined with the emotions accompanying a threat can make our ability to blame responsibly questionable.

Research shows that we often don't identify our enemies correctly. We tend to scapegoat. This word describes an ancient custom performed by the Jewish high priests in which they would lay all the blame for the people's sins on a goat and then drive that goat into the wilderness. We still do some of that instinctively.

Rather than identify the person who actually did the crime we will often identify:
- **Someone vulnerable** someone either physically weak or someone who can't fight back.
- **Someone already flawed** someone who has already done something wrong.
- **Someone close to us whom we might want out of our lives.**

If we look closely at this criteria, we will notice that the people who are most vulnerable, most accessible and often flawed are the people close to us. We will often blame our family, friends, the marginalized in our society, the police officer who is trying to help, and mostly ourselves.

Blame, which means to find fault with or to hold someone responsible for, is a powerful instinct. This blaming instinct directs our anger to the enemy target and demands that we expose or name the enemy. Confused blame, fuelled by our already strong emotions of terror and rage, can become a formidable force.

Confused blame likes a simple target. It doesn't like to deal with complexity. It likes to find one target and annihilate it quickly.

In our support group I'll never forget the night we went around the circle and all of us shared stories of innocent bystanders who had at a moment's notice become the target of our blame. One woman described how she had stepped on a bus early in the morning and the bus driver had very casually and politely asked her how she was feeling. She blasted him verbally saying it was none of his business. Another had blasted a friend, another a family member. All of us had stories of times when we had overreacted to a small incident to the point of absurdity. We laughed together in embarrassment as we pitied the targets of our outburst.

Self-blame or guilt is our defense line, a powerful instinct we use to hold ourselves accountable if we are responsible. We have what we call a conscience that monitors our own behavior. As much as we have tried to minimize the role of conscience in our society — usually because it is associated with the pain and discomfort of a guilty conscience — the need for a healthy working conscience is an absolute must for living in harmony with our own values, ethics and goals.

At an early age our conscience is programmed by adopting the values and code of ethics of those who care for us. Maturity is programming our own conscience. Every time I decide that I want to go on a diet and not snack in between meals, my guilt will kick in when I break that promise to myself. Harlan Wechsler says that self-blame or guilt is a guide to our moral wellness. "Guilt is a sign of something going on inside a human being, of something that is not right, that has to be fixed up." Guilt serves to flag every word that is less than truthful, every act that doesn't meet our standard and every thought that betrays our values. Without these helpful red flags, our lives would disintegrate into a free-for-all, an undisciplined muddle.

Unfortunately our guilt can become confused. In the book, *Giving Sorrow Words,* the author, John Adams, writes, "Most people are remarkably creative when it comes to finding reasons to feel guilty. They feel guilty about their actions and their thoughts. Sometimes they feel guilty merely because they are still alive and the other person is dead."

According to Marlene Young, director of NOVA (National Organization for Victim Assistance), there are three guilts which victims need to deal with: legitimate guilt, illegitimate guilt, and survivor's guilt. "Legitimate cognitive guilt is the kind that emerges when we identify our role in whatever happens and deal with the issues that we had some control over. Illegitimate guilt is the type of guilt that focusses on the should'ves, could'ves and would'ves over which we have no control. When survivors feel guilty for continuing to live, it is called survivor's guilt."

In our group we had plenty of illegitimate guilt or confused guilt. In one case a woman had told her fiancé that she would prefer to do laundry on a Thursday and not go out until Friday. The next day she discovered that he had been killed late Thursday night when he had wanted to be with her, and would have been safe doing safe things. She could not enter her laundry room for almost a year and had to rely on friends to help her to do her wash.

In my case, guilt visited me on the anniversary of the day that Candace went missing. I realized that what my conscience was telling me was that if I had picked up Candace that day, none of this would have happened. Candace would be alive. The end result of that line of thinking made me an accomplice to the murder. The feelings of that pain were incredible.

The power of confused guilt is not a thing to be toyed with. We need to take it seriously. Wechsler says, "People sometimes feel so guilty at these times that they take out their guilt by persecuting the members of their families. Because a man feels guilty about what he has done, he will blame his wife for every possible sin under the sun."

Redmond in her book, *Surviving: When Someone You Love Was Murdered,* says this survivor's guilt is very common. "Survivors express guilt and feelings of responsibility because they believed themselves to be in control and were, in fact, in control prior to the event. There is incongruity in this belief as it is proven invalid after the murder of a loved one. The criminal has erased the power and control exercised in carrying out the daily functions of living. The murderer not only took the life of the victim, but plunged the lives of the survivors into excruciating painful grief."

Underlying Reasons for our Blame/Guilt Confusion

Because we are often unable to immediately identify the primary cause of violence, we may remain confused.

We might not have all the research or investigative tools to know who really did the act. Contrary to what people say, some people do get away with murder, perhaps not in the long run but in the short run. And the need for "immediate" justice puts pressure on everyone to the right offender. If this is done irrationally, we can "wrongfully accuse" someone innocent.

Causes for most serious crime are complicated. A woman who has been abused all her life kills her violent husband in an explosive rage. We know murder is always wrong. But where does the blame lie? In the case of neglected children who grow up and commit criminal acts, where does the blame lie? With the children only? With the neglectful parents, the child and family service bureaucracy, or the state of poverty? Where do we begin with blame? Where do we end?

The offender can be overpowering. If the offender is powerful, threatening, unrepentant, resourceful, or a well-respected member of society, it's extremely difficult to lay blame. It might even be dangerous to blame that person.

Blame will find the target of least resistance — someone unable to fight back, someone already flawed, someone who has already done something wrong, someone expendable. We often scapegoat members of our families because they are safe. We know their faults, and their love makes them powerless against us.

Blame can be based on misguided belief systems that will make us take the blame for everything that goes wrong. Janice Lord in her book, *No Time For Goodbyes,* suggests some things we believe that are impossible and that create guilt:

- People who love each other should always be responsible for each other and be able to protect each other.
- If I had been a better person, this wouldn't have happened to my loved one.
- If I begin to feel better, it will mean that I didn't love him or her enough.
- It is not right that my loved one died and I continue to live.
- Good things happen to good people and bad things happen to bad people.

If we are guilty (bad) at least we can hang on to an old belief which makes some sense of our loved one's death.

Not only are we the victims confused, the media and people around us are often confused. As Janoff-Bulman writes, "For non-victims who attempt to make sense of criminal victimization, there is also a focus on what the victim could or should have done. In their attempts to maintain a belief in their own relative invulnerability, people try to distinguish themselves from victims."

Recently I picked up *The Globe and Mail* newspaper and was puzzled by the title "Door ajar in case of dead five-year-old." I wondered how an open door could cause the death of a little girl. My immediate thought was that she had probably wandered off. As it turned out, the little girl had fallen asleep, the door had been left open and someone had abducted her. Leaving the door open really had nothing to do with her death. Sleeping with the door slightly ajar isn't a crime. Taking a little girl from her home is. The article should have been entitled, "Man charged after girl found dead." These subtle attempts to blame the victims influence all of us.

Confused blame can often be traced to deeply hidden feelings of guilt. By uncovering our own guilt, we will be able to do the blaming more accurately, more rationally and with better judgment.

Consequences of Blame/Guilt Confusion

Blame and guilt serve as huge signs in our lives which are positioned to stop us from continuing to do something that is dangerous or unethical. If we are consciously or unconsciously blaming someone we love, we will find it very difficult to continue in partnership with them. If we blame our children for some misfortune, we will have a tendency to shout at them, neglect them, and abuse them. It is extremely difficult to cherish and treasure someone or something that we feel is hurting us.

In the same way, we cannot participate in any habit or action that we have guilt feelings about. A friend of mine had issues with keys and locking things. She kept dropping her keys, losing them and talking about them. It remained a mystery until we were able to make the connection between her son's death in an unlocked car and her guilt around keys and locking things.

We will be unable to go to places that arouse guilt feelings. If we blame ourselves we might become our own worst enemy. We turn all the anger, the guilt, the fear and the grief inward.

Confused blame/guilt can become pervasive. If guilt is not dealt with, it can become a way of feeling. We feel guilty about everything. If blame is not dealt with, it can become the way of dealing with everything. We have no friends; everyone is an enemy.

The tendency to blame the crime victim for the crime influences the rehabilitation programs for victims. Janoff-Bulman makes a strong case for this in her article, *Criminal vs. Non-criminal Victimization*. "There is substantial evidence in social psychology that the more individuals are blamed for their own circumstances, the less likely they are to receive help from others. Crime victims are likely to be in need of the greatest social support following their victimization, and yet it appears they may be likely to receive the least."

Untangling our Blame/Guilt Confusion

In her research Redmond learned "resolving guilt required understanding of each person's particular reason for self-blame rather than a blanket absolution." We need to go back to the source of blame and our self-blame.

Guilt and blame will need constant monitoring. Every time there is a loss, every time we feel fear or anger, we will be looking for something to blame for the injustices we are experiencing. As long as our world feels unsafe, uncontrolled, we will be instinctively looking for causes.

If we haven't been conscious of our blame and guilt, we might need someone to help us sort through these feelings.

Considerations

Cherish your instinct to defend yourself. Cherish your ability to discern those who are for you and those who are against you. We need to know who is life-giving and who is life-taking.

Monitor your guilt and blame. Ask yourself who you are targeting. If you don't know, ask a good friend if you are showing signs of blame confusion or guilt. It's amazing how often our family and our friends know this about us.

If you are showing signs of confused blaming or guilt, follow the blame and guilt paths to their sources. Who are you blaming for this violence? And why are you blaming this person? Are you blaming yourself?

Once you've identified the source, ask yourself if the source is in fact the person guilty of the actual murder. Think it through carefully.

During your analysis if you come across things that you have done in your life, where you behaved badly, acknowledge it. We all make mistakes, but a mistake prior to the murder or right after the murder does not make us guilty of the murder itself. Disassociate your own mistakes from the overall trauma and murder and deal with them separately.

If you can't do this by yourself, confess your guilt feelings to someone close to you. Integrate your feelings of guilt into your story, giving the reasons why you felt guilty and how you dealt with guilt. You can also apply your spiritual knowledge and background to it. Working through guilt can lead to an experience of renewal.

Think carefully again about the act of violence and identify all the people responsible for the violence and their subsequent failure to either contain the violence or prevent it. Blame responsibly. In the case of one murder, I remember the mother confessing her guilt feelings even though she had nothing to do with the act. Her son had been abusive and his wife had stabbed him to death. Together we went through the process of identifying all the people who had failed her son. We identified the father who had abandoned him, the social services who had only aggravated the problems, and a teacher who had failed him. We identified the woman who had married him and had heightened the stress in his life. As we continued to identify all the causes, we had to name her son and identify the mistakes of her son, and forgive him for the things he had done that had led up to the violence that had taken his life. We need to identify all the people who are guilty before we can move on to the next step of containing the violence and preventing it from happening again.

Remember that this isn't a one-time process. Confused, irrational blame is very much like weeds growing in a beautiful garden. We need to be constantly weeding. Watch out for the roots. Often by the time we've noticed the virus of illegitimate guilt or blame, the message has already become ingrained in our minds and will reactivate the old behaviors. Weed out the wrong messages constantly. Keep your garden tidy. A healthy accurate blaming instinct and an accurate conscience will be your friend and not your enemy.

*"Conscience is a great servant
but a terrible master.
It is somewhat like an automobile horn.
It is useful for warding off impending danger.
But if a horn gets stuck,
it's a terrible nuisance."*

—Rabbi Sidney Greenberg

9	TRUTH DILEMMA

Fragile Figurines

WILL IT BE ALL RIGHT? The tension choked us as we lifted the lid. Recently my husband began to experiment with clay sculpture. Out of his artist's imagination came these foot-high action figurines of farm boys captured in still life, illustrating life on the farm in the Forties. One boy is riding a pig; another is being chased by a white goose. The figurines are fun, cheery and delightful.

The process of making one of these figurines is tedious and challenging. First there is the preparation of the clay. It needs to be kneaded until all the air pockets are smoothed out; otherwise the figurine will explode in the kiln. Then there is the design of the figurine. Molded out of pure clay, which is really just wet mud, it needs to be braced and formed in such a way that it doesn't flop into a mass of mud again before the next day. After the basic molding has been done, the boy emerges — body, head and hair. Then there is the carving of the details; the hair needs to look like hair and the creases in the blue jean overalls need to look real. During this time, the drying of the clay has to be monitored. If dried too fast, the figurine will crack; if the clay is too moist, the figurine will turn back into mud. So it is wrapped, sprayed and let to dry — slowly, ever so slowly.

The color is perhaps the greatest challenge. It is impossible to tell what a certain color will look like from the applications. As the clay is fired and turns from mud into stone, something happens to the color. Yet the colors need to be evenly applied, perfectly edged — not one little crevice can remain untouched.

The hours are painstaking. I keep telling my husband that he should really try out the colors on something less detailed and advanced — but he is insistent. "If I've done it once and something happens in the kiln," he says, "I can do it again."

Yes — but the work!

The firing takes forever. Four hours of constant heat and then at least six hours to cool slowly. The slow cooling is another important test of our patience. If cooled too quickly, the beautiful figurines will crack.

Finally when we lift the lid of the kiln, we have no idea if there has been a hidden air pocket in one of the figurines which could have exploded the entire collection, whether they have cracked, or what the colors will look like. Anticipating the moment of truth is excruciatingly painful.

Data, Information, Knowledge, Understanding and Wisdom

There is probably no segment of activity in the world attracting as much attention at present as that of "knowledge management." The computer age has brought on the new problem of "information overload." Our own minds are still probably the best examples of efficient management of information.

According to system theorist, Russel Ackoff, the contents of the mind can be classified into five categories:

- **Data** — symbols. Data is raw. An example could be a spreadsheet of numbers.
- **Information** — data that has been processed to be useful which provides answers for the four questions: Who? What? Where? and When?
- **Knowledge** — data that answers the "how" question.
- **Understanding** — explores the "why" question.
- **Wisdom** — evaluates the understanding of the above information. Wisdom is the application of the acquired understanding combined with the knowledge.

Many of us refer to the entire process of knowledge management as finding the "truth." We need truth. All of us feel safer, more validated, more sure-footed, when we encounter all of the truth. Truth is like that perfect mirror that reflects back to us the reality of the way things are. No one can own truth. It is not exclusive. We each hold a part of the truth of what happens at any given time. My truth does not threaten your truth.

According to Webster's dictionary, truth means "the real state of things" or the "actuality of something." Truth is our reality check in everything we do. Truth is that over-arching word for describing the essence of what we experience and learn. It is the father of a family of words: information, inquest, facts, proof, evidence, meaning, definition, history, education, research, honesty, integrity, searching, learning.

Unfortunately, it is easy to fudge the truth. Counterfeiting happens in everything we value. There is fake money, fake designer clothes, fake ID, fake food, fake information, fake statistics, fake knowledge and fake understanding. We call some people "fake." In this day and age technology has given us the ability to technically enhance all images to the point where we know that probably every magazine cover is a fantasy. It shouldn't surprise us then that we are being flooded with "reality" programs on television.

TRUTH DILEMMA

9

After a murder or an act of violence, the truth of what happened, who and why, is often shattered into a million pieces. According to Judith Herman, "the perpetrator does everything in his power to promote forgetting. Secrecy and silence are the perpetrator's first line of defense." If this fails, an offender will attack the victim's credibility. "If he cannot silence her completely, he tries to make sure that no one listens."

Herman maintains that after every atrocity "...one can expect to hear the same predictable apologies: it never happened; the victim lies; the victim exaggerates; the victim brought it upon herself; and in any case it is time to forget the past and move on. The more powerful the perpetrator, the greater is his prerogative to name and define reality, the more completely his arguments prevail."

After a murder or any other serious crime, we need to know exactly what happened. In a *Newsweek* article published shortly after the September 11 terrorist attacks, there is a full-page spread describing the entire event; the buildings are diagramed, the collapse documented, the timing detailed. Not only do the victims of that attack need to know, we all need to know.

Murder is very much like a terrorist attack. One moment we can have a good handle on our lives. We can know where our loved ones are, where we are going, and what we will be doing the next day. We know the truth about our lives. The next moment after a murder, our lives can be shattered into a million pieces.

In order for us to pick up the pieces of our lives, we need to not only know what happened, we also need to understand what happened. We will instinctively need to collect all the pieces of the wreckage, lay them out like a giant puzzle, analyze the findings to identify the cause so we can fix it and create safety again. It's our way of solving a problem. In the case of murder, the problem is the biggest we have ever encountered; therefore the pieces are all extremely important.

The Truth and Reconciliation Commission was the perfect example of how truth helped create justice for victims. The South African Commission was charged with several tasks: to establish a complete picture of the nature, causes and extent of gross violation of human rights; to grant amnesty to persons who make full disclosure of all the relevant facts; to give victims an opportunity to relate the violations they suffered; to take measures of reparation, rehabilitation and the restoration of human and civil dignity to the victims; to report to the nation on its findings; and finally to make recommendations for prevention of such an atrocity in the future. Many people believe that this Commission prevented the country from disintegrating into a blood bath.

There are some who felt it didn't go far enough. To give amnesty to offenders without further accountability doesn't seem fair. Whatever the weaknesses, Gregory Jones says in his article on the South African Commission, "The very process of requiring personal, public confession requires an accountability that we ought not to underestimate. South African amnesty allows the perpetrators to go free, but it also has required them to confess the truth of what they have done. This involves courage, and it also enables South Africa and the whole world to have public reckoning of the past."

However, in the aftermath of murder, information is not easily accessible; the pieces are not easily obtained. Neither is the information we seek easy to deal with.

The cold hard facts of the murder can often be frightening and abhorrent. Our underlying question, "Why did this happen to me?" is a universal question that defies an answer.

Janoff-Bulman writes, "Victims are suddenly forced to confront the possibility of arbitrariness in life — the possibility that not only are events not predictable, but they do not make sense. Understanding the event becomes of paramount importance.... Why did this event happen? Why did it happen to me? How is one to understand the world in light of the occurrence of this event?"

Gwen Thiessen still finds it difficult that there are some pieces of the story missing. She finds it difficult that no part of her niece's body has ever been recovered. "That he (the offender) couldn't at least give us just one part of her — just one part of her so that we could say goodbye."

Their quest will continue because of this. In her impact statement Gwen wrote, "We are forever going to be attempting to find some way of living with the depraved and heinous details of Jodi's death. In daylight hours we try to function as 'normal' members of our family and friends, but feel totally set apart. In the darkness of night, we dare not allow our minds to slip into the replaying of horrific scenes of inconceivable brutality and appalling disrespect. Recovery from the devastation, pain, sorrow and insecurity seem unattainable."

Nils Christie in his paper on *Answers to Atrocities* writes, "Silence is one of the answers to atrocities.... Isolation of the victim is one of the major features in social systems where illegitimate violence is applied. There are no ends of attempts by oppressors to silence their victims."

And yet we need to have the truth known and spoken.

Underlying Reasons for
Truth Dilemma in Violent Crimes

Why is information and truth so difficult to access?

Often we, as victims, want to avoid the painful details ourselves. Our own fears can be our own block to pursuing our needs. We are horrified that we want to know the gory details. It feels so morbid — so abnormal. Friends of ours might show disapproval because of our interest; this might discourage us.

We might not be able to face the truth of the murder, because it might mean facing problems in our own lives. If we didn't have a good relationship with the person murdered, we might find it difficult to want to know the entire truth about the person and about what happened.

Some of the information is simply out of reach. It might be kept back legitimately because of the need for confidentiality during the investigation. However that doesn't mean it isn't important to us — or needed by us.

Some of the answers lie within the offender who is inaccessible. Many offenders are uncommunicative, evasive, or dead, killed by their own hand or the state. Victims who have access to their offenders often feel that the offender is not believable.

Because we suffer from trauma, our lack of concentration, the inability to remember anything, and the lack of ambition make it difficult to have the internal resources to find and obtain the needed information.

Sometimes we can lack the financial resources needed to access the information. Research might mean travelling, buying transcripts.

There is an overwhelming fear by professionals and caregivers of hurting the victims more; therefore, they protect the victims from information they think is painful. Unfortunately, by not giving us the painful information, they prolong the grief and accentuate the pain. We have a right to the pain that belongs to us.

Pain can be valuable. Lepers and athletes know the value of pain. It is often in our most painful moments that we grow. Even small discomforts like having our water turned off because of a water main break (which happened recently to us) can have value. Having to go out and haul water from a common water wagon provided a great meeting place for the entire neighborhood. Even though we avoid painful situations at any cost, most of us have to admit that it has been during the painful moments in our lives that we have the courage to change, that we become open to new learnings and are forced to cross otherwise forbidden boundaries. In the same way, we need access to the pain of a violent crime to benefit from the learnings.

Sometimes there is a conspiracy of cover up.

Some people lie. We ourselves might be less than honest with ourselves.

"You have an enormous feeling of wanting to understand and not being able to."
—Parents whose son was murdered

Consequences of Truth Dilemma

Not knowing the truth might hinder us from being able to tell our story in its entirety. Until we are able to tell our story we don't own it; we remain out of control of our lives.

If we don't know the answers to some of the "why" questions, we might not be able to feel safe again. We might constantly feel that we will be threatened again.

Most of us have fertile imaginations that, when fuelled with trauma, can create monsters out of the most ordinary people. Solid information of how the events unfold will help to contain our imaginations.

We can become stuck in the quest to know. We might spend a great deal of time researching the crime, trying to understand. I met a student who decided to study criminology because her mother was murdered, then realized too late that she wasn't suited for this kind of work. Searching for the meaning behind violence might keep us from doing what we were meant to do and living our own lives.

Accessing the Truth: Living with the Truth

Remember all of us are different in how we access truth. Some of us would rather have it given second-hand, already processed by a trusted friend. Others prefer to go and find out for themselves, to confront the hard evidence face-to-face.

We all learn in different ways; some of us prefer to read everything, or write it down. Some prefer to hear the truth orally and process it orally. Some might have to touch. Some rely on professionals to access the truth without emotion. Some of us need to hear it only once; some of us need to hear it many times before we can integrate it into our understanding. Some of us are more timid and need more time; some of us like to "get it over with."

But we do have some common needs. Most victims will need to know about the body of their loved one. Most victims who were able to view their loved one are glad they did. If you were unable to do so, you may have to find other ways after the funeral to assure yourself of the reality of the death.

Most of us will need to know some details about the crime — when, where and how it happened. Most of us will want to know how long our loved one suffered or how severe the pain was. Was the case handled in such a way that it prevented further pain, suffering or loss? Was the emergency response quick enough? We might need to see the medical examiner's autopsy report.

Most of us will need to know what is happening to the offender. Why did the person do it? How will the crime be processed through the justice system? Where is the offender being held? Some of us will want an ongoing report; others will want to stop their involvement after the trial.

Most of us will want to know personal information. Is there counselling available? Is there compensation for this crime? Is there time off from work to heal? Is the home safe to live in? Is everyone else in the family all right? What services in the community are available? How do we deal with the media? There are now practical guidebooks that answer these questions. Recent legislation has also mandated that criminal justice services provide this information for victims. Underlying our personal questions might be the basic question, "Why did this happen to me?"

At the best of times, it takes a great deal of courage to access the information that is both horrific and threatening. That's why we, as surviving victims, can easily be persuaded to leave "it" alone and to avoid pursuing answers to our questions. However, it is important to collect all the information possible. It doesn't mean that you have to read it all right away or spend hours analyzing it. But it might mean that you need to set up a box or a basket where you can place all the "papers" that contain the information you may want to look at some time in the future when you are ready.

Remember that sometimes denial takes as much effort as the accessing of truth and information does. At one workshop, a woman came up to me and told me that she knew the exact day the police report of assault was going to be shredded. She had been invited a couple of years ago to come and read it. She assured me that she had every intention of going to read it. "But I have a few months left," she said. "It's been bothering me all this time. I don't know why I didn't just go look at it a long time ago."

Considerations

Ask. Try to isolate some of the main questions you may have.
The better you can articulate your question, the more others can
help you find the answer. There is no such thing as a dumb question.

Be assertive. Remember you have a right to information about
your own life. If professional service providers are evasive when
you approach them with questions, be insistent.

**Be creative and pursue truth on all levels, constantly and
anywhere.** We learn about life in so many different ways. In the
stories of victims I have heard the most bizarre examples of how
people have found "answers" to their questions. However, all those
who came to some point of acceptance in the aftermath of
violence had one thing in common — they were all looking.
Sometimes it took a lot of time.

Plan ahead for hard answers. Remember that if you are accessing truth and processing it, it will take energy. For instance, if you are
anticipating a medical examiner's report, plan to have someone with
whom to debrief. Invite someone you trust to be with you. Have them
read it to you so you can have a buffer between you and the truth
until you are ready to access more information. Prepare to take
some time off after to "collect" yourself and process this new information. You might want to schedule an appointment with a trained
counsellor three days after you access the information just so you
have an inner timetable of how you are going to do this.

**The journey to find truth can also be found in other victims'
stories.** Read stories of other people who have gone through
similar experiences. This will provide you with a feeling of support
and also give you courage to know you are not alone. You might
find clues on how to deal with your own questions.

Remember no one person has all the answers for you.
I can't stress enough the need to gather around yourself many
people with many answers.

The process of gathering information is very individual.
People need different timing and access different truths. Some of us need to go right into the medical examiner's room and identify the body; some of us don't. Listen to your own heart.

Decide how you are going to organize your findings. This does not need to be elaborate — a box in the corner will do. If you find this difficult, you might want to find someone to do this for you. I think all of us know "newspaper clippers" and each family has a "storyteller" who is a natural researcher. Use these gifted people, affirm them, encourage them, and ask them to hold the information for you. Then when you are ready, you can ask to take their research and copy it for yourself. Or you might have them read it for you.

> *"Justice is knowing and acting on the truth and I don't know the whole truth."*
> —Man whose sister was murdered

"What is truth?
A difficult question
but I have solved it for myself
by saying that it is what
the 'voice within' tells you."

—Mahatma Gandhi

| 10 | UNCONTROLLABLE RAGE |

Migrating Geese

"THIS TIME I HAVE TO DO IT RIGHT," I said as we pulled two lawn chairs and a large loaf of bread from the trunk of our car.

It was towards the end of October, a beautiful warm autumn day that was coming to a graceful ending. A friend of mine and I had just a bit of time to feed the geese before they would return to their evening home, in a nearby swamp.

About this time every year thousands upon thousands of Canada geese, snow geese and ducks migrate through our city on their way to their wintering grounds to the south. Many of them rest for a day or two at a pond near our subdivision.

The first time we had attempted to feed the geese, we had done it all wrong. We had just walked right down to the pond's edge which sent most of them flapping into the air and on their way. Those that remained would have nothing to do with us.

This time we were going to do it right. We chose to come in from the west and follow the shadow of the trees to the pond's edge. We moved slowly. We whispered in hushed tones. We took our time and paused, allowing the birds to move slowly out of our path.

Finally when we were all set up, we started to throw crumbs into the pond. The seagulls noticed the free food first and swooped down to catch the morsels of bread in mid-flight. Their squawking drew attention to us and slowly, always with extreme dignity, the Canada geese started to swim closer, curious. Eventually they were all around us, begging for our food — ducks, geese and the forever annoying seagulls. We gave out the food slowly, watching them, enjoying them and catching a glimpse of their community living.

We had done it right. We had followed the code of bird feeders: move slowly, have food, talk softly, have patience, spend time among the birds, trust them, love them and they will come close.

Not every bird was following the rules. The seagulls often swooped too close to the geese and were hissed at. The seagulls would all converge on a piece of food and have to fight it out amongst themselves. Even the mallard ducks would make the mistake of moving into someone's territory and get hissed at.

It was a fragile moment. We were nervous about being so close. Then just as we were relaxing and enjoying this new-found intimacy with our wild friends, three children came running down the hill right into the middle of the flock, sending them fluttering into the sky.

They had broken all the rules. They had destroyed the moment. The peaceful feelings that we had so carefully cultivated had been replaced by the negative feeling of pure disgust.

Confrontation and Accountability

In order to live in peace with each other as a civilization we have developed a highly intuitive sense of right and wrong. We have carefully constructed a body of rules and laws, written and unwritten, a way of social control that governs absolutely everything we do. When we don't have these rules, we have chaos.

Where I work we have about fifty staff working in an open space environment which means we all sit in little cubicles and can hear each other talking. We share the same printer, copier, fax machine, computer system and coffee machine. To live in harmony we have set up a social contract. We have a staff manual that guides us through the bigger policies and issues. For the smaller things we resort to little notes and instructions. Near the copying machine there is a sign, "If you use this for personal use, put your money here." Another one says, "Don't use the blue paper for extensive runs, it jams the machine." It is our way of working together and management's way of having members contribute to the welfare of the office community.

But no matter how hard we try to manage this delicate balance of sharing and living together, at some point someone will fail to follow the rules. There is always someone who parks in the wrong stall, someone who borrows a book and doesn't bring it back or someone who doesn't pay for his or her coffee.

In our office the smallest infraction will elicit an e-mail — always gracious — asking us to keep the lounge tidy, put the newspaper back, submit our bills before the end of the month, refrain from using too much toilet paper and to record the mileage if we use the van.

Without confrontation we would never be able to maintain a well-run, peaceful working environment. Experts in conflict resolution have been trying to teach us that conflict is a natural and inevitable part of living together with others. A good conflict resolution process, holding someone accountable, talking about solutions, can leave us all in a win/win situation. It takes energy to confront someone if he or she has broken a rule. The emotion that helps us monitor the rules is the anger emotion.

When we confront someone with an infraction, we inevitably feel irritated. We nag, we confront, we accuse, we hold someone accountable, we criticize, ridicule, shun, guide, coach, police, guard, scandalize, defame, abuse, disparage, malign, revile, disgrace, shame, slander, dishonor, avenge, implicate, upbraid, condemn. There are many ways to let someone know he or she is stepping out of line.

As the boundaries and rules become more significant, guarding them is more critical to us. When our lives are endangered on the highway, we escalate into road rage. We will also rage if someone insults us, steals the love of our spouse, or in any way endangers our children. We will protect what we value with a great deal of energy.

"Anger develops as a natural response of the failure of others to meet with one's needs for love, praise, acceptance and justice," writes Richard Fitzgibbons in *Anger and the Healing Power of Forgiveness*. The victim's greatest contempt is often reserved not for the perpetrator but for the passive bystander. It is not only the offender that we might feel anger towards, but also towards those who remained indifferent to us and failed to help.

Anger has many faces and degrees of expression. It can be slight displeasure or annoyance, irritation, indignation, exasperation, wrath, hate, loathing, suspicion or furious anger. The more extreme states are called rage or vengeance.

Anger is a powerful source of physiological arousal. When we're angry our heart pounds, our blood pressure increases, we breathe faster, and our muscles tense as we experience the irresistible urge to do something about that which irritates us. The anger energy is stored in our muscles. Our body responds by glaring, flushing, paling, having chills and shudders, prickly sensations, sweating, feeling hot or cold, and losing control.

We become angry when we feel powerless, manipulated, and controlled. We feel angry when we are dishonored, insulted or when justice hasn't been served and someone has been unfairly treated, violated or abused.

We use anger for many good reasons.

- **We use anger to signal a warning to trespassers.** The raised clenched fist, the finger, the curse, the angry retort are all angry gestures that warn people that if they continue, they can expect the next level of anger.

- **We use anger to muster the courage and energy needed to correct a wrong, and if need be, to physically fight for our rights and our territory.** Anger also gives us courage. Anger reinforces our strength, gives us endurance, focus and the will to win. Anger often sharpens our wits, and gives us an ability to express ourselves. Anger makes us better fighters. We use it to protect.

- **We use anger to create boundaries.** In their adolescent years, teenagers who love their parents will begin to use anger to create the separation needed for healthy independence. Anger in this case is used as a boundary maker.

UNCONTROLLABLE RAGE

Rage or righteous anger is a natural response to a violent atrocity. But this natural anger we feel about an injustice can take on unusual proportions in the face of murder or a serious violation. We should not be able to read about the Paul Bernardo case without feeling a deep sense of rage. The problem is that this rage can quickly grow to unmanageable proportions.

This uncontrollable rage is not a rational emotion. It can begin to control us. Rage is characterized by revenge fantasies. Judith Herman states, "Some of us devise elaborate plans of torturous treatment. We delight in seeing the murderer suffer in an even more horrendous manner than one's own loved one did. These revenge fantasies, even though they are a normal reaction to something as horrific as murder, can frighten us when we feel them or when we hear someone else express these fantasies."

Lula Redmond observes that people surviving murder have "murderous impulses and anger." Often people who work with homicide victims complain about the anger in victims. As Redmond says, "One of the most difficult emotional reactions to understand by survivors, family members, friends and therapists and others who serve the victimized survivors is the intensity, duration and frequency of anger and rage. Anger is a normal healthy emotion.... For the homicide survivor, the normal anger of grief is compounded by the rage and desire to violently destroy the murderer of the loved one."

A friend of ours still has revenge fantasies eighteen years after the rape and murder of his sixteen-year-old daughter. Ray Hughes says, "You get mad at somebody but not with the kind of anger I have now. I could shoot a moose but it's kind of hard to go and gut an animal that was living. But with the murderer, the gutting would be easy — even before death when he would feel the pain. Then he would know just a little bit of our pain that we have for a lifetime. The murderer must know the meaning of life that he has taken and what that life means to us."

I was horrified too when I encountered this violence in myself. I knew it was something bigger than myself. About four months after Candace's death, a good friend asked me what it would take for there to be justice for me. I told her that it wouldn't be enough for that person to die because he would be dying for something he had done. Candace had been innocent. I was surprised at my answer. I believed I was anti-capital punishment.

I found myself continuing to search for that feeling of satisfying justice. I heard myself saying, "Ten child murderers would have to die, and I would have to pull the trigger."

What a shock! Since then I've come to believe that even the most decent of us will entertain revenge fantasies if the very core of our love and survival has been hurt.

Most of us don't act out our revenge fantasies, but that doesn't make the reality of them any less.

"Anger is our friend.
Not a nice friend. Not a gentle friend.
But a very, very loyal friend.
It will always tell us
when we have been betrayed."

—Julia Cameron

Underlying Reasons for Uncontrollable Rage

Murder violates every sense of right and wrong that we have.
It violates our boundaries, territories, our honor, our pride and
our trust. Most of all it threatens our lives, not just the life of the
one murdered, but all of our lives. The only answer to something
so violating in our society is good healthy righteous anger that
acts quickly to make things right. However when we can't act,
we feel disempowered. Our righteous anger, justified in the proper
situation, turns to uncontrollable rage.

**Most of us who encounter this rage are unfamiliar with the
intensity of this new emotion.** We don't know how to control it.
We try and squelch it ourselves.

**There is no acceptable way in our society to give expression
to this intense rage.** In times past if a clan of families experienced an insult or injustice, they could band together, declare war
and take care of the matter themselves. In that way they had
control over their lives and, consequently, control over their rage.

**The criminal justice system process maintains that to create
equal justice for all, it must remain objective and emotion-
less.** Instead of recognizing the natural anger expressed during an
injustice and helping the victim deal with his or her rage, there is
no place for emotion in the courtroom. The lack of understanding
for this justified anger only fuels rage.

**Rage is unacceptable in our society that requires us to be in
control of ourselves at all times.** Angry disruptions and protests
are frowned upon. We feel the disapproval of those around us
when we display our anger. Their lack of understanding only aggravates our rage.

Often our anger will be used against us to destroy our credibility. Victims are often described as "angry, vengeful, and irresponsible." This aggravates the feeling of not being listened to. Uncontrollable rage will only escalate this response. A child who isn't listened to will begin to raise his or her voice until the child screams and is finally heard. In the same way, rage not listened to will scream louder.

Consequences of Uncontrollable Rage

Venting of this uncontrolled rage is not productive. It is like revving the car continuously without putting it in gear. Constant venting actually encourages more rage and enhances it. We can become addicted to the state of being enraged and feeling powerful in that rage. The constant revving of our rage can cause extreme physical problems.

Uncontrollable rage at some point becomes impossible to manage and counter productive. One's ability to be logical, rational or reasonable decreases rapidly until it becomes almost nil. Good judgment drops as anger escalates.

However repressed rage can also cause physical problems in our lives. Rage can turn our minds into an internal courtroom where we can rage and debate the issues for the rest of our lives. The power of rage can deplete our energy.

If we can't do something about the causes of anger in our lives, the subsequent feeling of powerlessness and feeling defeated can lead to a place of depression. Anger can become pervasive. It will take over our lives and our expressions. Life requires us to respond in a variety of ways — sometimes in love, sometimes in grief, sometimes in fear, sometimes in tenderness. If anger controls us, we will respond in only one way with anger. We will see all the injustices in everything. There will be a beautiful rose and we won't be able to see its beauty; we will see only the thorns. Anger promotes a very narrow, unhappy perspective on life.

Uncontrollable rage is unacceptable in our society. Our friends and family feel justifiably unsafe around the intensity of this emotion. Uncontrollable rage feels dangerous to those around us.

They will begin to avoid coming close to us. Remember that rage is a relationship breaker which is why emotional anger targeted towards an innocent person can alienate that person forever. He or she will never be able to forget our anger and our display of aggression.

The worst case scenario is that, if we haven't gained control of our anger, we will abuse someone we love. Or we will have become what we have hated — an offender.

Attending to our Anger: Recycling our Rage

Don't be ashamed or alarmed about your anger. Julia Cameron, author of *The Artist's Way,* writes, "Anger is fuel. We feel it and we want to do something: hit someone, break something, throw a fit, smash a fist into the wall, tell those bastards. But we are nice people, and what we do with our anger is bury it, hide it, lie about it, medicate it, ignore it. We do everything but listen to it. Anger is meant to be listened to. Anger is a voice, a shout, a plea, a demand. Anger is meant to be respected. Why? Because anger is a map. Anger shows us where our boundaries are. Anger shows us where we want to go. It lets us see where we've been and lets us know when we haven't liked it. Anger points the way, not just the finger. In grief, anger is a sign of health. Anger is meant to be acted upon. It is not meant to be acted out. We are meant to use anger as fuel to take the actions we need to move where our anger points us. With a little thought we can usually translate the message that our anger is sending us."

It is the intensity of anger after murder that needs special attention. It is the "uncontrolled" anger, and the "unresolvable" anger that you need to be worried about.

To do this you need to apply your best thinking to understand the source of your anger. Identify the exact injustice, the exact betrayal, the exact moment of pain that arouses this anger. In other words, find your trigger point and instead of stifling or hiding or even ignoring your anger, know your anger.

Richard Fitzgibbons writes, "The experience of anger leads to a desire for revenge, which does not diminish until the existence of the resentful feelings is recognized and subsequently resolved. It will not be fully resolved until a conscious decision is made to let go of the desire for revenge."

Also learn that there can be no "irresponsible angry outbursts." Anger is no excuse for acting out your aggressions irresponsibly. Research shows that anger is not a knee-jerk reaction. Anger occurs only after we have processed enough information about a situation to interpret it as a betrayal or belittlement. This interpretation is grounded in our belief system which is crucial to determining our response. There is always a window of opportunity and choice in anger. We might not be able to control our feelings, but we are responsible for our actions. What we feel as uncontrollable anger can be controlled in expression.

Learn to recycle your anger into a creative energy. Direct it in positive useful ways. We will never be able to stifle our anger, snuff it out, or keep it hidden. The best thing to do with it is redirect it into something good.

The energy of anger can be compared to the force of electrical energy. With lightning that energy becomes a terrifying force of destruction. But when that same electrical force hums along the wires between you and a wild animal in a zoo, it is protection. It is an important, invisible reminder that some things need to be adhered to for all of us to live together. Anger correctly directed can create safety.

Give yourself time. Fitzgibbons writes, "Understandably, the more severe the emotional wound, the greater will be the time and effort needed to arrive at a control or resolution of the anger."

In the end you might have to let go of your anger. A Native American grandfather was talking to his grandson about a tragedy. He said, "I feel as if I have two wolves fighting in my heart. One wolf is the vengeful, angry, violent one. The other wolf is the loving, compassionate one."

The grandson asked him, "Which wolf will win the fight in your heart?"

The grandfather answered, "The one I feed."

Considerations

Identify your source of anger. If you don't know, ask someone else close to you if you appear angry. Ask them what makes you angry. Tell your story and stop and write down all the points in your story that make you angry. Begin to see if there is a pattern of who "presses your buttons" — from where your anger is coming and where it is being directed. Ask yourself if your reactions have integrity. Are you directing your anger towards your children when really you are angry at the police who mishandled the investigation? Are you still angry about an abuse that happened in your childhood? If your anger still remains a puzzle to you at this point, consult a professional counsellor.

Cherish your sensitivity to justice issues. Use your rage.

Set up an action plan to confront the injustice that enrages you. Is there something you can do to stop this injustice from happening? Most injustices cannot be stopped immediately. Can you set up a long range plan that might stop this from happening again in the future?

Manage your anger. Timing is everything in rage and anger. To gain control of your rage emotion put some time between your flash of rage and any action you choose to take. Remember that anger is meant to be acted upon, not acted out.

Remove yourself. If there is nothing that can stop this injustice from happening again and again, is there any way that you can remove yourself to a more comfortable and secure place? Can you lessen your exposure to the anger sources? Removal doesn't always mean physical distance. You might need to put emotional distance between you and someone who continues to hurt you.

Redirect your energy. If there is nothing you can do about the injustice that has directly happened to you, is there another cause or injustice toward which you can redirect your energy? Become active. Start exercising. Take up a sport.

Listen to your body. After experiencing an anger flash, learn how to calm yourself gently and slowly. Learn to relax. Take a walk.

If your anger still remains out of control, seek professional help through a support group. There are now many good "anger management" programs to help you.

"Rage — that's hate with a lot of chili sauce poured on it. "
—Man whose mother was murdered

CHAPTER 15: CREDIBILITY CRISIS OF
THE JUSTICE-MAKING PROCESS

Longing for Justice

THE TERRORIST ATTACKS AGAINST THE UNITED
STATES WERE NOT ONLY AGAINST THE STATE.
Soon President Bush was reaching out to other countries.
British Prime Minister Tony Blair became one of the
spokespersons in the move against terrorism.

Even though crimes of murder and other serious assault
crimes feel very much like a personal issue, they aren't.
Murder and serious physical assault are crimes against society,
the Queen (Regina) or the State.

The crime is bigger than us and our families, and this is
where it becomes complicated. Over the years the justice-
making process has been gradually taken over by the criminal
justice system.

Here I think it is important to review history.

History of Victimology

**In ancient times before countries were ruled by governing
bodies, murder was considered a personal attack and
avenged by the victim's family.** The killer's family was forced to
make things right because if they didn't, the result was a blood
feud — a vendetta — that sometimes lasted for generations. As
societies became more prosperous and more settled, the incentive
to resolve such conflicts peaceably grew stronger. Tribal elders
served as mediators. If negotiations broke down, the blood feud
resumed. The murderer's clan was responsible for carrying out the
settlement — for paying any fines and for ensuring good behavior in
the future. A murderer who violated the terms of an agreement
might be killed by his or her own family in order to keep the peace.

Punishment for murder varied among tribes. In Morocco, the Berbers forced the murderer into exile; the person could only return if the victim's family permitted it. In California, the Yurok Indians forced the murderer to compensate the victim's family.

This payment might be a string of seashells, red obsidian, a woodpecker-scalp headband, or a daughter. In East Africa, the Jolou often required not only the death of a man's murderer but also the impregnation of a woman from the murderer's clan by a member of the victim's clan so that the ghost of the victim might have a wife and children. A murderer's obligation to the victim's family, the need to appease the victim's ghost, and the threat of divine retribution are recurring themes.

Under Anglo-Saxon law, the murderer paid a mandatory fine called the *wergeld* to the victim's family. The exact amount of the *wergeld* was determined through an elaborate calculation of the social status of the victim. Everyone's life had a price that was eventually codified in the *Dooms of Alfred,* a ninth-century handbook of criminal fines. If a murderer failed to pay the *wergeld* within a year, he or she was deemed an outlaw — a person at war with the community — who could legally be killed by anyone. In addition to paying the victim's family, the murderer had to pay a fine called the *wite* to the local nobleman or to the King.

By the twelfth century the *wite* had grown so much larger than the *wergeld* that the nobles took the murderer's entire payment, usurping the monetary claims of the victim's family. The ancient relationship between the murderer's clan and the victim's clan was erased. A murder was now considered a breach of "the King's peace" — a crime against the monarchy. The victim's family no longer had a protected legal status, or a right to compensation, or any authority to determine the murderer's punishment.

Procedural Fairness

We want things to be fair. People who feel they are being treated fairly are more likely to comply with laws than people who feel that they have been treated unfairly is what Tom Tyler, author of the book, *Why People Obey the Law,* discovered in his study of people who appealed their traffic tickets.

His research showed that those participants who were, in spite of their strong arguments, fined anyway were much more satisfied in the long run than those whose appeals were dismissed because the police officer who issued the ticket didn't show to testify and they were absolved of having to pay the fine. Tyler suggests that, "Even though the outcome was negative, people's sense of procedural justice is high — they had their day in court and were treated with fairness and respect. It is often more important to people to maintain a sense of procedural justice than to have positive outcomes."

For us it's another reminder that we not only need good laws but also fair procedural justice in order for us to live in community life in harmony and peace. Good process is more important than good outcomes.

Justice Procedures

Criminal Justice System Here is an example of what is considered a progressive Victims' Bill of Rights within the criminal justice system. It will vary from jurisdiction to jurisdiction.
- The police and the Crown are required to inform you of your rights.
- You have the right to receive information about the legal process.
- You will be told the dates, the location and the outcome of the key court proceedings such as the preliminary hearing, trial and sentencing hearing.
- The Crown is required to consult with victims before bail proceedings, plea bargaining and sentencing and to inform them of all decisions — if you request it. Note: It is important to remember that while the legislation provides victims with a voice and the right to give an opinion, this is not the same thing as a veto.
- You have the right to a separate waiting area in the court building.
- You have the right to file a victim impact statement.

- Some compensation is available for counselling.
- You are to be granted some time off work without pay to attend the trial for purposes of testifying, presenting a victim impact statement or observing the sentence. The request must be made in writing.

It is important to remember that in the criminal justice system, the Crown Attorney is not your lawyer and that he or she represents the State first. This lack of voice has not gone unnoticed. David Epstein, a trial attorney says, "Judges, prosecutors, defendants, defense, counsel — they all know how to make their voices heard to some extent... but victims? They're a changing constituency. No one is really listening to them and their particular problems. Railroads for some time have not done much to please the customer. But airlines... compete in their services. Look at Dulles Airport. You walk in there and you're taken care of in a very few steps. There is someone to tell you what to do, to take your bags, to be polite. Our system has been behaving like a railroad, because maybe it figures the victim can't choose another court system. We've got to look at the victim like he's a customer who requires services."

William McDonald in his book, *Criminal Justice and the Victim,* confirms this. "It is a common complaint of all victims that they are treated like defendants, that they are only used for the information they can supply, and that their human needs are completely ignored by criminal justice officials."

Restorative Justice — an alternative justice-making process — Ideals. Here are examples of some restorative justice principles.
* Focus on the harms of wrongdoing more than the rules that have been broken.
* Show equal concern and commitment to victims and offenders, involving them both in the process.
* Work toward the restoration of victims, empowering them and responding to their needs as they see them.
* Support offenders while encouraging them to understand, accept and carry out their obligations.
* Recognize that while obligations may be difficult for offenders, they should be achievable.
* Provide opportunities for dialogue, direct or indirect, between victims and offenders as appropriate.
* Involve and empower the affected community through the justice process, and increase its capacity to recognize and respond to community bases of crime.
* Encourage collaboration and reintegration rather than coercion and isolation.
* Give attention to the unintended consequences of our actions and programs.
* Show respect to all parties including the victims, offenders, justice colleagues.

Even though the rhetoric and ideals of restorative justice are wonderful and worth promoting, the actual practices of many of the programs offering restorative justices processes are still struggling to live up to the principles.

The main criticism of these practices have come from victims of domestic and sexual violence, and victims of homicide and violent crime.

Stephanie Coward has explored some of this in her paper, *Restorative Justice in Cases of Domestic and Sexual Violence: Healing Justice?* She writes, "I found that women are not necessarily opposed to restorative justice initiatives per se. Rather, they are opposed to these initiatives as they are presently developed and applied. Many of the women consulted during this research stated that they had serious concerns with present restorative justice initiatives but that they would like to see them implemented in the future, after careful research and consultation has been carried out."

The concerns are that current restorative justice initiatives:

- do not take seriously enough the fears and vulnerabilities of the victims.
- do not sufficiently denounce the crime.
- do not address the power imbalance between the victim and offender.
- do not offer sufficient program experience and training for the facilitators.
- have not instituted the necessary program accountability and evaluative structures to deal with the issues of serious crime.
- remain more concerned with the integration of the offender rather than the rehabilitation of the victim.

Fourth Stage – Refer

Refer is the imposed stage on the Crime Victim Detour where the criminal justice system processes the crime. We are referred to the professional justice-makers. Often we find ourselves disengaged at this point because we become merely bystanders in the process.

Most of us are relieved — at least at first — that we have professional people looking after something so delicate and important for us. Referring our case to the professionals seems like the wisest thing to do.

Most of us couldn't take justice into our own hands for many personal reasons. The crime itself is completely disempowering. Because of the trauma it is hard enough to function, to get through the day; it would be impossible for us to organize a competent justice-making process. The justice-making process is out of the realm of our expertise, at least for most of us. Besides, the issues are so much broader than the effects of the crime upon our family. There are community concerns. There are also the rights of the offender.

In addition, it would take an enormous amount of time to organize a justice-making process. For us it might take a lifetime to muster up the energy, expertise and financial resources. Yet our need for justice is immediate. We can't get on with our lives until we have found a way to deal with the offender so that we can feel safe again.

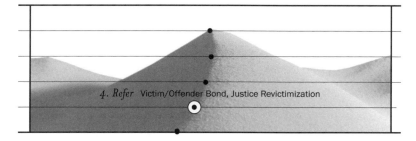

4. Refer Victim/Offender Bond, Justice Revictimization

Victim/Offender Trauma Bond All crime results in broken societal relationships. The more violent the crime, the more serious the trust issues become. Until there is some resolution, victim and offenders are often bonded together in an unhealthy way. As one father of a murdered child said, "It's like we are hanging on to the same rope in an endless game of tug-of-war." This bond can exist whether we know who the offender is or not or whether that person is alive or dead.

Justice Revictimization Our expectations for a balanced and understanding justice-making process are often disappointed in the existing criminal justice system that focusses more on determining the guilt of the offender than on the victim's needs for recovery.

It is extremely difficult to give our control over to the professionals in the criminal justice system and then realize that they have betrayed our trust.

"The only way out is through."
—Goethe

11	VICTIM/OFFENDER TRAUMA BOND

Backyard Massacre

IN OUR PEACEFUL FARMING COMMUNITY WITH LARGE DAIRY FARMS, THERE WERE NO ENEMIES, OR SO WE THOUGHT. Even though my father owned a small Shell service station, we still had enough adjacent land to "play" farming. Every spring, we would buy a box of delightful, tiny, fluffy, chicks which I would watch for hours.

One hot summer day I heard a dreadful cackling coming from the neighbor's yard. I ran outside. It was the most horrific scene I had ever seen. Our black dog had managed to dig his way under the chicken wire fence, stationed himself right in front of the door to the hen house and was killing the chickens. The chickens were helpless against his attacks. Barking madly, he would dart into their midst a vicious killing machine; feathers and blood flew in all directions. The place looked like a massacre. I think I could have understood if he took one chicken and ate it — that would have been bad enough — but he wasn't hungry.

Screaming at him to stop, I climbed the flimsy fence, jumped into the middle of the pen and flung my arms around the dog, holding him down. He wasn't a large dog, but it required all of my strength to hang onto him. He was unrecognizable — this usually calm dog, now bloodied and in a state of frenzied delight.

I held him down until the remaining panicked chickens finally realized that they were not in danger any longer and made their way past us into the safety of the chicken coop. Somehow I got him out of there, took him home and reported the incident to my father. I'm not sure what happened after that; hopefully my father compensated our neighbors for their loss.

But the neighborhood was never the same after that. Suddenly the natural boundaries and rules were no longer adequate. All the chicken fences had to be reinforced, including our own, and the dog had to be watched. He had changed from his role as a family pet into a chicken killer.

Community Relationships

We need community. Communities are places where groups of people share the same values or way of life. This can be any group of people who share the same interests — people who interact regularly, neighborhoods, towns, cities, regions, provinces, countries or even continents. Community can also be environmental, business or professional. Communities can consist of a network of people, real or virtual.

In Africa they have a unique word for community according to Archbishop Desmond Tutu. He describes the word *Ubuntu* as meaning "I am a person because I belong. The solitary human being is a contradiction in terms.... No one can be fully human unless he or she relates to others in a fair, peaceful and harmonious way. Anything that subverts this harmony is injurious, not just to the community, but to all of us."

In the West, we often wonder whether our need for community is as strong as it once was. Scott Peck in his book, *The Different Drum,* writes, "The reality is that we can never be completely whole in and of ourselves. We cannot be all things to ourselves and to others. We cannot be perfect. We cannot be doctors, lawyers, stockbrokers, farmers, politicians, stonemasons and theologians all rolled into one."

Peck even goes so far as to say that our happiness depends on community. "Do the work of creating community and you will obtain it.... Joy is an uncapturable yet utterly predictable side effect of genuine community." Research confirms this. Kristine Orth-Gomer of the National Institute for Psycho-social Factors and Health examined the lives of more than 17,000 people during a six-year period. She discovered a dramatically lower risk of death in those socially involved.

We are a communal people. Whether we want to believe it or not, we are all inter-connected not only in some mystical spiritual way but in a very practical physical way. We're happiest when we are accepted as belonging to the group of our choice, as our global community grows this is becoming more and more obvious.

Even though we might not be intimately involved with everyone, this community that we all hope to belong to is built on a network of relationships with each other ranging from a distant respect of strangers in our community, to more familiarity with neighbors, occasional contact with acquaintances, working with colleagues, or the more involved relationships in an extended family, friends, spouse, and children.

The stronger the relationships, the more we have in common, the stronger the trust. Most people work hard on these interdependent relationships that form community. We work hard to build credit, respectability, and trustworthiness. If we have achieved a healthy community, we know we will have peace and harmony.

Victim/Offender Trauma Bond

11

One of the most insidious, long-term results of murder is that we as victims can be bonded to the offender in a complicated, destructive relationship. We are so intimately connected in our communities that even when someone breaks the law we are still bonded to them until the issues are addressed.

But before we explore this bond more, we need to take some time to explore the concept of evil and the makings of an evil-doer. Evil is a term that is often used in victim language. It's a concept that is hard to understand. The most comprehensive definition of evil I've discovered is found in John Monbourquette's book, *How to Befriend Your Shadow: Welcoming Your Unloved Side.* Monbourquette, who is both a psychologist and priest, describes the difference between our shadow side and evil. According to him, "Our shadow was created through the repression of a whole set of feelings, qualities, talents and attitudes that we believe were unacceptable to those around us. Evil, on the other hand, is defined as the privation of a good that is owed: *privatio boni debiti*. Evil does not exist as such; in itself, it is non-being. What does exist is a deficient being or action: that is, one that lacks perfection it should have. Evil is named in terms of the realities of the affects. There will be as many different evils as there are realities affected. In the aesthetic world, it will be the imperfection in a work of art; with respect to health, it will be an illness; in politics, a social upheaval. With respect to morality, evil refers to an action that is not in keeping with its natural purpose; theologically, sin is defined as a break in relationship of love between a person and God."

According to this definition, in community, evil is that which breaks the trust and peace needed to sustain a community of people. The breaking of the nation's laws, such as, theft, assault and murder, are evil because they break the trust we need to live together.

When we encounter violence and murder, we not only need to deal with the evil act that has happened, we also need to deal with the evil-doer. Who are these offenders? According to the dictionary, this is someone who "manifests hostility toward, or opposes the purpose or interests of us" or our community.

"Little is known about the mind of the perpetrator," writes Judith Herman in her book, *Trauma and Recovery.* "Since he is contemptuous of those who seek to understand him, he does not volunteer to be studied. Since he does not perceive that anything is wrong with him, he does not seek help — unless he is in trouble with the law."

According to Herman, based on the testimony of victims and the observations of psychologists, the most consistent feature of the perpetrator is his or her apparent normality. We can never be sure who an offender is, or who a potential offender is. How much more comforting it would be if the perpetrator were easily recognizable, obviously deviant or disturbed. But he or she is not.

The legal scholar, Hanna Arendt, created a scandal when she reported that Adolf Eichmann, a man who committed unfathomable crimes against humanity, had been certified by half a dozen psychiatrists as normal. "The trouble with Eichmann was precisely that so many were like him, and that the many were neither perverted nor sadistic, that they were, and still are, terribly and terrifyingly normal. From the viewpoint of our legal institution and of our moral standards of judgment, this normality was much more terrifying than all the atrocities put together."

In Herman's study concerning perpetrators of hostage-takings, political prisoners and battered women, there is one common trait. Total control over another person is the common denominator of all forms of tyranny. "The erotic appeal of this fantasy to millions of terrifyingly normal men fosters an immense industry in which women and children are abused, not in fantasy but in reality."

Programs which deal mainly with perpetrators have classified the offenders into three general categories. The first is the situational offender. This offender has a lifestyle problem that led to the offense, such as drinking. Once this social issue is solved, the offender could be considered socially acceptable.

The second is the habitual criminal, those who have a criminal mind set. They thrive on crime, make their living on crime, and want to be criminals. These offenders' values and attitudes need to be confronted before they can be rehabilitated. These are the hardest to rehabilitate.

The third is the crazy-maker. These offenders carry dysfunctional lifestyle patterns which result in crime. They don't intend to "steal" but because they don't have resources or work, they tend to take what doesn't belong to them. The challenge with these criminals is to create stability in their lives.

Even though these are general descriptions for offenders of less serious crime, they can also be used to understand violent offenders. Understanding of the offender is necessary because whether we like it or not, we are bonded with them.

Founding president of Family Survivors of Homicide, James Kostelniuk, has written the story of his long-term correspondence with the man who murdered his ex-wife and two children in *Wolves among Sheep.* In order to understand, he began a correspondence with the perpetrator. He writes, "Though I grew weary of receiving these tedious and offensive letters and could have taken steps to ensure he no longer wrote to me, there was a part of me that did not want to lose the continuing opportunity to monitor him."

In our case, even though the offender has never been found, we are still bonded with this person in almost an extended "family" way. For instance, sometimes when I meet distant acquaintances I haven't seen for a while, they inquire about my life. They start with Cliff. And I answer, "Cliff is doing great (we're still together which is the real question behind the question), Odia is married to a Larry from Winkler, Syras is studying psychology, I'm writing," Then there is a pause. "Have they found anyone yet?" Instead of inquiring after Candace, they are inquiring about the offender. In our situation this course of conversation is a natural response to an unnatural situation so whether I like it or not, the "murderer" is still part of the family.

This unlikely connection between ourselves and the offender can leave us extremely confused, feeling controlled and vulnerable.

It's important to note that not only are the victims bonded with the offenders, often everyone who was primary in the experience of violence remains bonded somehow — like alumni of the crime. All of those who survived the atrocity together are often considered the "basic unit of survival."

To continue to be bonded with someone who is an offender forces us to become part of his or her dysfunctional world.

"Not all persons loaded with hostility are triggered, any more than guns are. But safety lies in taking care with loaded guns, grizzly bears and violent actors."
—Gynn Nettler

Trauma Hostage-Taker

In order to understand this Victim/Offender Trauma Bond, we also need to look at the trauma that binds them together. Sometimes the offender has little to do with sustaining the trauma bond, as in cases where the offender has been killed, yet the trauma bond continues. This can best be understood if we visualize the entire "aftermath of violence" as a force with which to be reckoned. All of the elements that we have described up till now take on the form of a Trauma Hostage-Taker.

We know this because victims often describe feeling imprisoned by the experience of violence. We say we are held captive in the aftermath of homicide which sabotages us economically, socially, psychologically and physically.

In this way the trauma bond of violence compares with the experience of those who have been taken as hostages, such as political prisoners, or people held prisoners in domestic captivity, slave labor camps, brothels, concentration camps or even in religious cults. Any kind of captivity that "brings the victim into prolonged contact with the perpetrator, creates a special type of relationship, one of coercive control," writes Herman. This bonding has been called "pair bonding" — survivor with survivor or survivor with perpetrator — "traumatic bonding."

In 1973, drawing upon the testimony of political prisoners from widely differing cultures, Amnesty International published a "chart of coercion" describing methods that enable one person to enslave another. Herman says that in the "accounts of hostages, political prisoners and survivors of concentration camps from every corner of the globe have an uncanny sameness."

These same coercions can be found in the aftermath of violence:

A hostage-taker uses fear to terrorize. It is not always necessary to use violence to keep a person in a constant state of fear. The threat of violence is used much more frequently than the violence itself.

A hostage-taker uses physical control to enslave a victim. The perpetrator will try to destroy the victim's sense of autonomy through physical confinement or control.

A hostage-taker uses social alienation and isolation to gain control of a victim. As long as the victim continues to relate to others, the perpetrator's power is limited. It is for this reason that the perpetrators isolate their victims from other sources of information, material aid or emotional support. For this isolation to be effective, the victim also needs to be removed from anything that reminds them of others. For this reason, the perpetrators often go to great lengths to deprive their victims of any objects of symbolic importance.

A hostage-taker uses manipulation to violate a victim's moral principles and betray his or her values. Psychologically, this is the most destructive. When victims are forced to violate their inner belief systems they feel ashamed and defeated. Their inner spirit has been destroyed.

Embodied in the aftermath of violence is a trauma persona that resembles a hostage-taker. We are terrorized by the experience, fragmented, wounded, disoriented, alienated, and disempowered. We are stigmatized and isolated. We eventually feel morally compromised by the crime. All of these words describe a hostage-taking incident.

Until we break this victim/offender trauma bond, we will never be free to recover from the incident, rebuild our lives or feel in control of our lives again.

Underlying Reasons for
this Victim/Offender Trauma Bond

The act of violence unites everyone who was touched by it.
Everyone participating in that moment of violence — the police
officers who investigated the case, innocent bystanders, the wider
community, the media and even our caregivers — can also be
caught in this bond. We become the "alumni."

During the act of violence, an unjust shift of power occurs.
The offender through an act of violence robs his or her victims
of the power and control of their lives. The police officers also
assume their role of officers of the peace, possibly taking power
and control from both the victim and the offender. Caregivers
might come in and assume another role. Until these power and
control issues are addressed, this power and control imbalance
remains in all of those who were involved. The roles assumed or
taken at this point of time will continue to play themselves out until
they are confronted.

**If we as victims were in a relationship with the offender
before the offense, we might find that the relationship
continues in another way.** For example, if the offender is our
spouse or our son or daughter, we might have grandchildren in
common. Because of this we might be forced to remain in contact
with him or her. There might be issues of ownership. There might
be issues of shared expense. Who should pay for the crime? Who
should support the grandchildren?

**There can be all sorts of conflicting emotions of compassion
and anger, understanding and confusion, attraction and
revenge, fear and power that are part of this trauma bond.**
All of these emotions which are directed toward the offender
remain with us until they can find expression in one way or
another.

We are bonded with the offender in our memories. This was
brought home to me when I met with lifers and realized that in
many ways we were part of a "surreal alumni" with the same experience. It was quite natural to form a kind of "support group of
like-experience" with them as we talked about the same trauma of

anniversaries, the same people involved in the investigation, trial, the same anger, feelings of going crazy, the same stigmatization.

We are bonded because we experience the same expectations from the community around us to "fix" what went wrong. The pressure to reconcile is strong. Society pressures victims to "forgive," to "heal" and to "move on." The victim might be tempted to be compliant for the sake of peace. Anna Freud identified reasons for this victim/offender trauma bond as "Altruistic Surrender" which is identification with the aggressor. "If you take on the values of the offender you don't have to be afraid of them anymore."

Victim and offender continue to remain part of the same community because they know the same people. Even if they didn't know each other previously, often during the course of the investigation and trial, they get to know the same people: the lawyers, media people, judges, service providers, police. All of these are channels of communication to remain connected. These are often leaky channels. Even if we don't want to know about each other, those around us might continue to "leak" information to us. Often people who want to help with this bond can inadvertently be the channels of further control and coercion.

Consequences of this Victim/Offender Trauma Bond

If there has been no justice-making process to deal with this bond, our resentment grows as we see or imagine the offender continuing to enjoy life and his or her freedom while we suffer traumatic consequences of their violence on us. Often the bond takes over our lives in many ways:

We remain fearful. The victim, who has faced death because of the offender, naturally associates this fear with the offender. Trauma fear, as we have said, is an extreme emotional response that isn't rational; it permeates the body and the mind. There are no bars strong enough to contain this fear.

We remain angry. There can be so much hate, hostility, hurt, fear and misunderstanding that the emotions themselves can obstruct any hope of thinking rationally about some practical considerations of dealing with the bond. Revenge fantasies might begin to control us victims and lock us into an agenda to defeat and hurt the offender. Judith Herman talks about the Stockholm syndrome — a specific form of victim/offender trauma bond. "Former prisoners carry their captors' hatred with them even after their release, and sometimes they continue to carry out their captors' destructive purposes with their own hands."

We remain dependent. The offender holds the key to our recovery. We might feel we need to know the truth about what actually happened during the crime because we need answers in order to piece our fragmented lives together. If we believe that the offender has the answers we seek, we remain bonded.

We feel disempowered — not in control of our lives. There is a continuing conflict of power and control. Unresolved issues that sparked the first act of violence might be heightened through the court process and continue to play themselves out.

Even when things might on the surface seemed resolved this insidious bond might still be lurking in our minds.

"Released prisoners often continue to track their captors and to fear them... the victim may continue to fear her former captor and to expect that he will eventually hunt her down, but she may also feel empty, confused and worthless without him," writes Herman.

Breaking the Victim/Offender Trauma Bond

Hopefully we can resolve some of our issues with the offender during a healthy justice-making process. In a perfect world, the offender after hearing our story of victimization will change, express genuine remorse, offer to look after all the damages that were done and then submit to a period of probation and supervision until he or she has proven to be trustworthy again. Once this happens we can relinquish our fears, our anger and regain trust.

But if we haven't had a satisfactory justice-making process, the bond might have even been intensified during the trial period. The natural response to dealing with this uncomfortable victim/offender trauma bond is to get rid of the offender. We want to lock the offender up and send him or her away for good. We hope that, by doing away with the offender, he or she can't affect our lives. Unfortunately, "out of sight, out of mind" often doesn't work with this bond.

While suffering the victim/offender trauma bond, we are usually too vulnerable to talk about "reconciliatory" forgiveness. Caught in this bond, we can easily be pressured into premature or manipulative forgiveness which can result in feeding the bond and empowering the offender's hold in our lives which could result in further destructive controls.

The only way to free ourselves of this bond is to break the hold it has on us ourselves. In order to break it we will need to deal with our fear, anger, mistrust, and dependencies. We will need to resolve the issues.

Considerations

First, identify if this is a problem in your life. Assess whether the bond is dysfunctional or manageable.

If it is dysfunctional, identify all the issues in this bond that leave you vulnerable. How does this person still control you? Do you have excessive fear or anger? Are there practical considerations or needs in this relationship? How can you deal with these vulnerabilities? How can you sever any dependency you have on this person?

Take steps to break the dysfunctional bond between you and the offender. Consult with others on how to do this. Withdrawing is one method. Confronting is another. But before you take action, ascertain realistically the nature of this bond. If the offender is obsessed with you, stalking you (which can happen even if he or she is in prison), you might need professional counsel on how to break this bond so that you don't accentuate the danger. Breaking the bond can be the most dangerous time in an unhealthy relationship.

If you need to confront the offender to work out some issues, there are many programs emerging which can help facilitate these meetings in a safe way. If you are vulnerable, be wary of the programs which have offender-oriented agendas. In order to assess whether they are offender-oriented, ask from where the majority of their funding comes and who usually initiates the contact. Insist on having a victim support person, someone who has been trained to understand victim needs.

Remember that breaking this bond might need more courage and attention than you anticipated. Often breaking this bond takes more than a "one-time" confrontation. This bond might need to be treated almost like an addiction. We might have developed thought patterns and dependencies that have become habitual in our minds.

Anticipate that any process this intense will take time.
Perhaps you will need to attend to this issue more than once. It is not a one-time solution.

Begin to fill your life with healthy contacts and people. Fill your life with symbols of your attachment to these people; pictures, photographs on the fridge, mementoes of your loved one and connection to the community are important. The more connected you are, the less hold the trauma bond will have on you. As we pointed out previously, our inclination at this time is to withdraw; therefore, it will take energy to cultivate healthy social relationships.

Often understanding this bond is enough to make it manageable.

"We would never have chosen these neighbors: life chose them for us.
But thrown together on this island of living, we stretch to understand each other."
—Anne Morrow Lindbergh

| 12 | JUSTICE REVICTIMIZATION |

Raspberry Patch Blues

I CAN'T REALLY BLAME ANYONE FOR NOT BELIEVING ME. As a child I hated picking berries. I found it tedious and boring, probably because I wasn't good at it. Inevitably after lunch when the sun was at its hottest and everyone was tired, I would begin to complain about a stomach ache.

"You're just trying to get out of picking berries," my family said — which was partly true — but the pain felt real.

Eventually I too began to dismiss it as my reaction to berry picking (which I continued to hate with a passion).

"Psychosomatic," my family said.

But slowly this mysterious pain grew until the gnawing ache turned into what I called attacks and until I could no longer pretend it wasn't there. During my first pregnancy these attacks, which lasted two to three hours, were unbearable. I would spend hours in the bathtub, hoping heat would soothe it, but nothing helped. I continued to tell my doctor but she couldn't find anything.

Finally, after the birth of my first child, I could bear it no longer. I insisted on more tests. I mentioned to my doctor that my family had a long history of gallstones. Although she said I was too young for gallstones, she agreed to have it checked anyway.

The tests revealed that I had a whole gravel pit of stones in my gallbladder. What a relief to know that the ache had a name!

In those days, surgery for gallstones was a considered a major operation. Although the surgery itself was painful, all I can remember is the relief; the ache in my side was gone. I couldn't believe the incredible freedom I had. I could eat anything, do anything, and still have no pain.

Suddenly the world seemed to have more color, more sunlight. I had been restored. I had been fixed. I couldn't thank my doctor enough.

Professional Ideals

"Very professional work" is a phrase of high commendation.
To be judged professional means to have achieved a level of
performance that commands universal respect.

In her book, *At Personal Risk,* Marilyn Peterson states,
"Contemporary professionals are secular shamans who preserve,
protect and treat our minds, our bodies, our souls and our relationships with each other."

She writes that the shaman's tasks have been parcelled out to
five disciplines: medicine, law, religion, teaching and psychother-
apy. Each has its own unique function and social responsibility.
While we may have modernized the shaman's function, our core
needs remain unchanged. We still need to trust those who can
help us feel safer, stronger, and less alone. We want somebody to
take care of the part of our lives where we feel vulnerable and
inadequate.

William Sullivan in the book, *Professional Ideals,* writes,
"Professionals are not expected to simply pursue their work as a
means to economic well-being. Professionals claim to provide
services for the public benefit beyond private gain or even at its
expense."

Peterson considers attorneys as professionals. "Lawyers attend
to the rights and obligations that enable us to live together in an
orderly fashion," she writes. "At their best, they protect the ideals
and principles on which our society is founded. They engineer the
parameters of what is allowed and what is not, constructing and
adhering to a set of rules that reflects our inherent sense of what
is right and equitable.... Theoretically they protect us from harm."

The professional's knowledge is a storehouse of resources for
us. Professionals hold the keys. They control the amount of information and explanations given to their clients. Since professionals'
knowledge and expertise light the way for us, most of us view
these holders as wise and masterly. Because of their value to us,
we set professionals apart and elevate them to privileged positions
of power.

Peterson writes, "Unlike the shaman whose powers derive from
spirits and whose reputation is established by fears of supernatural consequence, professional competence is derived primarily
from social attribution.... We grant professionals who enter our

lives major license to direct and even determine the flow of events that comprise our existence. In both subtle and overt ways, they influence and manage our choices. We empower them and reward them for their services by bestowing a host of advantages that demarcate their special and privileged role and further bolster their authority."

We give power to professionals out of our neediness. The more distressed we are, the more powerful professionals become.

In fact we project parts of ourselves onto professionals and act out our inner debates through them. According to Peterson, "With lawyers, we project our conflicts about good and bad, right and wrongdoing, justice and injustice." In other words, we suspend our own judgments to adopt the those of the professional.

Our Western society grants professionals a "significant degree of autonomy to make decisions that significantly affect each of our realities," writes Peterson. Because of our neediness we can easily become dependent on professionals.

JUSTICE REVICTIMIZATION

12

Unfortunately, the justice system has not been set up to meet the expectations of the victim. By not meeting these expectations, the justice system often revictimizes the victim.

The criminal justice system is there to apprehend the offender, to give the offender legal counsel if he or she is charged. The investigation team is there to collect evidence to prove the guilt of the offender. The guards are there to usher the offender into the courtroom, to reserve a place for the offender. The judge is there to declare whether the offender is guilty or not — no word to the crime victim. Then — if the offender is found guilty, the judge will sentence him or her for rehabilitation in a penitentiary where the offender is supervised and looked after for twenty-four hours of the day. In the courtroom there is no thought given to compensation or reparation.

As innocent citizens we envision the justice system in much the same way as the medical health care system. We are in an accident; the car has rolled over and we have two broken legs, internal bleeding and a concussion. Since we have such wonderful health care coverage, we assume the ambulance will come. We assume that we will be wheeled into an emergency room, and examined quickly. We assume that our injuries will be taken care of and that we will be put into in a white room with a bed after the operation. Drowsy with pain killers, we will sleep there until we are well enough to go home.

If we encounter a serious crime, we expect there to be a system in place to fill our justice needs in the same way. As victims we expect the professionals in law enforcement to console us over the loss that we have just experienced. We expect them to do a quick, efficient diagnosis of the crime and collect the evidence in a professional manner. We then expect to be ushered into a court-room with a sympathetic judge and hear a judgment that declares us as innocent, the offender as guilty with a promised compensa-tion package that will cover our losses. We assume that when we have left the courtroom we will feel restored, ready to resume our lives. That is justice.

Marlene Young, director of NOVA (National Organization for Victim Assistance) writes, "When a suspect is arrested, relief bordering on euphoria is common among survivors, who often believe that now everything is going to be all right."

Victims, according to Young, "... are almost always forced to learn that arrests do not necessarily result in prosecutions, or pros-ecutions in convictions, or convictions in stiff sentences, or stiff sentences ordered in stiff sentences served. Part of the survivor's unwanted education is that 'murder' is not what they or the lay public understand it to be — prosecutors, judges or juries may perceive the killing to be manslaughter or a negligent homicide, or even an accidental death."

Most crime victims are appalled to find out that they are not even represented in the courtroom as individuals. They have abso-lutely no position or voice concerning the proceedings. Just recently victims have gained the right to be consulted, but they still have no veto power over what seems their life. Their life is being exposed and their belongings might be used as evidence; yet they have no role.

As one woman whose sister was murdered says, "You trust that the judicial system is going to work. You trust that reporters have decency. You have incredible expectations of others' behavior that just doesn't happen. Now I have no trust in others."

Yet upon realizing this, most victims will not voice their displeasure loudly. Many of them are in such a state of vulnerability they cannot afford to displease the professionals. Often we as victims feel that we must not in any way jeopardize this divinely ordained justice system so as to cause a mistrial. We are intimidated throughout the trial, trying so hard to be the ideal victim; we feel that we must learn the role of appearing meek, accommodating and submissive.

It is often only after the trial — sometimes years later — that we realize that the whole experience has been unsatisfactory. We realize that somehow our needs were unmet, that we have lost in terms of confidence, reparation, and reputation. We realize that somehow we have been prosecuted by the defense, our loved one was somehow made to appear the villain, and we have been revictimized by the justice system we trusted.

"I thought that the criminal justice system worked. I now know that it is broken. It has so much need for change and repair that somebody needs to do it. I'm willing to take a shot at certain parts of it," says a man whose mother was murdered.

We may begin to become obsessed with the fact that we haven't had justice. It is not uncommon for victims to appear hostile and angry on television. Their language turns into a cry for "victims' rights." They participate in protest vigils, letter writing campaigns or angry telephone calls. Victims often begin to call for longer sentences, the death of the offender, and question the credibility of the entire justice system.

At this point, the rage that has been brewing beneath the surface can become uncontrollable. We can become bitter, angry, sarcastic. It feels odd to us who are usually mild-mannered, law abiding citizens to suddenly find ourselves fighting the law.

Mary Bessette, whose car was stolen by the same fellow who abducted and caused the death of her son, told me that the process for dealing with the theft and her demolished car was more sympathetic, more complete, more satisfying than the process that dealt with the theft of her child.

Because of the high expectations that have been ascribed to professionals by the public and maintained by the professionals themselves, failure to honor this public trust is seen as a more reprehensible betrayal than the acting out of the murder in the first place.

Underlying Reasons for this Justice Revictimization

We have inherited a flawed criminal justice system.

According to a Criminal Law textbook, the common law tradition found in English Canada derives from feudal England. With the success of the Norman Invasion, King William declared himself the "supreme landlord" of all England, so that all individuals who held land held the king's land. Over the succeeding centuries, the English kings slowly expanded and consolidated their power over the feudal landscape. Harms committed in disputes between individuals increasingly were seen to harm the *mund,* or the king's region. As a result, compensation was paid to kings, lords, and bishops, rather than to kinship groups. Originally, the King's Peace referred to his ability to protect his own person, but gradually it was extended to include the king's court, army, servants, hundred-court, and finally the four main highways of England.

The Norman kings saw themselves as the injured party when a crime was committed since the harm was against their peace. Since some crimes were now against the "King" or the "Crown," criminal law became a reality. The Crown replaced the victim as the injured party, and compensation to the victim's family was replaced by punitive fines that were payable to the Crown.

This is the criminal justice system that we have inherited. Increasingly it is becoming intolerable to think that only the "Crown" has been injured. Canadians are beginning to be disillusioned with the criminal justice system as a whole.

A publication of the Law Commission of Canada entitled *Engaging Canadians in the Renewal of the Law* states, "The Commission finds that many Canadians feel a sense of disengagement from the law, as if real life is outside the narrow scope of the law. Indeed the law is more often seen as an impediment to an improved quality of life, rather than contributing to it."

These historical roots of our criminal justice system have resulted in continuing revictimization of victims.

All serious crime is not only a crime against a person, it is considered a crime against the Crown. Yet victims feel an overwhelming responsibility for true justice to take place. The honor of their loved one is at stake; their own losses are at stake. To have this sense of responsibility and no possible voice in the proceedings makes us feel disempowered at a time when we need to feel empowered.

The justice-making process is there to deal with offender issues. The process isn't based on "unravelling the cause and effect of crime", but "the accused is innocent until proven guilty." The weight of proving guilt is on the Crown. It is all about proving the crime was done and who did it, not about solving the problem. Victims need to first hear the truth. Yet the proceedings don't start with a truth statement. They start out with a denial, "I plead not guilty." Instead of an inquiry into what happened, the entire process is motivated to defend the "accused." Victims aren't victims in this process, they are immediately seen as pawns in a case. They are used as "witnesses" which can be disempowering rather than empowering.

The process is incomplete. There is no place for a problem solving discussion. Because there is no extensive discussion about "why" it happened, there is no formal inquiry as to the cause of the misfortune. There is no place for the offender to give an authentic explanation of why he or she did what he or she did without it reflecting a guilty or not guilty plea; so therefore, the explanation can't take place. There is no place to address the safety issue between the victim and offender — except to throw the offender into jail. Prison might seem to be a solution, but not in the long run. I have heard too many victims say that the world isn't big enough for both of them, and feel tremendous fear even though the offender is in jail. The victim is never asked what will make him or her feel safe again. The offender is never asked if he or she intends to change, if he or she has learned from this. Victims need to be part of rehabilitation programs for the offender and themselves. After the sentencing, the offender is whisked off to jail and is dependent on the State. The victim's plight is ignored. The victim's losses are largely ignored.

The place of the trial is usually not victim friendly. It is not a place that creates trust for victims. "Theatrical" is how one victim described it. "It's like a performance." The judge comes in with a robe and everyone addresses him as "My Lord." The lawyers address each other as "My learned friend." Are they friends? If they are, it doesn't constitute a great deal of trust between the victim and offender who are warring with each other. And if they are not friends — if they are competitors — they are lying. Either way, it adds to the theatrics. Yet we enter the courtroom where we have entrusted our hopes for justice, the honor of our loved one, the privacy of our lives — and it feels as if we have stepped back into time. The medieval feeling of the place does not inspire trust.

There is no comprehensive service for victims, such as "one-stop victim services." We expect that justice is a coherent system, a unit. When we discover that a sophisticated tracking system for the offender runs through the justice system and that there is none for the victim, most of us are indignant at first, then horrified.

There is no independent counsel for us as crime victims.

Consequences of this Justice Revictimization

Often we are intimidated; so we comply. When the police tell us not to discuss the case with out friends, we comply. When the judge insists that there will be no display of emotion, we hide our feelings. Often we are called on to be a witness and are not allowed to participate in the proceedings. We don't protest. We trust that the professionals know what they are doing.

We are often overwhelmed with the formality of the proceedings and baffled at what is happening. The language is foreign. We feel uncomfortable in the courtroom, unable to hear because everything is directed towards the judge or jury. We feel we are unwanted.

We might feel extremely nervous about seeing the offender and remaining in the same room. We avoid eye contact. We might experience extreme emotions of rage and revenge. Often we feel diminished by the proceedings. We might feel that our loved one has become only a piece of evidence. There is no respect.

When we take the stand, we feel that we are on trial. We resent the accusations and insinuations. We feel vulnerable and unprotected.

Restoring Justice

Dealing with this element entails an action that goes beyond our own lives. In order for us to stop the justice revictimization, we need to make changes to the criminal justice system. But what changes should we make? Is it possible to make these changes?

Let me give you a story that will illustrate what I think we will need to do in order to heal the justice-making process. And yes — I think we can make some important changes. I've seen some changes already. We need more.

I remember picking up the phone late in the day. There was something hollow in her voice. "The second week of the trial flattened me like nothing ever has. I don't even have words." Then she proceeded to try to put the experience into words. She was right — the words weren't there — only the pain. But there were enough words for me to begin to feel her horror of the courtroom.

I was taken back in time to another room that had gone awry — the delivery room. It was more than thirty years ago when I was having my first child, during the years when the doctors ruled supreme. They thought that having a baby was only about delivering the baby safely. They sterilized the room completely, took total control, banned the fainting father, drugged the screaming mother, whisked the baby into the nursery as soon as they could and fed the baby sugar water.

It should have felt safe and right, but the entire time I was in the hospital I had nightmares that my husband wouldn't ever have a chance to hold our baby. I knew that something was not right. This artificial separation of our family unit at that critical moment was wrong. We had to go home to heal from the hurt that was done.

When I voiced my concern to some nurse friends, I was told that the delivery room could never be changed. I was told it wasn't good for the mothers to be aware and see how poorly the doctors behaved while they were delivering babies, flirting with the nurses, making snide remarks. It would never work to have fathers in the delivery room because some didn't want to be there. Such choices would disrupt the needed order.

But I'm sure we all know of the revolution that took place in the medical field. Midwives brought us the awareness that having a baby wasn't only about delivering the baby. It was also about creating family. They showed us that to create family we need a certain amount of blood, emotion, chaos and choice. Family-making is meant to be messy. Then we learned that we needed to customize the delivery room for the family, not for the doctors. Years later the delivery of my next two children was so different — so healthy by comparison.

I think the same scenario is happening in our courts today. In our attempt to create and deliver justice, we have concentrated only on determining guilt. We have given the courtroom entirely to the professionals who have made it into a sterile room of law and order. They have banned the fainting father from the room and silenced the screaming mother. More and more they are whisking the difficult decision-making process away from the public into the realm of plea bargaining, with the same intentions as the doctors in keeping the baby clean and safe, out of the weak mother's arms. Consequently, we now have offenders and victims experiencing the trauma of the courtroom.

We need the same delivery room revolution to happen in the courtroom. Justice isn't only about determining guilt, but also about creating peace and harmony between the victim and offender so that they can meet in the grocery store and not kill each other. Yet the courtroom is designed to keep them apart. More often than not, it enhances the anger between them, creates more friction, and heightens the conflict.

But I hear the same complaints. "The insensitive behavior of the law keepers is something we don't want to expose the victims to." "We can't cater to the different needs of the individual victims." "Choice would slow the process down." "We're not equipped."

Yet to create justice, we will need a certain amount of blood, emotion, chaos and choice. Justice-making should be messy. Victims and offenders are stakeholders in the justice-making. They have to take center stage again. It is where they belong. Just as we learned to customize the delivery room for the patients, we need to customize the courtroom.

Dealing with this Criminal Justice Revictimization

But until those basic changes are made, what should we do?
Realize that you are not alone in your discovery that our justice system is less than perfect. There are now more and more victim services that are beginning to understand the dilemma that victims face when they are entrenched in the criminal justice process. Seek out these services. Make sure that they are victim-centered services. This means that they are independent of the offender-based organizations in terms of funding and accountability.

If you are going into a preliminary hearing or a trial, prepare yourself for the disappointments. It is better to realize beforehand that you will not be officially represented in the courtroom. Then if you need support, consult with advocates or knowledgeable friends. Ask them to be with you during this time.

Anticipate what your needs will be before the trial. Do you think you will need a private room? What will you do during the lunch break? Who will phone in each day to find out what is happening? If you can't make it to the trial every day, will you need someone to attend for you? If you can't be assertive, find someone who can be. Find out what rights you do have, and then insist on them. Do not let anyone intimidate you.

Do not neglect your own healing process in the pursuit of justice. In the end, the person you loved is no longer here. Words can no longer hurt them. Remember it is you who is being hurt. In all of this you remain important.

You might want to address the injustices you experience by helping to change the system. Much has already been done to make some improvements but you might want to join others in advocacy work to make the justice system more just.

I am not clear at this point if we as victims need to work towards a complete meltdown of the courtroom as it currently is, so that it can become a friendly place for victims — much like the delivery room was made more family friendly — or if we need to find alternative justice-making processes.

Considerations

Educate yourself about each of the justice-making organizations that you encounter. Find out about them. Learn the new vocabulary.

If you need legal advice, ask for it. Be careful to not accumulate impossible debt by hiring a lawyer unless you absolutely have to. There are always other creative means to learn about the law.

During the police investigation, ask for information about how the law enforcement agency works. There are many handbooks available. If you can't read them, have someone read them out loud to you.

Become aware of the courtroom. Go a day early and walk around the place. Become comfortable with the washrooms, the parking lot, the cafeteria. Find a place where you can feel safe.

Generate support for yourself before the trial. Gather some friends; explain to them what you will be going through. Take along people who build you up — not tear you down. Plan a debriefing time with them after the court day.

During the trial, remain sensitive to your needs. If the proceedings become too quiet for you to hear, let the Crown know.

Prepare a media statement so that you will know what you are going to say to the media. Go over this statement with someone who has the ability to process things. Be clear. Imagine yourself the way you were before the injustice, what were your values then — keep them. If you have something prepared, it won't be as traumatic to see news reporters in the hallway.

Prepare yourself for down time. Going through all the processes takes an enormous amount of energy. Prepare to take a week off after the trial to "come down." Prepare for the sadness you will feel when it is all over.

*"There was a trial and the jury
found him not guilty.
I was devastated.*

*It was as if twelve people stood there
and reloaded the shotgun.*

*When I walked out of the courtroom,
I told the television reporter,
'When I left my house this morning,
I told my daughter that Daddy
would get the man who killed Mommy.*

*Now I have to go home and tell her,
I didn't.'"*

—Man whose wife was murdered

CHAPTER 18: DEALING WITH THE AFTERMATH

Ground Zero

SHORTLY AFTER THE SEPTEMBER 11 TERRORIST ATTACKS, I happened to tune into a talk show host quizzing a panel of experts on what they thought should happen to the site of the twin towers that had been so devastatingly destroyed. What would they suggest should be done with the site?

At the time of this discussion not all of the bodies had been discovered. It was much too soon to have that discussion, but they were trying. What do you do with the site of such an atrocity? Each of them mentioned that this site remained prime real estate land, strategically placed, and continued to be an important place for the people not only in New York but around the world.

All of them agreed that to rebuild the twin towers would be a mistake. They could not duplicate the past. Most of those on the panel felt it should remain a place of memorial for all the lives lost — a park perhaps, a place of art. Some felt the memory could be incorporated into something more commercial in keeping with the history of the buildings.

What to do? The place had taken on a new identity. Ground Zero had come to represent a place of war, a grave site, a glorious past that was gone, failure, terrorism, heroism and sacrifice by the fire fighters, tremendous loss of life and potential, friendship, drama.

The first stage is the clean up, but after that — what then? How do you recover the site?

If these are some of the questions we ask ourselves of a piece of land, can you imagine how difficult the questions and answers are when we ourselves are Ground Zero, the site of the violence that has occurred?

Recovering from violence is not a simple task.

Fifth Stage – Recover

After we've had extensive surgery we expect to eventually recover. In the same way, we are hoping to recover from this experience. We are anxious to get on with our lives by this time in the journey along the Crime Victim Detour.

We've already learned that the "method of choice," the criminal justice system, hasn't helped. Is there another method? Everyone around us is expecting us to function, to move on, to recover, but how do we solve this thing called the aftermath of murder and other serious crime? And even more important, what does recovery look like? What is the final solution?

Unfortunately, by this time, so much has happened in between — so much time has intervened — that we aren't even sure what "recover" will look like. We don't even remember what we were like before all this happened. Probably the greatest disappointment for most of us victims is to realize that even this part of the aftermath of murder, the healing, is not easy and straightforward.

Unsatisfactory Closure It is never over. The constant reminders of the crime, the unresolved issues, and the continuing losses can hold us hostage long after everyone else feels that it has been resolved.

Recovery Controversy The recovery process from something as horrific as violence remains unclear. What does "healing" look like? What does recovery look like?

Paralyzing Despair The cumulative effects of the fragmentation, traumatization, disorientation, disempowerment and unsatisfactory closure can cause a paralyzation often referred to as being "stuck." We can get stuck in any part of the journey.

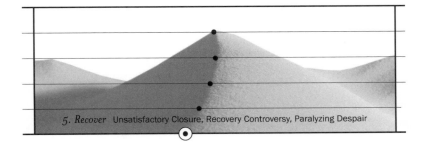

5. Recover Unsatisfactory Closure, Recovery Controversy, Paralyzing Despair

Dangers of Comparing our Recovery Process

After a murder, very few people bounce back easily and readily — but some do. If we compare ourselves to them, we might feel very discouraged. In this chapter, we are going to outline the many variables in murder and other violent crimes that do make a difference in our healing journey. For example, it will be harder to recover if the body of our loved one was mutilated after he or she was murdered.

The acceptability of our story is also key. Violence, like a suicide, has a great deal of stigma and blame attached to it. Some stories are more difficult to share in public. Not being able to share it as readily, feeling the stigma and guilt more keenly, might retard the healing process.

We also need to remind ourselves again and again that everyone is different and will deal with the tragedy in a different way. In our case I was the "social" one — able to communicate with others more readily and more acquainted with the "grief" and the victim stance. My husband was more task oriented, more research prone. We found that rather than compare ourselves to each other (we both had good times and bad times), it was more productive to help each other with our weaknesses in order to build strength.

The promise of answers can also be a very dangerous thing when we are dealing with something as complicated as the aftermath of murder. Even the suggestion that there are answers can put undue pressure on us as victims. Answers can be used as standards, and the minute there is a standard or expectation, those around us will compare us to the standard.

Most of the time (especially on our bad days) we fall short of the standards. This can lend itself to discouragement. Hope, as we mentioned before, is already a fragile thing with us; to have undue pressure might be the last straw for us.

Important Variables in the Aftermath of Murder

Few people handle trauma well. But there are some who do bounce back more quickly than others. What helps these people who bounce back more quickly than the rest of us?

1. CIRCUMSTANCES

Multiple murderers involved in the killing act of one victim
Perception of violence is multiplied by the number of people who participated in the violence. For example, if more than one person raped and beat a young woman to death, it seems more horrific to us than if only one person was involved.

The more people involved the greater the fear factor and the greater the disgust. "Someone should have been able to stop it," we think. The fact that the German people did not stop Hitler but followed his commands is a form of insidious complicity. Another complication of multiple offenders is that in defense arguments, the seriousness of the crime is seemingly lost in the discussion of who was the instigator. One of the perpetrators in the murder might also be described as the "victim" of the more aggressive offender. The significance of this argument can be lost on us as victims who see all participants, whether they are the instigator or accomplices, as guilty of the crime. If they didn't stop the violence and save our loved one, they are all guilty of murder.

Murder accompanied by torture or rape
Deliberate, inflicted pain and abuse before the killing makes the murder more difficult to accept. We seem to find a great deal of comfort in knowing that our loved ones haven't suffered, so information contrary to that can be very difficult to accept.

Murder following a kidnapping
Whether the actual time between the abduction and the murder is minimal or extends over a period of months or years makes a difference to the recovery period. The intensity of the search for the loved one remains indelibly impressed as part of the murder. Time spent "not knowing" is part of the remembered trauma.

Murder when the body is mutilated or not found It is important in our culture to give the body a proper and respectful burial. If the body has been mistreated, even after death, it affects us. We feel the dishonor of our loved one. To not find the body prevents closure.

Geographic distance of the murder The cost emotionally, physically and financially of remaining informed about the trial and investigation might be unaffordable for some victims. Being unable to participate in the immediacy of those events around the trial for instance keeps them uninformed and uninvolved. For those who are able to travel to the place of the trial, staying in a place other than the safety of their own home during the trial can be traumatic. The fact that the loved one was not on "safe home ground" might lead to guilt and blame.

Death by criminal negligence or vehicular homicide The hardest part of this kind of homicide is the public perception that the death was an accident. To us, the act feels like murder. If it continues to be seen as an accident, the impact of the death is more easily minimized and dismissed.

Murder/Suicide When the perpetrator has either been killed in the act of the murder or has committed suicide, this can leave us without definitive answers or without hope of ever getting answers. Often the case will not even go to trial. If there is an inquiry, both of the key players are not accessible. There is no satisfying truth-telling.

Murder where victim and offender knew each other well
Because of an existing relationship, the offender can more readily blame our loved one for participating, provoking or instigating the act of violence. If the offender is part of the family, we might find that we have not only lost our loved one, but we have also lost another member of the family to the prison system. We might feel the whole family fabric disintegrating. If both our loved one and the

offender were well known in the community, members of the community, church, faith groups and organizations might be very involved in the primary trauma of the case. The conflict inherent in the violence could tear our community apart.

Murder by mass or serial killers The enormous public curiosity about these killers can be very difficult to see or handle. These killers are often glorified. The victimized families might be bonded in like-experience with others who are very different in their response to the murder. Families might feel a sense of competition, comparison and favoritism by the court, media and the public. This would be very difficult to handle at time of heightened vulnerability.

Murder by a stranger These acts are the most senseless. Since the murderer does not have a relationship with our loved one, the murder is seen as a random act of violence, which makes everyone in the community vulnerable. There is heightened fear for everyone involved.

Murder of an emotionally troubled loved one When our loved ones are already stigmatized by society, for example if they were prostitutes or gang members, it is very difficult for us to see them portrayed as such in the media and blamed for their own misfortune. We know our loved one was going through a difficult time, but we don't see them as "bad." Our sense of powerlessness to help them during their lifetime will be accentuated after their death. This is probably the most difficult type of murder to deal with. Because of the blame and the judgment of our loved ones, we might not feel the support that we need from friends and community.

2. RELATIONSHIPS

The relationship we had with our loved one   If we've been experiencing a current good relationship with our loved one this can help us deal with the murder. If we were experiencing even a small disagreement with our loved one before their murder, their passing might prove to be more difficult.

If our loved one was our child, it might feel as if we have lost a part of ourselves.   It is not natural for children to die before their parents. As parents we feel that we are completely responsible for them. This is true whether the one murdered was a young child or an adult child. Our child is our child forever.

If our loved one was our mate, we might suffer many secondary losses.   Besides our mate, we might lose our place in a couple-oriented society. We might have lost our best friend, our lover, our co-parent, our breadwinner, or our main confidant. Suddenly being alone in making all of the major decisions might be traumatic enough in ordinary circumstances, but to face all the issues of death and murder might be overwhelming. It becomes complicated because there are three issues to deal with: the loss of a loved one, murder, and becoming a single adult again.

If our loved one was our parent.   No matter whether our parent is young or old, he or she is still our parent. We will feel the loss keenly. To lose a parent when we are a young child will of course be more physically traumatic than to lose the person as we are entering retirement. Murder will complicate the natural loss. We might feel very vulnerable, thrust as a child into an adult role, taking on responsibility for the justice-making as a parent would.

If our loved one is a sibling, this can be extremely complicated.   Again it depends on the relationship we had with him or her. Some sisters, who have always assumed a mother role with their younger brothers, can experience a grief very similar to that of a mother after the death of a child. If there was competition between siblings in the family prior to the murder, the competition can increase after the murder. If there was a certain estrangement between siblings, the grief might not be as intense as others expect it to be. There might be guilt because of lack of feelings. There might be resentment that the murdered sibling has again caused problems by bringing this unwanted attention to the family.

Dealing with family members might be difficult after the murder. We all react differently because of the relationship we had with the loved one.

One father, who misunderstood his son's reaction to his brother's death because it didn't resemble his own tremendous grief, was very upset. It created a huge rift between himself and his remaining son. When he realized that his son was mourning a sibling, not a child, the father finally understood the difference between their griefs. Before you judge the grief of others too hastily, take a moment to analyze the relationship. Sibling grief will vary from one sibling to the other because of the differences in our relationships.

3. RESOURCES

The resources that we bring to the experience of murder will be a strong factor in our ability to cope with the aftermath. Studies show that those who have more skills can often handle murder better.

Those who have communication skills find it easier to talk to those around them. A background in counselling and grief studies might be of help. However, some caregivers well versed in the emotional aftermath of trauma might find that they are helping everyone around them and neglecting themselves.

Economic resources might be a factor in dealing with grief. One woman told me she felt that she was able to grieve the death of her child more deeply and intensely because she didn't need to be employed and was able to devote all her time to attending to her grief. She felt that because of this she was light years ahead of those around her. Money can't solve our grief or take away our pain, but it can help us deal with it.

Education can be a helpful if it helps us access resources. It can also be a detriment in that we might approach things more intellectually and neglect our hearts. In grief we need to access our important heart knowledge.

Religious beliefs and ethnic customs will make a difference in how we deal with our trauma.

The emotional support we receive from our family, our friends, our colleagues, our employer, will make a difference in our ability to cope. The position you have in your career, in your family and in your community will make a difference. Having powerful positions can help us access certain information and resources. However we can't assume that a powerful position will be helpful. Others will assume that you don't need help, yet extreme violence makes victims of us all.

4. PERSONALITY AND GENDER

Our personality and our gender will make a difference in how we deal with trauma.

Different personalities handle trauma differently. Lewis Tagliaferre in his book, *Recovery from Loss,* says, "The personality patterns with which we approach other areas of life are also going to be involved in how we experience and handle grief." Using the Myers-Briggs Type Indicator, he does a comprehensive comparison of how our personality will affect the way we deal with grief.

In the same way, our gender affects us differently. Men often deal with grief differently than women. Whether this is genetic or socially conditioned isn't important.

Both men and women must face many of the same issues and learn to deal with them.

5. JUSTICE PROCESS

According to Janice Lord in her book, *No Time For Goodbyes,*
"the success you have in dealing with the criminal justice system,
insurance companies, and the myriad of other systems" will make
a difference in your recovery. Former experience with the system or
lack of it will make a difference.

6. ATTITUDES

**Attitudes in life that we have developed over the years
prior to the event will also determine our coping skills.**
The way you have learned to deal with stress will make a difference. Viktor Frankl in his book, *Man's Search for Meaning,*
describes two attitudes which helped him survive the atrocities
of the Nazi concentration camp in Auschwitz. "Cold curiosity
predominated... somehow detaching the mind from the surround-
ings which came to be regarded with a kind of objectivity" and
a strange kind of humor. "We knew that we had nothing to lose
except our so ridiculously naked lives."

7. MENTAL HEALTH

Our own mental health will make a difference. If we have
already been severely victimized by another serious crime or homicide, and then face assault, it will be increasingly difficult to deal
with each victimization separately and completely. Some of the
victims I have talked to over the years have a history of victimization. As children they were molested incestuously, then beaten and
assaulted. They've also experienced the murder of an uncle
perhaps, or a brother. When their own child is murdered, the final
murder and the resulting victimization is hard to disassociate from
the past trauma. The more "victim baggage" we carry, the more
difficult it will be to recover.

All of these variables — and so many more — will make a difference in how we respond to the aftermath of homicide and other serious crime. It might be helpful for you to take a moment and reflect on the variables in your case and how they differ from other members of your family. Were you more attached to the loved one or were you less attached? Did you have more issues? Were you at a more vulnerable stage of life? Were you feeling successful and optimistic when it happened, or were you already experiencing trauma?

In this section we have dealt with the variables in homicide but rape or any other serious assault would have many of the same variables. We could ask the same questions. Was the rape committed by one person or two? Was abduction part of the assault? Were there threats around the rape? All of the circumstances surrounding the crime will make a difference in how we deal with it later on.

"It is important to recognize that not everyone in a family will be working on the same task at the same time."
—J. William Worden

"But tears are my way of venting;
I feel a release when I cry.

I probably cry more than the average male,
but that doesn't bother me.

I do think my better friends are female
because women are so much better
at dealing with feelings.

The men I know who have suffered
the loss of a loved one tend to stuff it.

They think it's a sign of weakness to
cry or even show sadness."

—Man whose wife was murdered

| 13 | UNSATISFACTORY CLOSURE |

Car Whisperer

A GOOD MECHANIC CAN FIX A BROKEN DOWN CAR SO THAT IT RUNS AGAIN. But there are some who rise above; they are the ones who can make the engine purr.

My father owned a rural Shell service station in the heart of the Fraser Valley in British Columbia. As a young man he had opened a business repairing bicycles for the community but slowly as the means of transportation in the community changed from bicycles to cars so did his business.

Since we lived right on the same yard as the service station, as a child I was able to watch people bring their problems to my father. Some of the problems were small, such as a stubborn lawn mower that couldn't start. He dispensed with them quickly. For the more difficult problems, he would assume an expression of extreme concentration, and then begin to play with the machine. His fingers would stroke the outside of the car as he walked around it. Once under the hood he would begin to thump this, thump that. He'd put the car on the hoist and examine the underside. He would begin to attach new parts, screw this more tightly or unscrew that.

If he couldn't solve the problem before supper, he would sit all evening deep in thought. Sometimes he'd discuss it with Mom late at night. My mother who knew nothing about cars or engines listened to him intently. In the morning he would tackle the problem again till finally the car would run.

But for him it wasn't enough. With the car running, he would continue to walk around it, his head cocked listening. Then he'd fiddle with the engine, listen, and fiddle some more. He didn't stop till the engine hummed a song. Only when this true magic happened was he content.

But there was one thing he refused to learn. He was already retired when the computer age descended on us. As his children, we knew that he was quite capable of mastering a computer. So as adult children, we begged him to buy a computer so that we could at least begin e-mailing; he refused. We told him that it was as simple as following a recipe. Surely he could follow instructions — but he only shook his head.

And finally he told us why. "I can't fix it. What if it breaks? How can I use it if I don't know how to fix it?"

It wasn't enough just to use a computer; he wanted to tinker with it, and make it purr. That's what had given him joy over all those years.

The Successful Challenge and Conclusion

We love the word success. And we love success stories. Featured in a recent issue of *Reader's Digest,* there is the story of John Nash, the inspiration behind the successful movie, *A Beautiful Mind.* Nash, who suffered from paranoid schizophrenia, won the Nobel Prize in economics in 1994.

Nash's son, who also suffers from the same illness, says his father is now an inspiration. "He's a great hope for all of us. Anyone with mental illness can look at Dad and say it's possible to recover."

There are many stories of people we know by name, such as Helen Keller or Mother Teresa, that bring to mind tremendous challenges and beautiful strength. Most of the movies we see in the theaters are about someone facing a challenge and succeeding.

The flip side of that is that we generally don't like to lose — nor are we all that interested in losers. Sportscasters know this. The minute a team wins, they have a few gracious but sad quotes from the losers who are slinking off to the dressing room, then the attention is on the winners circling the rink — arms held high in victory. The reporters follow the winners into the dressing room, filming the flow of champagne. The success is analyzed, recorded and emulated.

Success doesn't come without hard work and preparation. We work hard at developing the winning skills, developing the strength and courage to come out on top. An athlete knows that winning involves fitness of body, soul, spirit and mind. Much is sacrificed in order to attain the win that will give us all the glory, power and influence that comes with winning.

For some the challenge has to be spectacular. They will climb Mount Everest, swim the English Channel, tame a lion, run a marathon, enter the Olympics or land on the moon. They tell us that being the best and completing these extreme challenges is worth everything that they have endured along the way.

For some of us even mastering the little challenges that come our way is reward enough. We are satisfied when we can write a list in the morning and have it all stroked off by the end of the day.

When we are winning, accomplishing, learning, and finishing well, we have satisfactory closure. We celebrate and move on to the next challenge.

Unsatisfactory Closure

13

In the aftermath of violent crime, for the crime victim there is no winning, no finishing, no accomplishing which makes it impossible to move on. The constant reminders of the crime, the unresolved issues, the unsolvable problems, the pervasive feelings of failure and the continuing losses can hold us hostage to an injustice long after everyone else feels that it has been resolved.

We yearn to find closure and to find a way of moving on, but because the overall impact of violence is so astronomical, the aftermath can never ever be contained. The continuing rippling consequences of the violence on a personal level, on the community and sometimes even on the national level defy any attempt to "put the event" behind us forever. Most of us will never find the closure we hope for.

This was brought home to me during a panel discussion that I facilitated. The evening had been designed to explore the issue of the victim/offender trauma bond; we had brought together three offenders and three victims of serious crime. It was a powerful presentation. As the panel members shared their stories the issues became abundantly clear.

The climax came at the end of the evening when one of the victims, whose husband had been murdered, began to list the ongoing losses in her life subsequent to the murder. It was a remarkable story. She had met with the accomplice of the crime and had showed extraordinary generosity to him. But as she was sharing openly with us, it was evident that her life had been abruptly and cruelly altered forever following the murder of her husband. She had lost an entire lifestyle, status, security — everything. Understandably, she was overcome with emotion as she painted the picture of the horror she had experienced. We were all in tears. This was the reality we were hoping to explore.

But the evening stalled when, during the question and answer time, one of the members of the audience rose to her feet and said, "I think this woman still has issues. It's been a long time since her husband was murdered. Why hasn't she experienced closure?"

The insinuation was clear. "Why was she still crying? Why hasn't she moved on? Why haven't you all helped her?" At the time I think all of us were a little horrified at the insensitivity of her question and we squelched it quickly. Yet the question is one we hear often. Is there closure for crime victims? And what does it look like? How can we live with the horror of violence that has the power to take us right back to the initial pain and trauma with the same intensity as it had thirty years ago? If we cry, does that mean we aren't over it? If we have anger, does that mean we aren't over it?

As one woman whose daughter was murdered says, "Closure. I hate that term with a purple passion. Some say when you finally have a trial and get someone convicted, you reach closure. I don't see closure coming. I mean you reach another state, but I don't think 'closure' is the term because you are never closed with what happened. You live that daily."

No matter how much we try, it is never over. Our lives have been forever altered. We have acquired a serious lifetime disability, and nothing will ever be the same for us. Even though the disabling losses of a violent crime aren't as evident as the severed limb of an amputee, the losses we experience are just as disabling and permanent.

We will never have closure — at least not the kind of closure in which the violent act of the past is packaged so carefully that there will never be any leakage into the present or future again.

Underlying Reasons for Unsatisfactory Closure

The reasons why we are not able to find satisfactory closure are too numerous to list. Each of the elements that we have described in the previous chapters is in and of itself a good reason for unsatisfactory closure. For example in the first element of story fragmentation, if we continue to have trouble telling our story without tears or continue to have questions about what happened, we have issues with our story. We aren't finished with it. We can't move on.

Other reasons we can't find closure are:

It is impossible to "forget" a crime of this magnitude. Once the story becomes public knowledge it becomes public property. The media remembers, the police remember and our friends and family remember. We face almost constant reminders. For example in my own story, almost eighteen years after our daughter was abducted, the case was recently outlined in our local newspaper.

The losses of the violent crime continue to affect us at the most unexpected and inopportune times. For example in my own story, when my family moved into our new house, which was a time of celebration and hope, I remember carrying the box of Candace's memories and broke down with a traumatic grief spasm that felt as if I was being pulled right back to the day we found her body. The shattered assumptions of safety will affect us for the rest of our lives. The losses continue and every time we experience the loss, we need to feel the pain.

The lack of closure in the justice-making process might continue to keep the case unresolved in our minds. Here is a list of some common scenarios of the investigation and trial process that leave victims feeling unsatisfied with how the justice system has dealt with the offender.

There may be no feelings of closure if:

- the offender is not found and the case remains a mystery
- the lack of evidence allows the accused to go free
- the trial is declared a mistrial allowing the offender to go free on a technicality — the accused pleads guilty and the case is plea bargained for a reduced sentence
- the offender is convicted and sentenced but during the investigation and trial there is no time when all the accusations against us or the life of our loved one are addressed and no vindication for us
- the personal cost we suffer feels like it outweighs that which the offender has to pay, and there is no compensation or financial help to cover the cost of attending the trial
- the offender commits suicide during the violent act or shortly thereafter, denying us the opportunity to know exactly what happened
- the offender receives a light sentence that feels like a slap on the hand
- the sentence which seemed reasonable when pronounced amounts to only a few months of incarceration with the rest being served on parole
- the offender applies for the faint hope clause and is released before we have even begun to get our own lives together
- the offender is executed (as in the United States) or put away for life, but we still don't feel like we can put our lives together because the person we loved can't be returned.

Eric Schlosser, in the September 1997 issue of *Atlantic Monthly,* quoted a victim who said, "You never bury a loved one who's been murdered because the justice system keeps digging them up."

If we haven't experienced a satisfying justice-making process, we will continue to feel the need for truth-telling. In order for us to regain a sense of closure, we will need a safe place where we can express our indignation, our humiliation, and our "righteous" anger. For us as victims, expressing these emotions empowers us and give us back the control of our lives. We need our story validated, our actions vindicated and our faith restored in the law and order of our country. Until this happens we will not feel as if we have been healed.

If we haven't discovered the answer to the basic questions of "Why me? Why did this happen?" we will not be able to put a plan of prevention into place. Without this plan, we will lack the confidence to put our fears aside and engage in the next challenge life has to offer us.

Probably the biggest reason we can't put this behind us is that eventually we become one with the experience. With time it becomes impossible to know what part of ourselves has either been made or destroyed because of the experience of violence. In order to survive, we have needed to integrate the experience into our lives; this in turn makes closure impossible. We can't move on; to do that would mean leaving parts of ourselves behind.

Consequences of Unsatisfactory Closure

Never experiencing a satisfactory closure leaves us particularly vulnerable to "justice fantasies." We might wile away the time, dreaming of the perfect ending. We might find great pleasure in dreaming that the offender is found, or that he or she confesses, is tortured and killed. We might find ourselves waiting for a long time for any of this to happen.

If we never gain control of our lives, we might become "control freaks" in our private lives. Having lost control of our lives once, we compensate by wanting to control everything forevermore. We remain in fear of losing more control.

We might lose respect for the justice-making process that cannot guarantee a satisfactory closure for us. Why should I be law-abiding if there is no justice? The tension with the law can cause us to get into trouble with the law and take on the role of the offender.

In our pursuit of closure we might lose our ability to enjoy the present. Many victims in this stage say that because they are so intent on the unfinished business at hand, they can't hear the birds sing. Some say that they can't feel. They grow numb — or they continue to rage.

We might feel that if there is no closure and no victory we lose the courage to accept another challenge. We are caught in an endless winter. We can't move on because spring hasn't come, neither has Christmas.

Finding Satisfactory Restoration

In order to deal with this element of unsatisfactory closure, the first thing we will need to do is "let go" of the idea of closure. For us "getting over it" isn't an option. However what we can do is integrate the horror of violence into our lives in a way that it becomes acceptable and even positive.

Integration means that we will need to accept the feelings of hostility, fear and guilt that are part of the event. We need to acknowledge them, understand them and slowly coat them with time, creative solutions, and goodness. Very much like the clam who discovers a grain of sand in its dwelling and begins to coat the sharp edges so it can live comfortably with the intrusion, we need to do the same. We might not be able to get rid of the horror, but we can become comfortable with it. Once we are comfortable, we can again move into the future.

For example, we need to become as comfortable with telling the events of the violence as we are about other parts of our lives. We need to accept the tears as normal.

We can begin to do this by reclaiming responsibility for our lives again. In the book, *The Grief Recovery Handbook,* John James and Frank Cherry write, "When we make other people responsible for our feelings, we also make them responsible for ending our feelings."

And we need to start as soon as possible. James and Cherry write, "Procrastination — putting off doing things that we're afraid of doing — is a favorite practice for everybody. We live with an attitude that there will be time in the future to take care of the things that we can't handle now.... Over time, we begin to make the death or other losses responsible for how badly we're feeling. As long as we believe that someone or something else is responsible, then we're helpless to recover."

Considerations

1. Embrace the horror of your experience. Make friends with the aftermath of violence that shadows you. Talk about it with others until it begins to feel normal.

2. Instead of trying to think of ways of "getting rid of your pain and fears" begin to think of ways in which you can recycle them. Is there is any learning or meaning that you might share with someone else? Finding meaning is one way of transforming the horror.

3. Make some practical decisions on how you are going to make your life better. You might not be able to solve the entire problem, but are there little problems that you can solve? Cut your problems into bite size pieces and tackle them one by one. You might not be able to forgive the offender, but can you begin to forgive yourself.

4. Strategize on how you can fashion your own justice process. What justice do you need? If you need to have a conversation with the offender, take the time to carefully consider how to orchestrate an encounter. One woman bought the transcripts of the entire trial (quite an investment and sacrifice on her part) and gave them to her son to prepare him for the fifteen year review. Since she was elderly, she didn't expect to still be alive at the time of the offender's parole hearing. In doing this she assured herself of a "future justice."

5. Allow yourself time to be frustrated when the aftermath of violence rears its ugly head. If you hear the name of your loved one over the media, don't ignore the sadness you feel. Continue to treat your losses as part of an ongoing mourning process. Don't put pressure on yourself to "get over it" and not cry anymore. Accept the fact that because of what you have experienced you will always be more sensitive to dangers or you might cry more quickly.

6. You might want to make the injustice you've suffered your cause. Many people have successfully turned their wounds into positive change.

7. Set yourself a future date when you will evaluate yourself and your progress. In the meantime give yourself permission to fall apart or keep busy. Sometimes it is only when we look back that we realize how far we've come. Then celebrate your progress.

"I know my life is worth celebrating, and if mine is, so is yours."
—Bryan Jay Cannon

"It doesn't close.

Were we going to stay together?
Were we going to get involved or
withdraw from society?

What did we want to do with
this tragedy?"

—Man whose daughter was murdered

14 | RECOVERY CONTROVERSY

Only a Thumb

CANDLELIGHT AND TISSUE PAPER ARE NOT A
GOOD COMBINATION. It was Christmas Eve — a long
anticipated moment when we were all huddled around the
Christmas tree. I had decorated the living room with candles.
The stereo was playing soft Christmas carols, and the gifts
were being opened with a flourish.

One piece of tissue paper fell close enough to a candle
to catch fire and burst into flames. A quick huff and puff by
all of us only fed the fire. The paper was ablaze. Since I was
closest to the door I grabbed the burning tissue paper — I
wasn't about to let it burn my children, the carpet or even
the coffee table — and ran towards the kitchen. (I am told
that this is not a good thing to do.) And as could be
expected, the rushing wind caused the fire to burn even
more rapidly.

By the time I reached the kitchen I could feel my thumb
beginning to sting. But again I wasn't about to drop the
paper on to my nice kitchen floor! I continued running
toward the sink and plunged the flaming tissue into a roaster
that was soaking in the sink. By this time the fire had grown
so large that it had caught the sleeve of my sweater. My
entire hand was stinging. But the fire was out — a smolder-
ing mass of hideous ashes submerged.

What a relief! But my hand. I pulled it out of the water.
The pain! We filled a bucket with cold water and plunged
my hand into it for relief.

It took a few minutes for all of us to recover. We blew
out every burning candle — even those in the ice lanterns
outside. I kept my hand in a bucket of ice while we continued to unwrap the gifts.

By the next morning, I had developed a blister the size
of a quarter at the base of my thumb. It turned out that it
was just my thumb that had been burned; the other parts of
the hand had only been singed enough to sting for a night.

The healing was remarkable. The blister served as a bandaid at first. I could see the progress daily. Then there was the itching. In six weeks it was completely healed. Now there is only slight discoloration to remind me that tissue and candles don't work well together.

Healing and Wholeness

The word "health" is derived from the old Saxon word "hal" from which we get the words "hale" and "whole." When we say "hello" to someone, it is more than just a greeting. What we are doing is saying that we hope that they are "hal" or whole.

Wholeness implies something organic. To say the wholeness of the body is organic means that if any one part of the body suffers, the whole body suffers. If every part of the body is healthy, we consider ourselves in good health. Our kidneys, heart, lungs, liver, pancreas, nervous system, and the other parts of our body are all designed to function together, and make up a wonderful unity.

The same is true of the psyche or personality. The personality is as varied and complex as the body. If a portion of our true nature is denied, we suffer throughout. Denial and repression do not rid us of the problem. Whatever we have denied suffers, and this suffering of the one part affects the whole. We cannot afford to exclude anything that belongs to us.

Our bodies, souls, spirits and minds have built-in healing processes. Most of the time, if we have a cold or stomach flu, we need only to retreat to our beds to rest and sleep to recover. Sometimes we need a little bit of help from the medical field, such as an operation or treatment, but doctors know that they are limited with their skills. They might set a broken bone but the bones must knit themselves.

RECOVERY CONTROVERSY

Recovering wholeness and healing from the wounds of murder and other serious violent crime is sabotaged and infiltrated with pressure and expectations from many different sources. We are not left alone to find our way. We find that even the "recovery" is full of controversy.

We saw this recovery controversy debate rage when President George W. Bush declared war on Afghanistan. He assumed that for healing and justice to occur he had to bomb Afghanistan and find Osama bin Laden. He sought healing through justice. Others like television talk show host, Oprah Winfrey, took the country through the emotional aftermath of violence. Archbishop Desmond Tutu took South Africans through the path of forgiveness with the Truth and Reconciliation Process to help them heal.

The debate on how to recover from violence can probably be found in these three positions: the pursuit of justice, counselling and emotional support, forgiveness and reconciliation.

The problem with this debate is not that there are the three positions, recovery probably includes all three. The problem lies in the "pressure" that is put on us to conform to one or another. But before we discuss that, let me review them in more detail.

The Justice Position. This position believes that the only way for a victim to deal with murder and other serious crime is to find justice in the traditional form of the criminal justice system. There are those who think that additional victims' rights will help the victim experience justice. There are those who advocate for longer sentences and changes within the Corrections and Conditional Release Act. Right now there is a heated debate between the criminal justice system and restorative justice initiatives on the role of the victim in the justice-making process. We've covered some of this in the previous chapters.

The Counselling/Support Position. This position believes that the only way a victim can heal is for him or her to receive counselling. This healing begins with trauma counselling after the event, continues with grief counselling, then might proceed to anger management. Belonging to a support group of like-experiences that focusses on the emotional healing is also seen as an effective way of healing.

The Forgiveness Position holds the view that the only way for victims to heal is for them to find resolution through forgiveness. Because this is a topic we have not yet explored, I think it is important to linger here for a bit and review some of the different definitions of forgiveness. Most of the writers I will be quoting are seen as authorities on the subject of forgiveness. In compiling these quotes, I just realized again why the pressure to forgive is so difficult and confusing. There is little agreement about what the word even means.

"Letting go" Forgiveness — The Canadian Dictionary defines forgiveness as "to renounce anger or resentment against." Another dictionary says forgiveness is "to give up the wish to punish." In these definitions, forgiveness has little to do with the offender. It is an emotional journey by the victim to release the entire experience from his or her life. It is a way to break the controls.

Richard Fitzgibbons in his essay, *Anger and the Healing Power of Forgiveness: a Psychiatrist's View,* confirms this. "In the process of cognitive forgiveness, an individual, after analyzing the origins of his or her pain, makes a decision to forgive, that is, to let go of anger or the desire for revenge."

Actually many victims who have experienced violence use this definition of forgiveness when discussing their path of healing. It's the one that I was most familiar with and the one I have described in my book, *Have You Seen Candace?*

Pardoning Forgiveness — The Canadian Dictionary also defines forgiveness as "to excuse for a fault or offense, to pardon, to absolve from payment of."

This definition is more difficult for victims of violence to incorporate. It might be hard to even conceptualize the idea of pardoning someone of murder for two main reasons.

First, we don't feel we have the right or the personal or moral authority to pardon murder. For example, I can't really pardon somebody for killing my daughter; only my daughter can pardon the person for taking her life. I can forgive the person for what he or she did to my family and my life, but that is different than forgiving him or her for killing.

Second, we are also not in positional authority to take on this role of judging or pardoning a murderer. Even though I do believe that we as victims need to play a more participatory role in the justice-making process, I also believe that assaults and violence are committed not only against an individual but against the society in which we live. As I have said before, we are all connected, and if someone takes the life of another person or physically assaults another person and jeopardizes the safety of all involved, the ripple effect of that act is widespread. If society is impacted, it also needs to be involved in the justice process. The pardon of a murder has to be a collective act that involves society as a whole.

Reconciliatory Forgiveness — In this understanding of forgiveness, the purpose and the main goal of forgiveness is to create peace between two warring parties. Howard Zehr, who is a strong leader in the Restorative Justice movement, writes in his paper *Restoring Justice,* "I urge that we continue to develop this school, redefining justice so that the goal becomes that of making peace. True justice is not achieved by raging a 'war on crime' but rather by building just and peaceful relationships."

This idea of forgiveness brings to mind the "safety" issues of violence. To reconcile means that we allow the person back into our lives. If we know this person to be a sexual predator or a serial killer, where does our responsibility lie? Allowing a sexual offender back into our lives might feel that we have to choose between our vulnerable children and the offender. Do we believe that people can change and become trustworthy? If we do believe this, what indicators of change do we need to monitor before we can build this trust again? How much time do we need to build our trust?

How do we do this when the person is in prison? Do we trust the people who monitor our prisons to remain objective?

Restitution Forgiveness — In this belief of forgiveness, the expectation is that the offender will provide restitution and payment for the crimes he or she has committed. As Archbishop Desmond Tutu writes in the Foreword of *Exploring Forgiveness,* "Forgiveness is not pretending that things are other than they are. Forgiveness is not cheap. It is facing the ghastliness of what has happened and giving the other person the opportunity of coming out of that ghastly situation.... You see if you have stolen my pen and you say you are sorry, and I forgive you and you still retain my pen, then I must call into question the authenticity of your contrition. I must...as part of the process of forgiving, of healing, of the willingness to make good...appropriate restitution."

The problems of this expectation is that many of those in prison don't have the means "to pay." Many victims who have been hurt do not want to be compensated by the offender because of the trust issues. To accept money might continue the victim/offender trauma bond that conflicts with the first definition of forgiveness which is the need to "let go."

Repentance/Forgiveness — The expectation in this belief of forgiveness is that we as victims do not need to consider forgiveness until the offender shows genuine remorse and asks for forgiveness. Remorse is key. The problem with this idea of forgiveness is how to know when the remorse is genuine. And what do we do with the desire to "forgive and move on in our lives" if the offender refuses to show remorse? We are then caught in the bond of victim and offender.

Loving Forgiveness — In this belief, forgiveness is learning to love again. "Forgiveness is a matter of a willed change of heart, the successful result of an active endeavor to replace bad thoughts with good, bitterness and anger with compassion and affection," writes Joanna North in her essay, *The "Ideal" of Forgiveness: A Philosopher's Exploration.*

Faith Forgiveness — This belief of forgiveness requires a faith in Jesus Christ. "The supreme lesson of the Gospel is that God so loved the world in its brokenness that He gave His only begotten and beloved Son for the restoration of the community He created. Christ's chief goal in His ministry was to have people experience the redemptive grace of the Kingdom of God. This grace is the result of the love of God," writes Lee Earl in *The Spiritual Problem of Crime: A Pastor's Call.* In Jeremiah 31:34 in the Bible we read, "I will forgive their wickedness and will remember their sins no more." In this definition God sacrificing his son is the model for the supreme act of forgiveness.

"Save the offender" Forgiveness — Inherent in this idea of forgiveness is the underlying belief that the overture of forgiveness coming from the victim has the power to change and transform the offender. Unless the victim forgives, the offender is forever held in the bondage of his or her evil act. "Forgiveness is not something that we do for ourselves alone, but something that we give or offer to another. The forgiving response is outward-looking and other-directed; it is supposed to make a difference to the wrongdoer as well as to ourselves, and it makes a difference in how we interact with the wrongdoer and with others. Even if the wrongdoer is no longer around — if he has since died, for example — our forgiveness is still directed at him as an object of our thoughts and memories, and our behavior would be different were it possible to meet him again," writes Joanna North in her essay, *The "Ideal" of Forgiveness: A Philosopher's Exploration.*

If we believe this, we feel we are directly responsible for the rehabilitation of the offender.

Person/Action Forgiveness — Another definition of forgiveness is that we don't forgive the "act;" we forgive only the "person." This is a way of not condoning the criminal act, but still redeeming the person. "When we are deeply hurt by another person we tend to think of him as a 'bad person,' as if his crime 'shoots through' or defines his whole personality. But in most cases, people are not wholly bad, and their actions result from a multiplicity of background factors. Reframing does not do away with the wrong itself, nor does it deny the wrongdoer's responsibility for it, but it allows us to regard the wrongdoer in a more complete, more detailed, more rounded way — in a way, that is, which does justice to the complexity of the wrongdoer's personality," writes Joanna North in her essay, *The "Ideal" of Forgiveness*.

Individual Forgiveness — This forgiveness allows for individuality. There is not just one way to forgive, but many. "In reality of course, each stage (of forgiveness) will be experienced in different ways by different people. Nor is there meant to be any suggestion of a specific time frame in which the processes occur or any exact matching between parallel stages at the same point in time. The process of forgiving another may be almost instantaneous or it may take time to achieve. In the same way the process of accepting forgiveness, both for oneself and from one another, is likely to take some time: indeed self-forgiveness ought not to be accomplished too quickly if one is not to be suspected of insincerity," writes Joanna North in *The "Ideal" of Forgiveness*.

All-encompassing Forgiveness — In this definition, forgiveness becomes a virtue like peace, love, and justice. It pushes us to taking "the high road" in life. "For Christians and non-Christians alike, the process of forgiveness enshrines common human values and virtues.... Through the effort to forgive and the effort to be worthy of forgiveness, we experience and put into practice the moral virtues of trust, compassion, and sympathy which are fundamental bonds of unity between all human individuals," writes Joanna North in *The "Ideal" of Forgiveness*.

Underlying Reasons for this Recovery Controversy

Recovering from violence is difficult enough, but when the recovery journey is examined and watched by the public, and is of concern to many others, this outside interest can become part of the controversy.

For example, it was of no interest to anyone how I dealt with my gallstone operation. But when my daughter was murdered, our attitude as a couple and our recovery processes were headlined in the local newspaper. People continue to be interested in our healing.

Why is everyone interested? Why is the recovery of victims of homicide and other serious crime of interest to the public?

I believe it is because crime victims are important to the justice-making process in the same way canaries were important to miners. When canaries were found in the Canary Islands and introduced to Europe towards the end of the fifteenth century, they quickly became popular not only for their bright yellow feathers but also for their lovely song.

In Germany the Tyrolean miners took them down into the mine shafts and used them to detect dangerous gasses that might be leaking. When the canaries stopped singing, the miners knew they were in trouble.

The main reason that the crime victim's recovery is so important is that we are the canaries in the mine shafts of justice. We are the indicators of how well the justice system is doing. We are the consumers.

The media knows that their public is interested in the reaction of the victim. The victim's voice, whether it be for revenge or forgiveness, makes headlines. The shrillness of the victim's voice, like a baby's cry, cannot be ignored nor should it be. The victim's voice is a powerful voice. The honesty, the pain, the suffering, the anger are heard.

Politicians know the power of the victim's voice. Some use it to make political points and necessary changes. The positive changes are always good. When they are not positive changes but rather popular ones, then we know that the politician is cultivating these changes, not for the common good, but for the assurance of a longer political career.

Service providers, counsellors and religious communities are extremely interested in the victim's willingness to forgive. The perception of being a healing agent is important to faith communities. They want victims to get on with their lives; for them this is "success." Forgiveness by the victim means their work is over.

Offenders need forgiveness. The need for redemption is a positive and necessary need in the course of rehabilitation, but becomes manipulative if the offenders seek redemption as a means of escaping responsibility for what they did.

The public does not understand the complexity of recovery. There is a segment of society who feels that if you "choose" you can get over "it." People do not understand the magnitude of the aftermath of violence. It's not a matter of "just choosing" to move on.

Before we move on we need to deal with all of the elements we have mentioned. We need to deal with our fragmentation, our fear, our grief. We need time. We need a fair justice-making process before we can feel safe to move on.

As victims we don't help the situation by joining in the debate. We add fuel to the controversy by stereotyping "good" victims and "bad" victims.

"You don't heal from something you are afraid of, you heal toward something you deeply desire."
—Dawna Markova

Consequences of this Recovery Controversy

Often we are pressured to choose a "way of recovering" that might not suit our needs. By identifying with one position or the other, we are forced to maintain that position. We become boxed in. I remember a conversation that I had with a couple whose child had been killed in a dreadful accident involving the deaths of a number of teens. Each set of parents had reacted differently; one had shown anger, another had chosen the word forgiveness, and another had dropped out of sight. Years later when I talked to the one set of parents who had been very vocal and angry in the beginning, they said that they were no longer "angry" but the community still saw them as such. The "forgiving" parents had experienced as much anger as the first. And the passive ones hadn't been passive.

Recovering with Integrity: The Blending

Each of these positions — justice, counselling/support and forgiveness positions — has its place, its positive aspects and its own controversy.

Most of us are a blend of the three. There is a time shortly after the crime where we might go through the justice stage. There is probably a time when we need to take time for ourselves and talk about the issues. We might discover tremendous healing in counselling or therapy. There might be a time when we "let go" and then we will talk about forgiveness. There is a time when we wonder about offenders. We might meet with them, hear their story and feel compassion.

And then there is a time when we just want to hide from the controversy and feel safest if we gain some anonymity.

The healing and wholeness journey insists that we re-examine everything — all of our habits, ideas, beliefs, values, passions, inhibitions, assumptions — until we find those things that are truest at the core, discarding everything else. It means exploring our questions until we discover how to create the kind of environment where we can again have integrity on a daily basis.

Probably the most important thing we can learn from watching the controversy around us is to find our own personal way of recovering from our losses. To blindly follow someone's suggested way of healing might have nothing to do with what we need to find freedom. Resist those who are trying to point you in one direction or the other. Understand that some of them have a lot vested in you choosing their way.

Redefine your recovery; it isn't about forgiveness or anger. It is about how you are coping. Here is a quick guide to know if you are doing okay — or if you need to go and get help. You are doing okay:

- if you are getting through your day, have a routine and can solve your daily problems
- if you are sleeping well enough to have energy in the morning, and if you are eating
- if you are having good moments among some of your bad moments, and you feel good enough about yourself to be hopeful about your present and your future
- if you are able to enjoy the little things in life again. Do you fill your lungs with good air once in a while, and stop to taste something divine? Can you enjoy pleasure and admire beautiful things?

Some of this is taken from Janice Lord 's book, *No Time For Goodbyes.* "No matter how 'all-together' you are, however, recovering from a traumatic and unexpected death will require a lot of patience and a lot of work. You will never be exactly the same again."

Considerations

Your recovery needs to maintain integrity. Remember that recovering from something like violence or murder is a long and difficult personal journey. You can't accomplish it in three easy steps or even fifteen. You will need to be real.

Remember that there might be a great deal of pressure on you to choose a certain process of recovery. Study the different positions and realize the complexity of them. All three have something to offer.

Resist pressure to conform to a certain expectation. To choose forgiveness just because it is the "noble" thing to do might be very harmful for your healing process. To choose anger just because it is the popular sentiment in the only group that you can belong to at the moment can also be harmful.

Resist being "locked" into any of these positions: justice, counselling/support or forgiveness. You might be floating between all three or two. Notice the changes in your position and allow for those changes. Even change groups as you feel positions changing.

Don't be afraid to become involved in the dialogue of recovery. Often the dialogue gives us an opportunity to tell our story, give our point of view and be heard. Be aware of the agendas of different interest groups but this doesn't need to stop you from participating.

Don't expect to find the definitive answer in any of these positions. Recovery of wholeness is not dependent on finding "the answer." There are many answers. It is not our responsibility to come up with the definitive answer for others.

Continue to relate to those who hold views different than your own. So often we as victims have been torn apart and kept separate because of these differences. Yet the common ground of our experience is so much bigger than the controversy. Strength will come when we begin to look to where we agree rather than to where we disagree.

Continue to focus on designing your own individual path of healing.

*"Healing is embracing
what is most feared;*

*healing is opening
what has been closed,*

*softening what has hardened
into obstruction,*

healing is learning to trust life."

—Jeanne Achterberg

15	PARALYZING DESPAIR

Sandals & Snow

TRAVELLING OVER TWO THOUSAND MILES
FROM THE WEST COAST OF BRITISH COLUMBIA
to the middle of Manitoba by myself wasn't that daunting
to me. "I've done it before," I told my nervous family as they
boarded the plane to fly home. We had just acquired a car
loaded with belongings. I was the only one who didn't have
a deadline to meet back home.

"Besides there's no snow in the mountains yet — and
there's simply no other way to do this," I said again and
again, waving goodbye.

The autumn colors were breathtaking as I zoomed over
the Coquihalla Pass. I felt as if I was skimming over top of
the world. The sunset was glorious.

I called everyone from Kamloops. "I'm enjoying myself,"
I said. "The weather is perfect. Just a night and a day and I'll
be home."

I was tired by the time I reached Golden, a small town
in the middle of Roger's Pass, so I stopped to take a nap in
the car. When I awoke a couple of hours later it was snow-
ing. I was wearing my sandals. My shoes were packed in the
back of the trunk. There was no way that I was going to be
able to unpack everything to find them.

"Not to worry," I told myself. I wasn't walking in the
snow. I was driving.

But it's very cold and lonely travelling by oneself in the
middle of a snowstorm through those mountains. When the
snow began to cover the highway, I latched on to a huge
semi-trailer truck and followed along behind. The truck cut
the wind and created sharp visible tracks. I was doing fine,
I kept telling myself.

As I approached Calgary, Alberta, the morning radio host
kept announcing, "First snow of the year has the city snarled
up in long traffic jams." So I took another nap at the first

truck stop. When I awoke in my cold car, nothing had changed. Calgary was still a mess. As I inched my way through Calgary I lost more valuable time.

The snow came and went the entire time as I travelled across the prairies. Around Swift Current, Saskatchewan, I was caught in a line-up for about two hours because of a dreadful car accident on Number One highway. The hastily fashioned detour around the mess of cars and trucks was worse than the highway. By this time my eyes were beginning to feel grainy. I was beginning to stop regularly for a cup of coffee and quick naps.

It was in Regina that everything changed for the better. Suddenly the highway was clear again — black and dry. I was into my second night on the road. The Northern Lights were dancing against the dark backdrop of clear sky and I could feel my spirits lift. Six more hours and I'd be home. The radio station blared with whatever music I could find, hard rock or western; it didn't make a difference. I stepped on the gas and the car moved easily and swiftly.

Brandon, Manitoba — four hours from my home — and it began to snow again. This wasn't supposed to happen! It was October! The tough miles were supposed to be in the mountains. The rest — travelling over the prairies — was going to be easy. But I knew the worst stretch of highway during a snowstorm (anyone in Manitoba can tell you this) is between Brandon and Winnipeg. I knew that if I didn't keep driving, I would become dangerously tired or, worse yet, not reach home before they closed the highway, which they often do. I was so close.

Yet the miles and miles of ice and snow, the constant skidding of the car with my heart in my throat, the hours and hours of staring into the bright sun, the gallons of coffee, and my continuing feeling that I had worn the wrong kind of shoes, all added up. I stopped. It was one disappointment too many. There wasn't enough coffee or chocolate to lift my spirits. I was so close to home; yet I was seriously wondering if I could make it. I was worn out. I pulled over to the side of the road and cried.

Hope and Meaning

Hope springs eternal. Hope is something that comes with life. We can't live without hope. Hope, according to the dictionary, is "a feeling that what one desires will happen." Hope simply means we believe that something good lies ahead.

"No one can live without hope.... To lose hope, means to become either totally disheartened to the point of considering suicide, or fearful or aggressive," Adrio Konig said in his address to the International Chaplaincy Conference in South Africa.

Hope is the fundamental belief that: there is meaning to life; that everything happens for a purpose; that every individual born in this world is important; that there is a justice which rewards what is good and punishes what is evil; that life will unfold the way it should; that life will not give us something we can't bear; and that life is worth the living, whether it be good or bad. These are not unrealistic beliefs. We have heard them often described by those around us. They are ideals that have survived the ages.

When these beliefs are challenged, hope is what keeps us going. If we don't have hope, we are susceptible to death. A famous study called "Broken Heart" surveyed the mortality rate of 4,500 widowers in the six months following the death of their wives. The widowers had a mortality rate forty percent higher than other men the same age.

Prisoner-of-war accounts indicate that some POW's may die for no apparent reason other than the loss of hope. Harold Wolf, a noted psychologist, has said, "Hope, faith and a purpose in life, is medicinal. This is not merely a statement of belief but a conclusion proved by meticulously controlled scientific experiment."

Hope is not the same as wishful thinking, for that implies a denial of reality. It is more than optimism. Hope gives us the courage to continue to live even in adversity.

"Hope is part of the imagination. Hope is what propels us into the future," writes Dan Allender in *The Mark of Evil*.

I never knew the importance of hope, till I felt despair. Despair is when we've had too many unexpected setbacks. We've run out of energy.

Paralyzing Despair

As a result of the aftermath of violence, many victims find that their hope has faded — or has disappeared completely. They have realized that they "can't move on." They are stuck in a paralyzing despair.

The crime, which has become central in our lives, is like a huge parasite in our souls, drawing its nourishment from us, imprisoning us so completely that we lose sight of all else. We can't see past it. Our energy is gone. We have lost hope. Despair, according to the dictionary, is the "loss of hope."

When we are faced with a perceived insurmountable obstacle or a neverending painful emotional state, we are susceptible to paralyzing despair. It can be compared to a major depression. "Protracted depression is the most common finding in virtually all clinical studies of chronically traumatized people," writes Judith Herman in her book, *Trauma and Recovery*.

"If hope is lost, then one is cast into a mechanical, rote existence that sees each day as nothing more than a repetition of what has come before. Lost hope spells the loss of vitality, passion and creativity. Once people lose hope, they become robotic serfs, that any person or regime can easily control," writes Dan Allender.

Depression of this magnitude includes all of the characteristics that we have described in the elements. This is the bottoming out. In this depression we will continue to be tearful, irritable, and brooding. We will have anxieties, phobias, and be plagued with obsessive rumination over past events. We will have excessive worry over physical health, headaches, or joint, abdominal or other pains. We will experience difficulty in intimate relationships, less satisfying social interactions and difficulty in sexual functions. There may be marital problems, occupational problems, academic problems, alcohol or other substance abuse. The most serious consequence of paralyzing despair is the attempted or completed suicide. There may also be an increased rate of premature death from general medical conditions.

It is no wonder that we do land up here. After a serious crime, we have experienced the fragmentation of our words and story, the trauma, the losses, intrusive memories, loss of our self-image, loss of faith, the guilt, constant humiliation, lack of information, the neverending justice process, and the chronic rage. We are haunted by fear of the offender.

I'll never forget meeting a woman from Colombia who described her life as a young bride, full of hope and promise. She had married a successful politician and expected life to be easy. Her first-born child died; she was distraught. "But I handled it," she told me. Then her husband's career collapsed and with it, her marriage. "But I handled it," she told me.

Then she needed to flee her country. She lost everything and became a refugee here in Canada with her three remaining children. She was a single woman having to support a family in a strange country. "I studied and became a social worker." She remarried.

Then her oldest son was murdered. And she lost everything again. She lost her career, her new house, her husband — and was aware that she was losing the love of her two children. This time it was her anger, her fear and her inability to reach out to those around her that were driving everyone away. It was her inner feelings of despair that were defeating her.

*"Hope means to keep living
amid desperation and
to keep humming in the darkness."*
—Henri J. M. Nouwen

Underlying Reasons for Paralyzing Despair

In identifying each of the elements throughout this book,
we haven't discussed what it looks like when the elements get
tangled up with each other. Since none of this is an exact science,
I'm not sure we really know what it looks like. But if we were to
imagine, here are some combinations of the different elements.
These are only suggestions.

If you combine terror trauma with disabling harm, you might
have crippling anxiety attacks.

If you combine uncontrollable rage with justice revictimization
and with the victim/offender trauma bond, you might have insistent revenge fantasies.

If you combine grief displacement with uncontrollable rage,
you might not be able to control angry outbursts in the courtroom
or anywhere else where you feel your loved one is being maligned.

If you have uncontrollable rage, spiritual crisis and blame
confusion, you might be very angry at the church or faith community.

If you have story fragmentation and identity devastation, you
might be suffering from lack of confidence.

We have good reason to despair. Our story is shattered.
The sadness is overwhelming. Time has no meaning. We feel
like social misfits. We feel an estrangement from God. The spiral
of losses continues. We have no energy for rage; instead we are
irritable all the time. We feel guilty. We are absolutely powerless
to do anything about creating justice for our loved one or for
ourselves or anyone else.

Consequences of Paralyzing Despair

Being stuck here is dangerous. Studies of returned prisoners of war, battered women, captives, survivors of homicide show that people coming out of such violation all have high suicidal tendencies.

Being stuck means we have lost our freedom. I've heard so many victims say that they also received a life sentence with the death of their child.

Here are some of the symptoms of a major depression. Major depression is different than the normal depression of sadness after the loss of a loved one. If your are experiencing these nearly every day, call a doctor.

- Depressed moods most of the day, feelings of sadness or emptiness or irritability.
- Diminished interest or pleasure in all, or almost all, activities of the day.
- Significant weight loss when not dieting, or weight gain, or increase in appetite (a change of 5% in a month's time).
- Insomnia or hypersomnia.
- Feeling restless or slowed down.
- Fatigue or loss of energy.
- Feeling worthless or guilty.
- Diminished capacity to think or concentrate. Being indecisive.
- Recurring thoughts of death, suicidal thoughts, or suicide attempt, or specific plan to commit suicide.

We can also look at this state — this abyss — in terms of the elements. We can get stuck in each element.

- Desperate to heal our story, we can become obsessive about the telling of the story and certain parts of the story. When someone asks us we will linger on the parts of the story that make us feel good. We will tell our stories to strangers. Many of us will write out the story and try to publish it. We tend to dominate social times with our story. I've seen some victims sabotage the entire agenda of a meeting or a visit with his or her story.

- In order to deal with our fear, we can become fanatically obsessed about creating safety for ourselves. If we need a "security blanket" of some kind we will buy it, no matter what the cost. If we think gun controls will make our lives safer, we will lobby strongly for gun controls.

- In order to deal with our grief, we might feel the need to enshrine our loved ones. We might inappropriately wear picture buttons of them. And some of our friends will accuse us of spending too much time visiting the cemetery.

- In order to deal with the anxiety over our inability to control our mind and our time, we might begin to micro manage our lives. We will avoid any kind of trauma trigger. We will be afraid to watch certain movies, read certain books, travel to certain places or hang out with certain people. Anything that might threaten our control over our emotions and our thoughts becomes an extreme threat. We can become control freaks.

- In order to deal with our spirituality crisis, and our questions about God, we might throw ourselves into "spirituality." We might take great pains to "forgive." Or we might avoid any contact with religion or spirituality. We might feel very angry whenever anyone mentions God — especially when they talk about a "loving" God or praying to a God to help them or say that "all things work together for good."

- In order to deal with any problems we have with friends, we might abandon our old ones and become very active with a support group of people who have also experienced traumatic loss. We might not like to be called "victim" and react strongly. We don't know how to introduce ourselves or where our story is appropriate. We constantly wonder: Are they are "for us" or "against us?" We might suffer from lack of confidence. We are no longer sure of our place in society.

- To deal with our shattered assumptions we might fight hard to retain our work and work hard. We might over commit to prove we can do it. We might become obsessive about the safety of our family. We might sue and demand that we be fully compensated.

- After we identify the primary "cause," we might become crusaders to make this a better world. We might fight for our chosen cause at the expense of our health, our friends, and our families. We might punish ourselves.

- To answer our questions, we might spend a lot of time and money doing research. We might buy the court transcripts, and hire private investigators.

- To deal with our rage, we might entertain revenge fantasies. We might seek ways of getting even. If we are unable to hurt the person who hurt us, we might find a substitute and make someone of that "kind" feel our anger and rage. We might vent our anger on the extended family or on anyone who reminds us of the offender.

- In order to deal with the offender and make this world safer, we might need to agitate for longer sentences and stricter parole procedures.

- We might fight for victim rights in the courtroom. And we might not do this in a rational informed way; we tend to do this with voices of rage and frustration.

Dealing with our Despair: Finding Hope

Those around us are often more aware of our inability to get on with our life.

If you recognize yourself as being "stuck," this might be a time for you to seek help if you haven't already. Having normal sadness, anger, or grief is never a problem, as long as we are working towards solutions. Not moving and not being able to get out of bed in the morning means that we are in trouble. We need help.

It is also not uncommon for many of us to get stuck for decades. Some of us remain stuck in one part of the detour, simply because there is no way out. There are no answers to our problem.

However there might be other reasons:

- We might be stuck because there are some people around us who don't want us to move. They are stuck and they want us to keep them company in their "stuckness." This is not a good enough reason to remain stuck.

- We might feel that to move on somehow means that what we have experienced isn't serious. We might think we will feel guilty if we move on.

The most important factor in starting to move is to "want to." Remember our lives are important too. Being stuck for too long makes us another casualty in the act of murder and violence. Giving up, letting go, moving on, starting over, forgiving, are not words of defeat, guilt or weakness. On the contrary, these words can give us back our freedom.

Considerations

Begin to look at how to empower yourself again.

Look for things where you can be successful. When we are depressed, we need small challenges that can reinforce our confidence again. Review the places where you are stuck and make small changes in each one of them. Don't expect much of yourself at first but celebrate the little progress that you do make. When I was trying to write my first book, completing just one sentence was a moment of great celebration.

Don't let others evaluate how you are doing. Learn to assess yourself. If you are feeling good about it, it is good. No one else knows what you are up against.

Reassess your friends. Are you hanging around people who are always putting you down? Are you sticking close to family members who are holding you in one spot, contributing to the lack of growth in your life? Begin to look for people who make you feel good about yourself. You might want to get a pet who thinks the world of you.

Make an effort to find a group of people you can socialize with that is supportive. Depression and getting stuck make us want to withdraw when we need to get out. Even going for coffee at the local mall and "people watching" is better than sitting at home, isolated. Notice those who are also lonely and "stuck." There are many of us who fight depression.

Begin to watch your thought processes. With what are you filling your mind? Are you reading only "escapism" material, watching only "escapism" programming, dreaming about too many unrealistic goals? What can be healthy distractions for someone living a busy life can become addictive and unhealthy for someone who is fighting a depression. Spend your resources wisely. Read good books, watch educational television and buy little things that will help you put value into your life. You might want to go back and reassess the core values you held previously.

Do something — anything. Take a walk. Light a candle. Avoid eating and drinking too much. Take baby steps. Talk to someone about your depression. Name it, claim it — and then look for professional help.

Forgive yourself for not being able to transcend this impossible hurdle with flying colors. Most of us can't. The aftermath of murder is a formidable foe.

If you remain stuck too long, seek professional help.

"All that the downtrodden can do
is go on hoping.

After every disappointment
they must find fresh reason to hope."

—Alexander Solzhenitsyn

Part Two

THE NEVERENDING JOURNEY

Profusion of Color

THE BACKYARD WAS A LITTERED WASTELAND.
We had just moved into a new house that had been
neglected for years. Our two adult children eyed the yard
with interest. "Can we help you?" I hesitated for a moment.
I had plans. But their eagerness was so evident. Why not?
I asked myself. What harm could they do? "Sure," I said.

They were delighted. In February, they bought the seeds.
"Will they grow?" I asked.

"Mom, plants want to grow," my daughter said. "You
have to remember that. They want to live."

As soon as the snow melted, we began to haul in the soil
— six truckloads I think it was and three of rock.

"Rock?" my husband shook his head in disbelief.

"For the pond," my son said.

The seedlings grew beautifully, taking up much of the
basement floor. But by the time they were ready to plant, the
constant watering had washed most of the names off the
plastic labels.

"How are we going to plan which plants go where
when we don't even know what they are?" I asked. "We need
a plan. We need to make sure the flowers match in color, in
texture. The tallest need to be in the back…."

My son smiled and said, "All flowers look good
together. We need to let them choose their place. Just let us
do it."

The flats of seedlings, thick and toppling over, looked
daunting.

"There's too many," I said.

"There's never too many," said my daughter. "We hate to
see the bare ground underneath the plants. We want a profusion of color."

And profusion it was. Somehow or other, the plants all
came up in the right place at the right time. The rich soil,
the perfect timing of the rain, the beautiful sun — and those
little plants flourished.

Our neighbors peered over the fence in awe. "What are the names of all those plants?" they asked. "I don't know," I said.

It was a summer of pleasant surprises. The joy of the children, the amazement of our neighbors, and the gorgeous, original, spectacular garden was all mine to enjoy.

We gazed with love on our little garden.

The Stare

I remember so clearly the first time I read the list of the fifteen elements of the Crime Victim Detour to my husband. He was quiet for a long moment then said, "That is the worst list that I've heard for a long time."

I was a little surprised by his response. "But is it right?" I asked, looking for affirmation.

But that wasn't his concern. He was recalling the journey. He just stared off into space.

After the terrorist attacks on the World Trade Center, it was reported in the newspapers that members of the general public came to look at Ground Zero. It was said that they just stood there for long periods of time, in silence, staring at the grotesque twisted iron and rubble.

"I don't know what the gates of hell look like, but it's got to be like this," said one onlooker. For those of us who haven't been able to visit New York, we stare at the pictures. The images are burned into our memory.

This trance-like stare has been well-documented in many atrocities as well as in natural disasters. People need to look. People need to stare at the place of loss. When a hurricane ripped through the little village of Gimli close to where we spent our summers, we went to look at the disaster the wind had created. We stared at one exceptionally large tree snapped off like a twig, an overturned shed, litter scattered in the most amazing places. We were awed at the unbridled force of nature.

Some are offended by this stare, calling it idle curiosity. Some call it morbid fascination — and perhaps it is. But more than that, it is a natural reaction. When something unusual, something so out of the realm of our experience and understanding happens, we need to absorb it into our lives. We need to stare at it to remember what it looked like, to see it as it is, to read the story of what happened, to burn it into our memory as a warning, and then to incorporate it into our lives.

Reading through the fifteen elements of homicide and serious crime often brings about the same reaction. We just want to stare at the list for a while. We need time to absorb the anguish and horror of the titles as we begin to understand how this applies to our own lives and those around us. Our lives have become Ground Zero. We need to "live the horror" by looking at it until we can live with it.

Allow yourself to stare if you must as you read this book. Over the years I have taken many people through this dreadful detour of crime victimization. Often I have caught them staring with horror at the list and I wonder why we continue to expose ourselves to the horror of this. I certainly wouldn't write this if I wasn't convinced that the only way we can really get through the aftermath of violence is to become knowledgeable about what has happened to us.

Models of Survivors

At this time it might be important for you to know that there are others who have been at this Ground Zero and survived.

Here are examples of how people used the element that hurt them the most or where they were stuck to build something beautiful.

The national bestseller, *When Bad things Happen to Good People* by author Harold Kushner was written because of a tragedy. Kushner writes, "Aaron died two days after his fourteenth birthday. This is his book, because any attempt to make sense of the world's pain and evil will be judged a success or a failure based on whether it offers an acceptable explanation of why he and we had to undergo what we did. And it is his book in another sense as well — because his life made it possible, and because his death made it necessary." The writing of the book was his way of dealing with his fragmented story.

Eddie Burtinshaw, a twenty-year-old was killed when a thirteen-year-old boy gunned him down. Because his mother was afraid that it would happen again, she was instrumental in changing the laws so that a child could not walk into a store, pull a gun down from an unlocked rack, load it and shoot it. She was able to change the laws, so that now all firearms in stores need to be locked up. She knows that the world is a safer place because of her tragedy. She dealt with her trauma and her fears in a positive way. Many have made the world a safer place because of their own fears.

One man whose adult sons were killed in a car accident recreated the entire Bayeux tapestry — a cloth embroidered with pictures telling the story of William the Conqueror and the Battle of Hastings. The only change the father made to the original tapestry was the addition of the names of his sons and the dates of their deaths.

Charlotte Wolfrey became an advocate for change in her community in Labrador. "I know that it was too late to save or do anything for my daughter but I want at least to do something for somebody else's daughter, to be able to call the police and have them respond in a reasonable time.... I'm an advocate not just a parent of a murdered child." There are many who have dealt with the devastation of self-worth and change of identity by changing from being a victim to an advocate.

For Rev. Dale Lang, his mission is one of prevention. "I've been in about fifty different high schools now across the country. I think that if the young man who pulled the trigger on April 28 would have had one or two hugs from a teacher, if he had one or two more kids that actually spoke decently to him instead of picking on him, it would have been enough to keep my son from dying. I hope that I never hear about another young person being killed by another young person, because every time I hear that I know the pain."

The organization Mothers Against Drunk Drivers is a perfect example of how genuine outrage against an injustice, in this case the irresponsibility of people who drive when under the influence of alcohol, has been used for positive change. The organization's public awareness campaigns, their expression of constant and persistent outrage, their presentations and panels of victims have changed our lives. Now we constantly hear the term "designated driver." We know how alcohol will impair our driving.

Carol Pearce, whose journey of healing after the murder of her husband has been one of spirituality, faith and forgiveness, met with the man who was an accomplice in the murder. "If we don't forgive our fellow man, then how do we have forgiveness from God? That's my simple belief. When you believe that, then God works that forgiveness in your heart." Carol quilted a lovely wall hanging which represents the sharing of our stories. It is currently displayed in the front foyer of our office.

Priscilla de Villiers worked tirelessly in creating CAVEAT, an organization that contributed much to the victims' rights movement. Her message was, "If another child disappears, we are accountable. I feel most Canadians should be accountable. I feel that if you allow innocent people to be hurt and be victimized, it's your shame, because you're allowing it to happen." She helped create a more sensitive justice system that will help bring closure for many.

Nicholas Wolterstorff in his book, *Lament for My Son,* turned his despair into poetic prose. It is a work of art. He writes, "I buried myself that warm June day. It was me those gardeners lowered on squeaking straps into the hot dry hole, curious neighborhood children looking down on me, everyone stilled, wind rustling the oaks. It was me over whom we slid that heavy slab, more than I can lift. It was me on whom we shoveled dirt. It was me we left behind, after reading psalms."

Lesley Parrott's eleven-year-old daughter Alison was raped and strangled. Lesley was awarded one of the YWCA's Women of Distinction Awards in Toronto. The July 1999 issue of the *Report on Business Magazine* provides the commentary, "One of the Women of Distinction was Lesley Parrott, who turned the personal tragedy of the murder of her daughter in 1986 into a dignified intelligent force for change. She won the communications and community service award for achieving something one would think nearly impossible given her circumstances: outstanding work in her business, advertising. With the help of colleagues in the industry, she designed the STAY ALERT.... STAY SAFE program for schoolchildren that operated right across the country."

Intervention and Recovery

I have a friend who told me one day that she had never made things happen in her life. "Life happens to me," she said.
Knowing a little about her life, I would have to agree. She's been fortunate to have many good people in her life who have nurtured her along the way. The happenings in her life have all been good.

That's how our garden grows. The seeds are planted, cultivated and there seems to be little intervention. My husband just putters every day, watering, pulling out a few weeds and the plants grow. Without much effort on their part, the plants thrive.

But what if the life that happens isn't good? For instance when our garden suffers a storm, my husband goes out and takes special care of the plants. He stakes the taller plants.

In the same way, if violence happens, we need extra support, care and intervention.

In watching victims and listening, I would say there are four main interventions that they have used that have been helpful for them. These interventions are significant "happenings" of their own making. After violence, healing doesn't just happen with time. It takes more than the passing of time. The negative that has happened in their lives has to be balanced with the same amount of positive happenings.

The first intervention is that of justice-making. This is the intervention that we have explored thoroughly in this book. It is the preferred intervention. It is common sense that when there has been an injustice of such severity as violence that the healing process should include a justice process that rights the wrong. The Crime Victim Detour follows this line of thought and ends in paralyzing despair because we often fail in our justice-making processes. Even though the system has failed us, we still can't ignore it as a legitimate process of recovery. We must insist that the criminal justice system become a viable means for victims to recover from injustices.

In this book, I haven't paid as much attention to the following three interventions but they are still important to recognize. Perhaps at another time, we can explore them more.

The second intervention is that of choice. I have heard many victims describe a moment in their lives when they made up their minds to "move on" with their lives. This was not an easy one-time choice. I do not want to imply in any way that we as victims can just choose to let it go. This intervention is one of determination, willpower that probably looks very much like the choice of an alcoholic to not drink again. To "let go" of the aftermath of violence takes that much commitment and probably needs as much continued support as an Alcoholics Anonymous (AA) program or a Weight Watchers program.

The third intervention is that of creating meaning. Many victims spend a great deal of time examining the injustice until they can find a lesson to learn, a lesson to help others learn, or some means of transforming the evil that was done to them into good. They emerge with a cause. We call these people survivors. This intervention takes tremendous amount of energy, creativity and stamina.

The fourth intervention is that of faith and spirituality. This comes out of a deep sense of hopelessness and brokenness which results in a victim reaching out to a Higher Power. This effort is not as concerned about healing from victimization but in transcending the wound. This intervention cultivates the belief that there is a justice system of a divine nature.

Even after having named these possible interventions, we need to realize again that none of these are a "one-time" choice or event. They all entail a process that needs to be incorporated into our lifestyle. Often we are a blend of the four.

"We are meant to be real,
   and to see and recognize the real.

We are all more than we know,
   and that wondrous reality,
   that wholeness, holiness,

is there for all of us,
   not the qualified only."

—Madeleine L'Engle

The Journey

ANTICIPATION WAS TRULY PART OF IT. My father would wake up at 4:00 in the morning and start carefully packing the roof-top carrier with all the tenting equipment. For months in advance my parents would plan our two-week summer vacation; by the time the day came, we were beside ourselves with excitement.

The night before our departure we could hardly sleep. One wake-up call and we'd scramble into our clothes and race downstairs to find Mom packing the car trunk with our clothes and the food. We would pile the comforters on the back seat — this was before sleeping bags were invented — then off we would go in our 1953's robin blue Bel-Air Chevy with my parents and the baby in the front seat and us three girls in the back, sitting high on a cloud of comforters and pillows.

We would meet up with my aunt and uncle whose children matched our ages and drive hard. At the end of that first long day's drive we already knew the routine. The fathers would unpack cars; the moms would begin the meal, and the older siblings would set up the tents. That meant that us younger ones were free to be the scouts. Off we'd go. The first things we needed to find were the washrooms, then the closest source of water for the cooks and the woodpile for the fathers.

After finding these things we'd race back to camp to alert the others of the whereabouts of these important facilities. Then off we'd race again to find the lake. There was always a lake. We would have to find it, test the temperature, ascertain the beauty and accessibility. Then back to the campsite we would run to tell the others of our findings. Then we'd put on our bathing suits and head for the lake.

The next day, we would pack up early in the morning, drive hard all day in search of the perfect lake. We found some good ones, even quite wonderful ones, but never the perfect one. We never did find it. The next summer we'd go on the search again.

Quest for the Perfect Ending

In writing this book I have consistently used the metaphor of a journey to describe the aftermath of violence.

However this journey through the aftermath of violence hasn't been anything like a summer vacation; it's been a journey through the abyss of pain and suffering.

An important part of any journey is the quest for and anticipation of finding the ending of that quest. Even during our summer vacation, as we neared the end of the day, the inevitable question was "Are we there yet?"

I think we are at the point where we ask: What is the real goal and destination of this journey through the abyss of the aftermath of violence? Does this journey ever end? What does the ending look like? What does healing look like for us? What is the name of the place we want to reach?

For every kind of injury, disease or condition there seems to be a chosen word that best describes the healing process or closure — the destination. With a natural death, the word I've heard used to describe healing is "acceptance." With alcoholism, it is "recovering." With rifts in relationships, it is "forgiving." With people suffering from cancer, it is "remission." With those who have had a surgery, it is "healing." With spiritual apathy, it is "renewal." With broken bones, it is "mending." For chronic pain, the word is "coping." We "restore" offenders. We "redeem" a failure. We "correct" an injustice. Victims who have suffered sexual abuse prefer the word "surviving." We "manage" our rage. We "heal" a broken heart.

You might notice that often the chosen word that describes the goal also reflects the process. The word we choose needs to respect the struggle, add a little bit of hope, but not minimize the condition. For example, it feels untruthful to say that someone can be completely cured of alcoholism, because if they do slip, the process is clouded with feelings of failure. The word "recovering" anticipates a lapse in drinking and prepares us for it. By using this word it ensures support for the duration of the process or recovery through the good and bad times. It would be cruel to say of someone who has just lost a limb that they are healed. The wound can heal but the person will need to go through a rehabilitation program to learn to deal with the lost limb. Since the loss is permanent, words such as "accepting" or "managing" are more appropriate.

In most cases of serious crime such as murder, it's been very difficult to find the words to describe the healing process simply because there are so many aspects of the healing journey that relate to other issues. In the journey through the abyss, there are the issues of mourning the loss, of trauma, of anger, of justice, of harm. Each one of these issues anticipates a journey all its own. The appropriate words for these might be to "accept" the loss, "confront" the fear, "manage" our anger and "correct" the injustice.

In my own personal journey, I used different words at different times. At the outset, when facing the huge justice issues and realizing that there was no justice, we gravitated toward the word "forgive." When I started working with other victims of homicide, I realized how offensive the word was for them. At one point I felt comfortable with the grieving words such as "closure" and "acceptance." But that only identified the process of dealing with the losses. Very early on, I felt the word "integration" described it best. We needed to integrate our story, our lives, ourselves and the experience.

All of the above words are good. But we might find that they are inadequate. Words such as "miraculous healing," "transcending," "transformative," and "forgiving our enemy," can be used in such a way that they push the victim into unrealistic expectations. When others use these words, we can feel judged if we haven't arrived at the goal described in the word. But then again, any word can feel harsh when we are sensitive about wanting to heal and not being able to.

The Neverending Journey

The cruel reality of our journey is that the journey we are on might never be over.
This became obvious to me when I picked up a book about our family tree compiled by an uncle. He had done a beautiful job of detailing the names, relationships, birth dates and deaths of everyone in our lineage. There beside Candace's name were the words, "murdered November 30, 1984." At first I was hurt and furious at the insensitivity — the label. But then I realized that changing the words wouldn't take away what happened. Candace's murder is part of our family history — a very important event. For those who come after, the story will be important because of its long lasting effects on our lives.

The effects of murder visit future generations. One time as I described this during an interview, I noticed the interviewer blanch slightly. Later he told me he realized that his grandmother had experienced the murder of her son, his uncle, and that he could now see the effects of murder were visiting the second and even the third generation in his family.

In the United States during the time of slavery, the slaves found comfort in a spiritual song, "We shall overcome." In the aftermath of violence there are the same feelings of being out of control of our lives, of being imprisoned, of being held captive. The promise that we will "overcome" is comforting and possible.

Embracing the Journey

During our time on vacation, I always noticed the moment when we began to "embrace" our holidays. At the beginning of our vacation, my father drove hard, still working off the adrenaline from the vacation preparation. We needed to accomplish something; we needed to drive a certain distance each day. We were conscious of time, routine and cleanliness.

As the vacation progressed, we noticed that the time on the road driving each day became less and less. We would spend more and more time at the beach till finally we would spend full days at the beach. No one cared what time it was. Our bodies knew when we were hungry. At first we would sweep the tent free of sand every time we entered; eventually we would sweep once in the morning, once at night, if that. As we relaxed into the rhythm of those wonderful hot summer days, the vacation became easier, more enjoyable.

In the same way we need to embrace the journey. We need to relax in the rhythm of the aftermath of violence. We even need to relax at the bottom of the valley and look up — only then will we be able to see the stars in the darkness.

We know that we can't see far into the future, but we know that if we keep moving, we will find our way.

When we embrace our story, we are in control of our story.
When the story becomes an integrated part of our lives, we can tell our story coherently and fluently. We can talk about ourselves in terms of whatever role we play — parent, sibling, spouse. We can talk about our successes and our failures. We are no longer afraid of the emotions that surround our story. We don't mind feeling the sadness in the story or facing the guilt. The story has become part of the landscape of our hearts.

When we embrace our fears, our fears become less intrusive.
We have managed to shrink our fears into manageable and realistic proportions. We still have fear — we might even have more fear than those around us because we know that something bad can happen to good people — but fear no longer hinders us from living. We have faced our mortality. Fear has become a tool to help us live better, to value life more, and to recognize valid risk. It no longer controls our lives. We can sleep well and wake up with renewed energy.

We have embraced the pain of grief. We have completed the grieving process and we are able to talk about our loved ones in the past tense. We will never forget our loved ones. Sometimes we still experience their presence, but their memory no longer holds us to one spot. We have moved from focussing on the losses to looking for opportunities. We are developing new friendships, loyalties and relationships.

We have mended the fragmentation of time. We are able to embrace the past, the present and the future. We have organized our past, and can remember it chronologically. We are managing the present. We have regained some of our short-term memory — not all of it — but most of it. We have learned the value of lists. We can complete tasks and establish some kind of routine in our lives. We are hopeful about the future.

We have embraced the power of our spirituality. Our God, our Creator, our Higher Power, who might have seemed distant and remote during the crisis, has come close again. Our image of our God has changed during the experience. We might still have many questions about the "control issues," but we are content now to leave those in the hands of the theologians. We have realized that "control" isn't that important. We have become comfortable living with the mystery of the Higher Power in our lives. We have learned to trust again that our God guides us and communes with us. We give ourselves space to develop this new inner strength and commune with God.

We have embraced our new self. We're not as sensitive anymore to the approval or disapproval of those around us. For example, we don't react when someone introduces us as the "parent of a murdered child," words that link us to a very public crime. We know we are more than the crime. We know we haven't lost. We are the sum total of many identifiers in our lives — parent, spouse, sibling, colleague. When people call us a "victim," we don't think it describes us completely as a person. We know the truth of who we are in our hearts.

We have embraced our responsibility in stopping the cycle of endless losses. The harm is a scar but not an ongoing loss. We have made the necessary changes to make ourselves feel comfortable again. We might have had to change jobs, change houses, continue our education, remodel our home, or downsize. We are doing "work" again. Our days have a structure once more. Our bills are paid. We are satisfied with less. We have learned that it is more important to be "free" from the controls of the crime than to fulfill our justice fantasy. Justice looks different now. Living well is the best justice.

We have embraced our own guilt feelings, confronted them or acknowledged them. We are also managing our blame. We have learned that nothing is as black and white as we thought. We know that the offenders need to take responsibility for their choices, as we need to take responsibility for ours. We believe that there is always a window of choice. We know that taking responsibility for the good and the bad in our lives frees each one of us.

We have embraced the truth of what has happened to us. We are surprised how the information came to us. We thought it would be through diligent research, or in the courtroom, but it was almost as if the information we needed found us — as we waited. We were also surprised by what information gave us the most comfort. We realize that even though we were searching for the hard facts, it was often the offhand comments of friends that helped us make sense of the murder. We might not have all the details of our case; there are things that still puzzle us, but we have a greater understanding of human nature now. And in hindsight, that is what we were looking for all along.

We have embraced our anger and have gained control of our rage. We have learned to use this anger energy in positive ways, it has sustained us when we had no other sources of energy. We know what our anger triggers are. When we listen to the news, read a newspaper or watch television and see the continuing revictimization of others, we feel a surge of anger. We know what harm violence can do. We wish it would stop. We know why other victims rage and we remain sympathetic. We even understand the offender better now. Not that we condone violence — but we understand. We find comfort in creating change.

We have embraced the limitations of the offender. We know that we are no longer under any physical or emotional threat from the offender. The issues between us have been resolved either emotionally, spiritually, socially or physically. We know that we will never meet this person on the street again, or that, if we did, we would be able handle it with dignity and composure. We have learned to live in a world where offenders and victims live together.

We know the importance of continuing to confront inappropriate and abusive behavior while supporting and celebrating good behavior.

We have embraced our disappointment in professionals.
We have realized that they are vulnerable human beings under their cloaks of professionalism. There were some who were helpful, others who weren't. We learned to distinguish between the two. We learned to seek out those who could help, and to disregard those who were less than helpful. We have gained knowledge of how the different institutional systems work. We are no longer dependent. We have found other ways to vindicate ourselves, find dignity, tell our story, write the impact statement and find meaning.

We have embraced the limitations of our justice system and no longer expect there to be a grand and wonderful "closure." We have accepted the fact that life is not fair. We know that we will never receive "closure." We have accepted that. Justice is an ongoing issue. We know that complete justice hasn't taken place but we are no longer driven by that agenda. We know the need to have a healthy justice system for others and work towards that end. We realize that instead of expecting justice, we need to create justice for others.

We have embraced our own process of recovery. We are determined to design our own healing journey. If we need to cry, we cry. If we need to withdraw, we retreat. If we need to vent for a bit, we choose a safe place to do so. We can confront those around us who want to put us into a box. We have learned to educate others about our own journey.

We have embraced our sadness and pain. We have sat in the ashes of our disappointments. We have understood that it is all right to be sad. We have realized that despair left unattended can be dangerous. We have learned to recognize the signs of danger. We value our hope and take care of it.

We have embraced the journey. We don't sweat the small stuff anymore. We choose our battles. Even in our battles we have learned to relax. We are no longer obsessing about closure; we are relishing the beauty and exhilaration of the struggle. It is the climb, not reaching the summit, that is important.

The Seasoned Traveller

During the first year of our marriage, we lived in Vancouver, British Columbia. Every day I had to take the bus from the south end of the city to the heart of the city. The first time I took the bus was nerve racking. I had to learn the fare and the route. I even had to learn what clothing was appropriate for the bus ride. Mostly I had to remember to take an umbrella with me, even if the sun was shining in the morning. It didn't take long until I'd get on the bus, open my book and not look up till I was one stop away from my work. I just knew where I was.

The difference between the inexperienced traveller and those who are seasoned is that inexperienced travellers are constantly anxious about their whereabouts. They've forgotten to take their umbrella. Seasoned travellers are prepared for the rain; they can enjoy the scenery or a good book as they travel along.

The same applies to travelling through the aftermath of violence. We will pass through the elements of the aftermath of violence more than once. We will visit our grief, our guilt, our blame and our rage. We will encounter heightened fear and endless questions. It will never be over. And eventually if we keep moving through and not getting stuck, we will become the seasoned travellers of the aftermath of violence. We will become relaxed in the dark journey. We know we will never arrive. But that becomes less and less important. It is the journey that is important.

As we conquer and survive we will gain a new sense of pride and accomplishment. As one victim whose son was killed said, "I feel almost invincible. I have survived the worst thing that could ever happen. All other problems pale in comparison. If I could survive that, I can survive anything."

Selected References

Allender, Dan B. *God and the Victim.* Washington, DC: Prison Fellowship, 1997.

Bard, M. and Sangrey, D. *The Crime Victims' Book.* New York, NY: Brunner/Mazel, 1986.

Bourne, Edmund J. *The Anxiety & Phobia Workbook.* Oakland, CA: New Harbinger Publications, Inc., 1990.

Cameron, Julia. *The Artist's Way. A Spiritual Path to Higher Creativity.* New York, NY: G.P. Putnam's Sons, 2002.

Caruth, Cathy. *Trauma: Explorations in Memory.* The John Hopkins University Press, 1995.

Christie, Nils. *Answers to Atrocities.* Jan. 23, 2002.

Coward, Stephanie. *Restorative Justice in Cases of Domestic and Sexual Violence: Healing Justice?* Ottawa, ON: Carlton University, 2000.

Earl, Lee A. *God and the Victim.* Washington, DC: Prison Fellowship, 1997.

Fattah, Ezzat A. *The Sad History of Victim Assistance. Caring for Crime Victims: Selected Proceedings of the Ninth International Symposium on Victimology, Amsterdam, Aug. 1997.* Monsey, NY: Criminal Justice Press, 1999.

Fitzgibbons, Richard. *Anger and the Healing Power of Forgiveness. Exploring Forgiveness.* Madison, WI: The University of Wisconsin Press, 1998.

Frankl, Viktor E. *Man's Search for Meaning.* Boston, MA: Beacon Press, 1959.

Guggenheim, Bill & Judy. *Hello from Heaven.* New York, NY: Bantam Books, 1995.

Herman, Judith Lewis. *Trauma and Recovery*. New York, NY: BasicBooks, 1992.

James, John W. and Cherry, Frank. *The Grief Recovery Handbook. A Step-by-Step Program for Moving Beyond Loss*. New York, NY: Harper & Row Publishing, 1988.

Janoff-Bulman, Ronnie. *Criminal vs. Non-Criminal Victimization: Victims' Reactions. Victimology: An International Journal,* vol. 10, 498-511, 1985.

Janoff-Bulman, Ronnie. *Shattered Assumptions*. New York, NY: The Free Press, 1992.

Juda, Daniel P. *Hearing the Horror: A Comment on the Final Report of the APA Task Force on the Victims of Crime and Violence. American Psychologist,* 415-416, April 1987.

Kiemel, Ann. *magic of life. I Love the Word Impossible*. Wheaton, IL: Tyndale House Publishers, 1976.

Kostelniuk, James. *Wolves Among Sheep*. Toronto, ON: HarperCollins Publishing Ltd, 2000.

Kushner, Harold S. *When Bad Things Happen to Good People*. New York, NY: Schocken Books, Inc., 1981.

Lord, Janice Harris. *Beyond Sympathy. What to Say and Do for Someone Suffering an Injury, Illness, or Loss*. Ventura, CA: Pathfinder Publishing of California, 1989.

Lord, Janice Harris. *No Time for Goodbyes. Coping with Sorrow, Anger, and Injustice After A Tragic Death*. Ventura, CA: Pathfinder Publishing of California, 1991.

McDonald, William F. *Criminal Justice and the Victim*. Beverly Hills, CA, Sage Publications, Inc., 1976.

Meda, Andrea & Thompson, Kathleen. *Against Rape.*
New York, NY: Farrar, Straus and Giroux, 1974.

Molloy, Michael. *Experiencing the World's Religions:
Tradition, Challenge and Change.* Mountainview, CA:
Mayfield Publishing Company.

North, Joanna. *The "Ideal" of Forgiveness: A Philosopher's
Exploration. Exploring Forgiveness.* Madison, WI:
The University of Wisconsin Press, 1998.

Parkes, C. Murray. *Psycho-social Transitions: comparison between
reaction to loss of a limb and loss of a spouse. British Journal
of Psychiatry,* 127:204–10, 1975.

Paterson, Morton MacCallum. *The McGeachy Papers.
Toward a Justice that Heals,* vol. 1, 46–47, 50–51, 56–57.
The United Church Publishing House, 1988.

Peck, M. Scott. *The Different Drum. Community Making
and Peace.* New York, NY: Simon and Schuster, 1987.

Peterson, Marilyn, R. *At Personal Risk: Boundary Violations
in Professional-Client Relationships. New York, NY: Norton,
W.W. & Company, Incorporated, 1992.*

Redmond, Lula Moshoures. *Surviving: When Someone You
Love Was Murdered. A Professional's Guide to Group
Grief Therapy For Families & Friends of Murder Victims.*
Clearwater, FL: Psychological Consultation and
Education Services, Inc., 1989.

Ross, Jerilyn. *Triumph Over Fear: A Book of Help for People
with Anxiety, Panic Attacks and Phobias.* New York, NY:
Bantam Books, 1995.

Schlosser, Eric. *A Grief Like No Other. The Atlantic Monthly.*
vol. 280. Boston, MA: Sept. 1997.

Sullivan, William. *Professional Ideals. Work and Integrity:
The Crisis and Promise of Professionalism in America.*
HarperCollins Publishing Ltd, 1995.

Tagliaferre, Lewis & Harbaugh, Gary L. *Recovery from Loss. A Personalized Guide to the Grieving Process.* Deerfield Beach, FL: Health Communications, Inc., 1990.

Taylor, Daniel. *The Healing Power of Stories: Creating Yourself Through the Stories in Your Life.* New York, NY: Doubleday, 1996.

Tutu, Archbishop Desmond. *Exploring Forgiveness.* Madison, WI: The University of Wisconsin Press, 1998.

Tyler, Tom R. *Why People Obey the Law.* New Haven, CT: Yale University, 1992.

Wiederkehr, Macrina. *A Tree Full of Angels. Seeing the Holy in the Ordinary.* San Francisco, CA: Harper San Francisco, 1988.

Wolterstorff, Nicholas. *Lament for a Son.* Grand Rapids, MI: Wm. B. Eerdmans Publishing Co., 1987.

Zehr, Howard. *Changing Lenses: A New Focus For Crime and Justice.* Scottdale, PA: Herald Press, 1990.

Getting Through the Maze
A Guidebook for Survivors of Homicide
By Sue Simpson

An excellent resource for victims and service providers
alike, this handbook is conveniently organized to aid
the reader in navigating through the bureaucratic maze
of the Canadian Criminal Justice System. Comprehensive
and detailed, this book gives an accurate reflection of
the process in a very considerate and compassionate
format. Key points of information are offered about the
police investigation, media, justice system, corrections and
parole and compensation. The second section deals with
these areas in more detail, using a question and answer format.

125 pages (spiral) $9.75 Cdn/US $6.75 Victims' Voice, 2002 ISBN 0-9688385-6-1

Have You Seen Candace?
A Mother's True Story of Coping with the Murder of her Daughter
By Wilma L. Derksen

With soul-wrenching honesty, this book describes a
mother's agony and hope in the midst of the search
for her abducted daughter. The book spans the events
and learnings of one year, beginning with the day that
Candace disappeared and ending with the anniversary
of that day. The story reveals both the earnest goodwill
of a supportive community, the life of an average family,
the horror of the aftermath of murder and the way one
family tried to cope. Not only is it a book of insight, it
remains a tension-filled story.

270 pages (softcover) $17.50 Cdn/US $11.75 Amity Publishers, 2002 ISBN 0-9731557-1-X

Available directly from the distributor:

Kindred Productions   **1-800-545-7322** toll free
169 Riverton Ave.   or 204.669.6575
Winnipeg, MB R2L 2E5.   custserv@kindredproduction.com

Also available through your local book store.